HARP & ALTAR

Writing from the first six issues

Edited by Keith Newton and Eugene Lim

ellipsis
· · ·
press

ISBN 0-9637536-4-9
ISBN-13 978-0-9637536-4-9

Edited by Keith Newton and Eugene Lim
Cover design and book design by Michael Newton
Cover image by James Gallagher, from *Kennedy Cards*, 2006
Permissions can be found at the back of the book

Harp & Altar
www.harpandaltar.com
Brooklyn, New York

Ellipsis Press
www.ellipsispress.com
Jackson Heights, New York

Printed in Canada by Westcan Printing Group

Contents

MANIFESTO

"The poet is of no party."— *Baudelaire*

Our manifesto is an act of substantiation.

We reject all forms of futilitarianism, in whatever disguise.

We believe that comedy is the song of the village and tragedy the song of the goat.

We believe what is written in the books, but now we want to see for ourselves.

The single idea, beating on the same doors in vain.

The analogue and the invention.

The death cell.

The first permission.

Though we watch the stage for things to happen, though our minds wander.

By ourselves in the green field, playing our diversion.

Though the story begins with the loss of a home.

Out of the machine, we shift restlessly in our seats.

hart!

IT WAS A NICE TWO-SYLLABLE NAME. Hart Crane. Even one. He was the son of a candy-maker, the one who invented life-savers. Hart Crane drowned, so that was pretty strange. I read everything he wrote which was only White Buildings and The Bridge which I found a little impossible. And then the fat biography and his letters. I had never read anyone's letters before. I was 27. It was good being a journalist or whatever I was now because I could *do* all the reading that was too much in college because now I was getting paid to know. I could see in my reading that Hart was trying to write the great long American poem and I think it was beyond him. Not because he wasn't great, but the long poem idea seems a little stretched thin and who needs it, really. But Hart kept finding patrons and getting grants. He was like a comic ingénue. He winds up completely isolated on an tropical island in a hurricane or else getting thrown out of Mexico on his Guggenheim he was such a drunk. Meanwhile, writing writing the bridge. Why has no one ever made this film. He was a very familiar man. I felt I knew him. A prematurely white-haired fag, shy-faced and handsome. Wearing one of those Russian sailor shirts he was always leaning against a tree or posing in a group, distractedly touching his own face. He seemed to be gazing into another world. My father looked that way in our family pictures. I figured it meant you were gay. There's one of me when I was thirteen sitting with all of my friends and I was doing it. Looking right through the camera, back at myself but pleased. Usually the other people in the picture seem to be actually in the world. They're stopping the balloon from floating off.

He was a great poet of love. Hart produced in a flicker the blue of veins he spied in a lover's breast. His rapid twists of attention took your breath away. To him poetry was film. Even lighter. Watching a man's hands grow not quite thing-ified but resonant—meditative. You *got* there by looking long. All that looking was compressed in a poem. He published his first one in *Poetry*, came to New York and got a job in advertising through a friend of his father's. And that young, 18 or 19, already Hart was a total drunk. They gave him the perfume account because he was "a poet" i.e. fag. Even leaving open vials on his desk to inspire the young poet who stumbled in sick in a dirty shirt, and then shoved the disgusting shit out the window by his desk, ending *that*. I thought about going into advertising briefly not cause of Hart but because of Eddie. I think I always liked ads.

Hart published a poem called Chaplinesque and he and Charlie Chaplin go out on the town. Charlie didn't drink, but Hart must've been charming, not just terrible, and together they were at a bunch of parties in the village. Imagine some party where he and Charlie Chaplin stroll in.

Allen Ginsberg and Robert Lowell were talking at a party at Allen's one night. Lowell was scary. Manic eyes, big glasses, white shirt, of course. Allen wore a white shirt too but Lowell's just took up more space. Gregory Corso yells at Lowell you're talking to us like we're in school. I mean at the reading. Allen yells shut up Gregory.

I went to a giant party in Tribeca one night and Robert Di Niro was there. He was wearing a beret and a plaid flannel shirt. He looked like all of us only a little more deliberate. I was tripping my brains out. It was bright.

I said, are you Robert De Niro, the actor. He paused, waiting.

I am Eileen Myles, the poet.

He smiled very sweetly. At which time about a million women swarmed him. I toured with Jim Carroll. We didn't really hang out. Except one night we split a pint of ice cream in our hotel. That meant that Jim took a knife and cut the pint in half and we each went back to our rooms, yelling down the hall at each other about the night we split a pint in Milwaukee.

I don't think you were supposed to become as steeped in your material as I did with Hart Crane. I attached my homosexual poet to him and took a ride. Planes overhead, a train hurtling along its tracks. They had so much time back then and they were meanwhile very interested in speed. They thought the future would be amazing and it is, don't you think.

I'm thinking about a line Hart Crane wrote two different ways.

"The Bridge of Estador" is the name of the poem the good version's in. It was just one of those back of the book poems. Really cranky. In many ways Hart was like any weird guy—or the poem was like what you'd find that was great in the back of anyone's notebook. It was *subtitled* "An Impromptu, / Aesthetic / TIRADE."

> High on the Bridge at Estador,
> Where no one has ever been before,——

Then a few lines below, is the killer: "But some are twisted with the love / Of things irreconcilable,—— / The slant moon with the slanting hill," and then he follows it up, getting all echoey and vatic: "O Beauty's fool, though you have never / Seen them again, you won't forget."

Twisted with the love of things irreconcilable. That was it. That was being gay for me—the slant moon with the slanting hill. The line just never undid itself for me—it's unbelievable—and every time it ripples in the exact same light.

Hart tormented by the love of a remote (but certain) resemblance that you could not consume but could only view. That got under my skin. I just sat at my typewriter and felt. I thought about Rose. I'm your sister, Eileen, she whispered. What did that mean? I didn't think incest was so bad. If you loved somebody. She said no. I flipped the pages. He liked sailors.

To write the Crane piece I took a ton of amphetamine. I had this doctor in Queens. Yet I was a drug coward—too afraid to go days on end. I'd go three or four—live sleepless and sad. Accomplishing rote kinds of work in bursts of energy. Cleaning house. It was ridiculous. The very thing I took it for, to write, was in fact entirely sabotaged by the drug. I was like a needle at the final cut of a record just perched there skipping. I had already read everything by him and about him. I was full. And there I sat. Couldn't go out: nope I'd say on the phone, sipping a beer at my desk, or a cup of coffee. Uh-uh. I am working. I'm doing my Franklin Furnace piece. What are you doing these days. I'm working freelance. Got a piece from Franklin Mint. Yup. Thought you said Franklin Furnace. Yup I guess that is what I said but it's not what I meant.

Hart Crane's mother came to visit from Ohio. And she talked a little about staying in New York, which must've been scary. Grace Crane in New York. Uh oh. Hart was *her* family name. He was Harold originally. That's who probably got the advertising job. C.A.'s son. Harold Crane. Why don't you call yourself Hart. Hart Crane sounds more like a real poet. She was smart. I bet it was her idea to put the Maxfield Parrish on her husband's candy boxes.

So the mother and son went shopping, got him socks and a winter coat (which he lost in the waterfront bars on the first cold night). They looked at those wan Preston Dickinsons at the Daniel Gallery on Madison, came downtown on 5th Ave. talking about the paintings and later heard some music. It was just like in Cleveland. Hart went with Grace as a teenager to hear Gertrude Stein.

She went back to Ohio and he took the Staten Island Ferry with a couple of friends. He loved it out there. Leaving the land, hovering in New York Harbor the eerie shimmering place with green liberty holding the giant flame. It was a great day and Hart was one of those kids everyone really loves. He was still really funny when he drank and his friends all encouraged him. Hart was a genius. He wrote his mother, staunchly, about the trip:

I have never felt as encouraged, as free or as clean. Think of me often as such or not at all, for I hope you will understand me.

RYAN MURPHY

All Saints

1.

I can't stop thinking of the nothing I want.
Five past eleven on a Monday.
Which is also awful.

Like sun through the smokelight,
or a phantom limb,
her hair a kind of feathers.

Visibly shaken. Heat scales
an advent of August.

More rope.

Or we can ballantine,
bask me in your light
of shipwreck:
stipple and shell and shall.

I mean, how often
can one remember one's posture?

2.

St. Brendan, you heartstar
you graygreen spire,
I can't stop thinking of the nothing I want
to do.

This is how things appear
from the celebration of the bicentennial.
And the rigging over Rose Wharf.

I don't want to seem intrepid
sailor, we are friendless one and all.
O privateer, whistling in the courtyard
birds, sunflower and candles.

    3.
Like sun through the smokelight,
the game called on account of fog.
Children with popsicle
hands waving in the fog horns.

The body, strung vibrant
with rigging,

daisystar, ark on a hilltop,
Spanish lights in suburban
backyards.

Bundle and squirm
we came with cacophony,
the light of shipwreck.

    4.
The incoming tide
like a bowl of nickels.

We struggle and chime.

St. Andrew, you graygreen
spire. Gloucester harbor,
splinter through the courtyard
gates. Sunflowers, candles.

5.

Vigorous and charming
the baseball hats and commemorative
coins of the bicentennial.
The rotting hulls of the last tall ships.

Daisystar, pulled by the plague
of storms and foglights,
sinking fast, amongst calls for

more rope.

I am some sad potatoes.
Which is also awful.

It is Monday, the same Monday
or another Monday come around,
and the petulant lights of the churchtop
warn off small planes

like a children's book lighthouse.

JOANNA KLINK

Northern

With the onset of darkness it calls. The clipped
shapes of the note flair out, somewhere at the woods'

sharp edge, into senselessness. A fine rain
suspended in the air unrelieved. Night-winged,

with large forward-facing eyes and in truth I have
never heard it—though it calls. Though I could

scarcely make it out from the narrow bed,
though a brief rain fell inside the room

and the brushwood miles away made a leaping weir
in the stream and the shape of a swallow dove

over reeds of wheat that swayed, though there was
no wind, somewhere behind its eyes

or brushed the discs of feather on its face
and I could not understand what I had lost,

having not heard it or cared, having moved
through the rooms of this house for several hours,

months, turning off hall-lights or the stove or turning
over in my head what I no longer believed,

unwell but for the whites of my eyes where once
the sun could be seen rising in winter as now it

calls and the call breaks easily in all directions
and slips beneath the hovering maple trees

and I think it must pass over beetles, minerals,
wildflowers and thin bones, over pale-and-dark

needles of pines, highway bridges, boatlights
on muddy rivers and the untallied golds of farm-

fields where seeds float, low piano notes
over lakes of air into which rooted things

rise, and yield, like the arable blues and blacks of
foredawn and the blue tint of the cloth awning

over the man's face turned down to the street in grief,
and had I known I would be so long here

I would have seen that certain rains never
do sink fully into the ground, felt the shape-shifting

speech of leaves was part of who I was and
wondered a little longer about the source

of the rainbed and the two irises suspended in
each of our eyes' black liquid and the flowers

in lake ice in a northern wilderness where an owl,
unable to adjust, unable to open its throat, sings,

regardless of what I thought or had sensed, through such
merciless blankness, ceased to sound long ago.

Said

Said of them who went to the village for sun or quiet and found quiet.
Said of them who slipped into another's house and spoke in low notes so as not to be

   announced. In all their concealment the house in stone

   ———————————————

chipping off the slough of months, the house in stone and its indiscernible
      track inside their chests like the dust from the stone walls and its indis-

cernible track on their lips and wrists, said of them who knew the days were brief

though they announced a life went to buy pears from wooden carts
and went to buy bread from the old woman in the store with iron grates

————————————

or lemon tarts to be eaten in the stone house to which they fled with their books in hopes of
      home in all their concealments from each other said *I will be here.*

Who heard them heard through the silence of thick stone the smaller silence inside
      and the occasional shoe-pat from the sidewalk or heater-knock, for it was still winter

despite the nearby sea and sun, the thinning forms of themselves as they spoke or ate or
                                                                    read grow

                              ———————————————

full in the fullness of that measure said to touch those who have passed through long
      pain and seen themselves under the fine white dust of certain ceilings

as they are, alone, with their impulse to conceal what has grown dense in proportion to the
                                    daily disappointments went

on in that house as the weather warmed and the street-stones warmed under the fretted
      red roofs feeling *I will be here.* How many of you would have stayed

————————————

knowing some conviction of inner emptiness was made raw by the presence of each other

    and spared only by the presence of each other in fractions of hard gray-

                        breaking ten-century-old

                        stone in bits and

                              dusts from the very

---

walls and words in patterns they spoke with the old-sweet shyness held in each

throat beneath each hour marked twice, once by the village church-bell peal and once by a

                        distant village church-bell peal's delay?

Said of them who went to the village: *they were there.*
As one who prays might press his head to stone.

SHANE BOOK

from The Collected Novellas of Gilbert Ryle

They Are Not Motions, Suites, Cabins

I was drawing fewer iguanas, bees,
asps. I was sticking to a murder,
a last hunger. Nothing swinging.
"He, I." and then "Don't." with a shard
of coral, wrote her, on the lens of the ski
mask in the painting titled:
"On the depth and privacy of his Yes."

They Are as Robinson Crusoes, Commanding

Sick on a quay. Quay-sick. There was sickness
on the quay. On the little cement area, a mass
laying on of hands. Over the spacious abacus
he sung out nine untested terrors. Hay strands
tied on. A pair of parakeets bolted
to a wave. From a blue mug, a hat trick
of notes left sticking straight out of the meniscus
of the cooling Paraguayan tea.

They Cannot Be Taken to Bits

His manhandle was ever "Bat and Toe."
This freedom, he thought, is what makes
his subliminal feel relationship to it
profound, a farther land ever-shimmering.
From somewhere nearby, core odour
of day-lily. He set off in pursuit. He kept
a trio of daggers under his dirndl
for just such emergencies.

They Come Home in a Torrent of Laughter and a Nubian Eunuch-Powered Litter

1

Sea algae and sea-era dust.

2

Loosed postage randomly pasted as an old tableau vivant I always held me
over,

3

over on a wall of the old chateau—a high-test

4

contusion of refugeed bees milling round for a chance to beat out
beats on the taut skin

5

of my only wholly tuned conundrum. Hold me, I've been put on hold.

6

Low in panoramic dale or hoarse from attempting to wail, those I ran me from

7

was guests, centipedal nodes vastly scurrying.

8

From where may I not pour me over, a wispy helmsman
nearly undone in fevered looking? Of sea algae pairs

9

trying it out in a porous land. Of chain-excesses hand
in hand with the first ferocious noseeums.

10

Of a season.

11

A singing bridge scuffed then scuttled by a roar of cleats be a wriggling
troubled bowl,

12

be a bad hole.

13

With a lung-full heaped full of ballast for scope,
I come in low

14

over the false-eyed leafy copses

15

bent in for the lack or how two who love do a deal
to steal a moment in

16

from the sea of throws.

ZACHARY MASON

from The Lost Books of the Odyssey

The Iliad of Odysseus

I HAVE OFTEN WONDERED WHETHER ALL MEN ARE COWARDS LIKE I AM. Achaea's flower, the chosen of Ares, disciplined, hard-muscled men who do not know what fear is—all a fraud, a conceit for bards and braggarts that has nothing to do with the vapid squalor of war.

I have no talent for martial arts. I was the despair of the arms master but I was the heir and to his sorrow he was in no position to give up on me. When I dropped my practice sword, hit myself in the head with my spear or broke down in frustrated tears, he would smile grimly and with forced good cheer say, "*Anyone* can learn to fight with enough application." And, lo, the good man was right—despite my clumsiness, fat, stiff muscles and inclination to cry under stress I did eventually attain a modest standard of skill at arms, thanks mostly to my father watching our practices and encouraging the master to beat me bloody if I gave anything less than my absolute best. And beat me he did, and often, though to his credit I do not think he relished it. After a whipping he would help me up, dress my wounds and say, "Sorry, boy, but it's your father's orders and you'll get worse than that when you go to war." I dreamed of coming into my title and having him flogged and enslaved.

The exception to my general military ineptitude was with the bow, at which I excelled. When I pulled the string the world became quiet and I was aware only of the target, which I regarded with interest but no malice as my arrow all but invariably found its mark. Unfortunately for me this only exacerbated my reputation for effeminacy—as it allows one to strike from safety, the bow is a coward's weapon, the sort of thing used by nomads and Asiatics. I could shoot rooks in the eye at a hundred paces all I liked and still be despised.

My shameful aptitudes did not end with archery—I was also articulate. I have never been at a loss for a tale, lie or synonym. I could recite the epic of Hercules after hearing it just four times. I was ideally suited to be a bard, a profession fit only for villains, wandering masterless men who live at the pleasure of their landed betters, as my father reminded me when I broached the idea. He and his men would say things like "We are here to live the stories, not compose them!" Sing, Muses, of the wrath of god-like shit-for-brains, hereditary lord of the mighty Coprophagoi, who skewered a number of other men with his pig-sticker and valued himself highly for so doing.

When I was twenty Agamemnon the High King came to the island to raise an army. His brother's wife had preferred a sloe-eyed prince with a palace to her lawful husband, a Spartan King who lived in a mud hut and slept with his pigs for warmth. Privately, I saluted her common sense.

My father volunteered me to lead our troops. Age was slowing him down and he had lately been transferring more administrative responsibility to me but I hadn't expected to be war-leader so soon. I had been making a point of carrying myself as I thought a battle-hardened hero would, loudly scorning danger, and though I thought my act was transparent enough for a child to penetrate it seems I had convinced both my father and the men in the guard—they gave a cheer when they got the news and immediately started divvying up old King Priam's daughters and treasures.

Refusing to go to war was impossible. The only excuse would be madness or infirmity, and it would have been very suspicious if I were struck by a terrible disease just when it was time to sail. At this point a man of the common run would have realized the situation was impossible and bowed to fate but my cowardice made me capable of the extraordinary.

My father threw a feast in the High King's honor and I got my first good look at him. I knew his reputation as a warrior but in his face was a willfulness such as I had never seen. He looked like a man who would lash out with all his strength if even minutely crossed.

I played the part of the young-buck-keen-to-make-a-name for all I was worth. How eager I was to leave boring, quiet Ithaca, see the world, win renown by feats of arms and so forth. Looking distant for a moment, I said, "And Troy is a long, long way away? If a man took ill there I suppose he would have no option but to stay and fight?" and darted a quick, inquisitive look at Agamemnon. Palamedes, Agamemnon's lieutenant, a bald, silent man who thought much and spoke little, looked at me as though I had suddenly become interesting.

After a few minutes I made myself look as ill as possible and made my excuses. I went out, closed the door behind me, and, taking a deep breath, fell down thrashing, my heel hammering against the floor. The door opened—there were Agamemnon and Laertes, Palamedes and the arms master, all the men I had grown up with looking down at me as I writhed on the ground, saliva dribbling down my chin. Through my convulsive chattering I growled, "Close the door. Close the door!" Abashed, they did, leaving me to complete my fit in private. After a minute I desisted, sick with relief.

The next morning I showed up for arms practice as usual, face ashen, very grave. Father was there, all but unmanned with grief—his son was damaged goods, all but unmarriageable and not fit for battle. Agamemnon clapped an avuncular hand on my shoulder and asked me how I did. Palamedes asked if I ever felt the touch of god when the fits came on me. I knew that seizures were often preceded by epiphanies so I reluctantly admitted that I did—sometimes, I told them, it was as though Pallas Athena herself spoke with me while my spell played out, whispering secrets in my ear. It was the first thing that came to mind. I had their rapt attention, which made me confident and, like a fool, I embellished on my intimacy with the god. Agamemnon smiled and I was horrified to see in his face an emotion I had thought alien to him—generosity. "My boy, your luck is in. Palamedes here was telling me about the warrior Laon, who suffered the same disease you do, but it never slowed him down, not for a moment. So you see, there is no need to be concerned. And I'm even told its lucky, the god's-touch disease. And for this campaign I believe we'll be needing all the luck we can get, ha ha!" He clapped me on the shoulder again and went off to see about his ships. Palamedes smiled at me before following him and I decided that if I got the chance I would kill him.

I had hoped that the war would be short and I could return with an undeserved reputation for bravery. Spirits were high, in the beginning. Agamemnon and his lieutenants expected a quick victory but it was soon evident to me that there would be no such thing. The Trojan walls were high and thick, our siege engines were grossly inadequate and there was not a single skilled sapper in the army. The Trojans were as aware of our weaknesses as we were ignorant of their strengths—they would only sally when they could bring overwhelming force to bear at little risk to themselves. Most of the time they were content to let us spend our strength against their impregnable walls.

Their city was larger and their fortifications stronger than anything in Achaea—I realized that Agamemnon was basing his strategy on his experience attacking the little towns on the Attic coast. I was the first, but by no means the last, to realize that our failure was certain. I tried to persuade Agamemnon and his cronies with artful words but they scorned me, wondering rhetorically which campaigns I had fought in and whether I wouldn't rather skulk off home, leaving honor unavenged and glory lying in the dust? In vain I argued that honor could as well be served without wasting time, men and matériel.

The camp smelled of unwashed men, which was bad enough, and made worse by drunk soldiers who couldn't stagger the hundred feet to the latrine trenches. Only I seemed to mind the stench—the others breathed it in as though it were perfume. They were content to spend every night drinking and lying about their conquests of cities and women. During the day they fought and those lucky enough to survive came back to camp to repeat the cycle the next day, world without end.

Many times I was on the verge of just leaving and sailing back to Ithaca. I did not flee only because I would have lost all face with my father and our subjects. As father and I know, and as we try not to remind them, there is no good reason for our subjects to pay their taxes, row our ships, fight our battles or tip their caps to us other than tradition and the threat of violence (which is implicit, nicely civilized and glossed over with older, better families like mine). Much as I loathed the war there was at least the prospect of a tolerable life afterwards. My father would have disinherited me if I had shamed our house and I would rather have died than come down in the world.

I have speculated that brave men do not exist, but Achilles son of Peleus was an exception. The young chief of the Myrmidons was built like a mountain but fleet as the wind. Women found him comely but he reserved all his affections for two young men, Patroclus and Antilochus. In combat he was the most cold-blooded and terrifying man I have ever seen. I took to following in his wake on the field—I earned the first notches in my shield by finishing off the Trojans he wounded. Here, I thought, was a man who was in his way as different from the common run as me.

I made him my study. He was devoted to a sea goddess, Thetis, in front of whose portable shrine he sat for hours each day in silent prayer. I watched him train with Patroclus and the Myrmidons. He came to practice early and for every javelin his men threw, even the champions, he threw three. He was, in his way, as relentless as death. Cultivating him was easy, as the other chiefs found him stand-offish and abstemious and he had few friends. It was easy to draw him out—I got the sense that he liked to talk about himself but rarely got the chance. He told me he had been blessed by Thetis at birth and made immortal, immune to every weapon. But for all that, his immunity was limited—the day of his death was already fixed by Fate and not even the gods could change it. He therefore intended to win what glory he could in his set span of days. I questioned the value an immortality that lasted exactly until one died but his fatalism was impregnable and he laughed at me and called me a sophist.

The war dragged on for years. Only our numbers kept us from being routed. We lost five men for each one of theirs, which was, alarmingly to my mind at least, considered an acceptable rate of attrition, as we outnumbered them ten to one. I did not wish to number myself among the sacrifices and therefore became a skilled tactician, anticipating the places where the Trojans would attack and being elsewhere. From time to time I would guess where the Trojans would be weak and ambush them, just to avoid getting a reputation as a man who avoided trouble. Over the years lines of tribal authority weakened and men with knowing eyes and similar dispositions gravitated to my troop.

I was with Achilles when his fate found him. Hector, the mainstay of the Trojan army, had appeared in the thick of battle, scattering Greeks before him. Achilles went straight to meet him but his bodyguards were shot with arrows and he found himself more or less alone (as always, I was hanging back, waiting to see what developed). Egged on by Hector, the Trojan rank and file hurled themselves at Achilles, overwhelming him. Moved to a rare feat of self-exposure I cried out, from a certain distance, daring them to come over and fight me—I had a clear path back to the encampment—but they ignored me. Achilles never shouted for help but burst out of them, spear whirling, killing many and, best of all, putting his spear through great Hector's jaw. The remaining Trojans fled, then, but instead of pursuing them Achilles stood there leaning on his spear. I approached and found him grey faced, his left foot soaked in gore—he had finally been wounded and it was a bad one, the tendon in his left ankle slashed through. I put his arm over my shoulder and helped him hobble back to camp. The doctors dressed the wound but it got infected and when I went to visit him I could smell the gangrene. I pled with him to have the leg off as the physicians said he must, or die, but he refused, saying death was better than life as a cripple. Within days he got his preference.

This was five years into the war. Any sane man would have called it a loss, or perhaps found some way to construe it as a victory, and gone home, but Agamemnon was immovable. I was not the only one who tried to talk him into decamping but we might as well have debated with a stone.

I decided to end the war on my own. Knowing we would never take the city, I decided to go straight for the war's cause, so one night I put on beggar's rags and snuck into Troy with a bag of gold and a skinning knife. I went to the palace and lingered on the steps, begging alms of passersby (many of whom I recognized from the field, none of whom gave me a second glance). Helen passed by with her maids, all slaves, three Achaeans among them.

That night I slept under an abandoned market stall, stray dogs and adulterers padding by me. The Greeks probably thought I had deserted but I was both braver and more treacherous than they supposed. Early the next morning one of the Achaean maids came out to do her marketing. I fell into step behind her and, when opportunity arose, dragged her into an alley with my hand over her mouth. "Don't scream, sister," I said in Greek. "I have gifts, first gold and then your freedom, and in exchange I only want a little gold of another kind." I told her what to do to earn her passage home. She said nothing but took the bag and the knife and I saw in her eyes that she was a viper, that she hated Helen and her bondage and would do the dreadful thing I asked.

I crept back to the Greek camp and was asked no questions. The next night the maid was dragged to my tent by a guard who had found her wandering within our perimeter. She gave me a dark canvas sack within which was a mass of tangled, blood-spattered blonde hair with chunks of scalp still attached. The tone and richness of the hair identified it as the locks of none other than Helen of Troy, late of Sparta, no longer the most beautiful of women in respect of her recent death and mutilation but for all I knew the most lovely of ghosts. I noticed the brown crust under the maid's fingernails and called for a bath, telling her the hot water would wash away her bondage as the sea would wash away all indignities over the course of her imminent trip home.

That evening I called a general assembly. With the heat of the bonfire on my back and the eyes of every Greek on me I told them that in one of my fits Athena had revealed that though Troy could not be taken, the war could be won. My announcement was greeted with hoots of derision. Loud voices wondered how this was possible. I shouted, "By bringing an end to the cause of this war, to Helen of the house of Tyndareus!" And I held up her hair, instantly recognizable in the firelight. A moan went up from the men and Menelaus leapt to his feet trembling, knocked over his wine-cup and called for a sword, a sword. I threw her hair at his feet, saying "Your wanton wife is dead and there's your honor cleansed. The war is won, let us go home." The Spartans gathered around him and some fool put a blade in his hand. The rest of the men gathered behind me, homesick and warsick, and turned hard gazes on the Spartans.

I had hoped that the Spartans, outnumbered, would back down. Menelaus and Agamemnon would bear me a grudge 'til the end of their days but let them, in everyone else's eyes I would be a hero—Odysseus, who had won the war at a stroke and abased the High King's pride. Unfortunately I had underestimated Spartan discipline and the hold the Spartan kings had on their men. They got their arms and my followers got their arms and battle was imminent when the Trojans attacked.

There must have been a spy in our camp—they could hardly have found a more vulnerable moment. We were disorganized, distracted, half armed, at odds with each other and tightly clustered. They rushed us from all sides. The fighting was bitter and in the first minutes I thought we would be overwhelmed. I fought my way away from the bonfire and found a store-tent to hide in as shrieking filled the night behind me.

The night passed with glacial slowness except when I cut the throat of a Trojan soldier who came in looking for spoil. I had hoped that our numbers would outweigh their initiative but by the time the false dawn lit the sky things were not much quieter—the Trojans were making an all-out effort to break us. It is strange to say that it occurred to me to find my men and rally them to the banner of the Laertides but I quickly suppressed this pointless impulse.

I borrowed the dead Trojan's bloodstained cloak and helmet, reluctantly left the relative security of the tent and made for the camp's edge. Trojans saw my helmet and assumed I was one of them. Greeks made to attack me till I hailed them in their own language. I passed a few knots of melee, my brothers in arms doing noble deeds and dying. I was terrified for my own life and did nothing to help them, though the circumstances of their deaths are etched in my memory. I clambered over the rude timber walls at the camp's boundary and dropped down onto the sand below. From within the wall came cries of agony and the roar of flames—the Trojans must have gotten at the ships. Without, all was peaceful—a wide empty beach stretched before me and Troy was just visible on my left. It seemed unnatural that I could leave so easily. I threw my borrowed helmet into the surf and started walking.

After an hour the war seemed as though it had been a dream. I looked back and saw black pillars of smoke over the camp and over Troy.

I took stock of my situation. I had a sword, bread and a bag of silver. I was on a coast where I had no friends and many enemies, though few of them knew my name. Having no alternative, I kept walking south along the shore. I had heard of a city not far from Troy and in two days reached it. The guard at the gate asked me who I was and what I wanted. I had a mad impulse to say, "I am a sinister-minded foreigner who has lately been making war on the principal city of your country in hopes of rapine, pillage and blood-soaked revenge," but instead said I was an itinerant bard hoping to sing for my supper. The guard looked at my sword and said I carried a strange sort of lyre. I replied that bandits abounded, many of them desperate and dangerous renegades from the war up north, and I had discovered by trial and error that it was more effective to hit them with a sword than a musical instrument. Indeed, my lyre had not survived the first trial but I was pleased to say my sword was in good shape even after many encores—my most popular ballad was "Feint Toward the Heart and Slash the Hamstring" but "Throw Sand in Their Eyes and Stab the Sword-Hand" was gaining popularity.

I found a place with the lord of the city. I had been afraid it would be galling to sit at the lower table but in the event found a bard's station unobjectionable—I was given all I needed and there was no offensive familiarity. At first I sang the old stand-bys—"Theseus in the Repeating Labyrinth," "The Tale of Medusa's Shade," "Athena's Lover" and the like. I had the rapt attention of everyone from the lord to the potboy. Even the dogs under the tables watched with heads cocked.

Refugees trickled in over the following weeks and from their accounts I pieced together the story of the war's end. The Trojans had overplayed their hand—they set fire to the Greek ships but in their race to the shore left many Greek soldiers behind them, intact and desperate. Diomedes, an independent-minded Greek general, wrote off the ships as a loss and had his soldiers mount up and race for Troy, emptied of men, its gates hanging open. The Greeks erupted into the city and gave vent to their rage. When the Trojans saw the smoke they rushed home to stop the sack and hours and then days of vicious house-to-house fighting followed, until Troy and the Greek ships were all in ashes, the soldiers slain or scattered, both forces broken. The only Greek ship to survive was Agamemnon's, which has been anchored out in the bay—he and a handful of men sailed away that night, their sails filled with the spark-laden wind pouring out of the burning city, leaving their countrymen to get home as best they could.

I was concerned that the refugees would recognize me but no one thought to look for a Greek captain in the face of the bard sleeping on sheep-skins by the hearth. Still, when a month had passed the city was thick with displaced Trojans and I decided to go.

There were few bards that far out on the periphery of the Greek speaking world and I flourished. I never failed to get applause when I gave them the classics and soon became confident enough to invent material. I never went as far as sussing out the local headman's lineage and singing a paean—I preferred to keep an emotional distance from my patrons. I took to telling the story of Odysseus of the Greeks, cleverest of men, whose ruses had been the death of so many. (In the same moment I formulated this epithet it occurred to me that it was Helen's treacherous maid who told the Trojans when to attack. I wondered whether she were wealthy now or dead, or perhaps both, lying in a beehive tomb with gold and wine jars piled around her.)

It was when I was a guest in Tyre that I first heard another bard singing one of my songs and it occurred to me that I had in my hands the means of making myself an epic hero. What good is the truth when those who were there are dead or scattered? So I rearranged the events of Troy's downfall, eliding my betrayals and the woman-killing, and made a good tale out of it. My account of Odysseus's heroics changed according to my mood. Sometimes I led the defence as the Trojans went to burn the ships, sometimes I put myself in Diomedes' boots and led the counter-attack on Troy. Sometimes Athena loved me so much that she shattered the Trojan curtain wall with a thunderbolt.

Diomedes' cavalry, the maid's bag of gold and the hours hiding in the airless tent combined somehow to give me the idea of Greek soldiers ensconced in a treacherous wooden horse. The ruse appealed to me and though I could never come up with a fully satisfactory reason why the Trojans would blithely drag a suspicious fifty foot tall wooden statue into their city, I glossed over their deliberations and the story was well received. I told the story so many times that I sometimes thought I really remembered Menelaus breathing fast and shallow in the stuffy darkness of the horse's belly.

I traveled widely and won much acclaim. I lived among other men but was not of them and this suited me precisely. On the island Chios I bought a gentleman's farm where I passed the winters. There were women, sometimes the same one for years, but I never married any of them and their names ran together.

In the tenth year after leaving Ithaca I realized I was done with singing and with new shores and cities. I gave the Chian farm to my woman at the time, and there were no hard feelings when I left for port and hitched a ride on a Phoenician trader bound in the general direction of home. At sea I lay on my back on deck and stared at the grey skies while composing an account of the last five years. From a muscle-bound Scythian brigand who had caught me stealing cheeses from his cave I made a one-eyed cannibal ogre. From the cold winters on Chios when I spoke with no one but my lover I made island imprisonments with kindly witches (there are, as far as I have seen, and I have seen much, no gods, no spirits and no such thing as witches, but I seem to be the only one who knows it—the best I can say for the powers of the night is that they make good stories).

At last the traders dropped me on the Ithacan shore and I hid my chests of gold in a cave I remembered. I cast my old cloak into the woods and using a tide-pool for a mirror shaved off the beard I had started when I landed on Asian shores. Clean shaven, I looked absurdly young. I strode off to my father's hall and the predictable kerfuffle ensued—amazement, tears, glad reunions, questions, more tears, feasts, speeches. Tedium. I played my part as best I could but just wanted it to end so I could spend my remaining years with sword and harp on the wall, making loans at high interest and fathering sons. I never sang again, fearful of being recognized, but I got some second-hand fame as a patron of bards. I was most generous with those who had my songs word-perfect.

Victory Lament

MY BIRTHRIGHTS WERE GREAT STRENGTH, copper beauty and an enduring sadness. My mother Thetis told me I could not die and indeed though the years withered men like autumn leaves I persisted. Just as my body stayed young so did my temperament—I wandered from Gaul to India and back, taking great delight in seeking out the best fighters and cutting them down. One year a new star appeared in the sky and I decided to go to the imperial court and appropriate its significance for myself before the astrologers arrogated it to flood, locusts or plague. I won an audience with Emperor Agamemnon by thrashing the sixteen spearmen who stood scowling before his summer palace. I sketched the shadow of a bow, smiled up into his darkening countenance and proposed a wager. I would engage his two greatest champions both at once—if they won, I would be his slave and set his perfumed foot on the necks of nations but if I won I would loot what I liked from his palace. The vizier Odysseus whispered worriedly in His Imperial Highness's ear but Agamemnon brushed him aside, smiled at me hatefully and summoned his paladins—Ajax, built like a mountain, who drew his strength from the deeps of the earth and Diomedes, who was so fast he moved in a blur and had crossed blades with the gods.

The fight would have been disappointing had there not been the emperor's impotent fury for relish. When I tired of the hollow sound of their skulls knocking together I dumped them before the throne and claimed my rights. I loudly announced that I would start my pillaging in the harem and strode straight past the eunuchs with their cruelly barbed halberds and up the long stairs to the high tower where Agamemnon, ever fearful of cuckolding, kept his women.

I had not meant to do more than provoke him into seeking out the greatest champions to kill me—that way I would know once and for all if I had any equal in the world. Agamemnon lacked invention—it must have been Odysseus who advised him to weld shut the doors to the harem tower that first night while I was distracted. The walls were five feet thick and the windows no wider than arrow slits. There was no way to get to the roof and no way out except the fused iron doors—I was stuck. The girls must have been expensive, as they kept passing in food and water. They were a delight at first, but soon became tiresome—always a hothouse of intrigue and gossip, the harem's suddenly absolute isolation brought out an absolute cattiness. There was nothing to do but practice the sword and meditate, day in and day out.

A year and a day after I had been locked inside the harem there was a shriek of metal and I went down to find them prying open the door to my prison. Odysseus was there holding a white flag of truce. Behind him were fifty men with nets and bolos and a hundred archers with what I could tell even at a hundred paces were poison tipped arrows. Odysseus apologized for the mixed reception—he had wanted to talk to me but Agamemnon would not permit the gate to be opened without all this, he said, gesturing to the pale, trembling soldiers behind him. He sat down beside me on the stairs and poured arak from a copper flask. I had not tasted spirits since my confinement and drank happily. Odysseus expressed his opinion that I had come to court not so much for conquest as in hopes of finding a worthy enemy. If this were the case, I was bound to be disappointed—the late Ajax, undefeated prior to his death at my hands, was the strongest the kingdom had to offer. I could always set myself single-handed against all the Emperor's armies but at best that would be like a lion fighting a swarm of biting ants.

He said I had chosen poorly by going to the harem—had I gone to the treasury instead I might have found the secret panel set in the floor that led to a maze of caverns in one of which there was a cedar chest guarded by tiny white spiders (their poison of staggering virulence) and within that chest found what he had brought me today, a small key of black and twisted iron. This was the key, he told me, that opened the gate the gods had locked behind them when they tired of the world and finally left it to its own devices. It had been held close by the Atreides dynasty since time out of mind, as much to keep the gods out as mortals in. Odysseus freely admitted that he wanted me out of the kingdom but said that the only way to do this was to see that I got what I wanted, elsewhere—he told me to go and seek a match among the gods because I would not find it among men.

I set out for the iron gates of heaven, which as is widely known are a thousand miles north and a thousand miles east of the mountaintop grave of the philosopher Lao Tsu. In time I found them, set in a high glacier on a mountain peak where blizzards never let up shrieking.

I unlocked the great black iron door with Odysseus's key and opened it onto a staircase that led up indefinitely into a still, starry night. I trudged upward for some indeterminate duration, the night unchanging around me. (I still don't know how long it took. Now and then my mind would turn from the task of putting one foot in front of the other but I pulled myself back from the brink of reflection, knowing it would lead to despair.) At last I reached the top and found a silver gate that was the twin of the iron one, though it had been so long since I left the Earth (it was invisible behind me and had been time out of mind) that I wondered if the first gate had been a dream. I smashed the silver gate with my fist and burst in on an astonished heavenly bureaucracy, blue-skinned ministers of celestial protocol gaping at me from between their desks' towers of memoranda. For all their surprise, retaliation was swift and comprehensive—slavering, white-tusked demons bayed insults and hurled burning brands, a grim-faced god with the Milky Way in his quiver shot stars at me and mad-eyed devas attacked from all sides at once and no side at all, and through it all the Emperor of Heaven for whom the world and all the worlds were as baubles in his hand did not deign to turn his august eyes in my direction. Here, finally, was true power to oppose me but to my lasting sorrow I had forgotten what failure was and my blade flickered through the hearts of my antagonists until I came before the Emperor of Heaven who continued to disdain me even as I cut through his excellent jade neck. He came crashing down from his high throne, mountain ranges wearing away on the distant Earth as he fell and fell and fell. Now I have taken his throne and read his book and the now docile devas flit about my shoulders, waiting, perhaps forever, for me to impart my wisdom, which is that I have learned nothing, know nothing, wish I had never picked up a sword, left my hut, been born.

JARED WHITE

The Deer and the Hedgehog and the Gardener

Herein we describe plants as a function   of desire. This
Demands   a story of intellectuals in the fields

Of good old Mister Roderick, Johnny   Come Lately and
Sir Manqué. Rounding the bend   we come to a Roman Aquaduct

And ducked   under the arch. This deserves a dozen replays
In the media   having graduated from the library

To the inner ear   just shy of the cerebellum. If the book said
Keep your thoughts   to yourself, do. The plants are deafening

And if you hear these uneasy   noises, we may blush.
All the definitions involve shaking   us awake from imagining

And no one likes to be awakened   to actual facts.
That is why you're here and why we   are tending the tomatoes.

Otherwise all we'd eat would be rice and millet.   Indentured
Servitudes.   Have you come around and kicked the tires?

There's a passage in which the plants   did it by themselves
And even still there was a tendency   to make arrangements.

The gardener worked hard to make sure   everything is very beautiful
And edible also. With elbow grease the former   starts including me

With my dreadful innovations. Who dreads the legumes   of a mere
Roderick? I can always become   more hifalutin in passing

These annuals and those   London planetrees. When you remember
Unfortunately you don't actually   remember. The story

Buries the story with this particular shovel.   By the hazelnut grove
We were educating   each other to our likes and dislikes, refinements

While Evelyn loved Roderick on her days   off. We laugh at such
Staff setups. From this angle you can see   the newest cultivars.

Even no one tending   is almost someone. For a while at least
We can nibble through. Is this boulder ersatz or   just too heavy?

I'll never tell good parks   from the woods and good gardens
From a salad. The forest   as we walk forms rows of trees.

Let us then derelict our duties. This must be the mulch   and this
Your meditation rock. See here the Roderick   last seen

Mistaking poetry for fiction.   In the greenhouse he would not
Have erred. We call this the school within   the schools

Like at the gates of the garden I wondered   what were for.
Breezes that shook us in our travels   shock us with their gentleness

As we stroll under the galleries to where it was   we were going anyway
In conversation. How do you always do everything   so slowly?

JOANNA SONDHEIM

from Vera

between us and the river
    V., heavy-lidded, her shocked companion.

if there were horses, either stock-still or backwards in flight,
a shimmering at in our favorite hour, an automobile has arrived.

as a result, the ladies sleep and pale.

    through evening's sultry sediments,
V.'s fingers follow where the light goes.
    or the rumor of appearance?

the shriek is humored, the wail less so.

upon returning, our plot of land and the house's movements across it.

V. suggests there's been a change.

if this is the wind, we'll start with Mister ___, his courage is astounding.
by his faulty stature, his feeble feet. V. tying and tripping, giggles at the loss.

through the crack in the door
the moor, its wild wind, some
grassy tugboat, moats, the holes wind up
and

these ladies vanish in any case, such wealthy skirts,
flyaway tendrils, the gloves and jewels we gathered on the stoop.

V. taps her nails on the balcony, or the noise I admire.

sometimes music in another wing, that flight, and solitude.

spinning, if they've fainted, it's a difficult find,
Vera takes one under her arm, drops a precious vase,
giggles with her lady friend.

in another story, lady slamming doors and outside the dry weather
starts small fires on the porch.

     V. naughty, the room is very cold, but a consuming breeze, and our lady
per usual, a heap on the floor.

there is work to do, a tear in the drapery.

     if there is sun on the other side, and the animals that appear.
     H. might alert a stampede, he might sit and drill holes in the frozen lake.

     H. watched I didn't leave, and so walk circles near the window.
     notice things moving in the grass below, notice the grass below is moving.

where the whistling originates, a wind tunnel, or:
the slippery tide in the hallways,

       ,,.one got loose in the drawing room, I follow
       the fingers that brush my cheek,
Vera's laughter, hasten in bolting the shutters.

there was one morning, H. watched the dog shivering in the corner,
a city park that is close by has flooded, H. watched damp birds in the window.

     I dream that the house has been haunted, wake to find colors above my bed
inside of a sweet thrill, V. snaps her fingers and dances in a surrounding room.

brushed as if a glacier,
  , lady's hand lies slimly,
the meaning of all this nonsense?
      tut tut, but
surprised she found her skirt lifting on its own.

      ghostie Vera is making lace
for the windows. her tiny needles.
in the library,   a secret desk drawer.

the youngest in the room keeps track of indiscretions.

many animal analogies, one for things smaller than eye level.

a house that is nothing more than hallways,
     how dreary! a couch is for collapsing,

Vera, her handkerchief, from nowhere, to the chest.

BRONWEN TATE

Feasts of the Calendar Year

Icons follow over arch
of door of wings.
            Events lead to events.
More modern varnish. Your solemn
            overarching.

        I
On the table different instruments.

Embrace under canopy
your moment of travail.

We will not address you again.

        II
Not beeswax he swallowed.

A heavier lifting,
domed rejoinder.

Hope your mother meant it.

        III
Does she hesitate in giving?

A hand could flutter
if imperfect.

See her already up the stairs.

        IV
More of a crowd than I would allow.

All the gesturing
sprigs point to season.

Wash the painful possibility.

V
Burnished symmetry and unequal fishes.

Submission hovers,
a hand nears touch.

Mystery may come still into water.

VI
After so much waiting, recognition, spark.

A voice coming
forth out of rust.

Depart in peace our tired dismissal.

VII
If we count back as we have the habit.

Assent is a lily,
a breath.

Already quickening under the folds.

VIII
Branch underfoot a leaf, your coat.

Eye, a gate,
needle, a kneeling camel.

Celebration as deliberate blinders.

IX

Who is looking up, and if not up, where?

Disciples,
your flimsy sandals.

All the lands and seas still to go.

X

When touched the tongue or the ear.

Stop in the street
to understand.

The sudden flame of it.

XI

Hurled from the rocks by force of vision.

If follow
was not clear.

Hide your face from what is.

XII

Is sleep an assumption?

Strange separation,
small, lifted away.

And they left staring at what is not.

ROBERTA ALLEN

Forbidden Territory

IS IT IMPORTANT TO CONSIDER why I want to write about my ex-boyfriend's family? If my ex-boyfriend didn't mind my writing about his family or if I could disguise them in such a way that my ex-boyfriend wouldn't recognize his family, would I still want to write about them? Isn't at least part of my interest in writing about his family the fact that I promised *never* to do so? Is going back on my word a measure of my immaturity? Will reading this to him assuage any guilt I may feel? I know it's possible for some writers to create characters purely from imagination, but it feels unnecessary to fill the world with more fictional characters when there are so many characters who are not fictional and should be written about exactly for that reason, and because anything can be made-up, but the things that happen in real life—for example, the invasion of toads in a Chinese village right before the big earthquake, which, according to the inhabitants, was a sign of impending doom or, years ago, the spontaneous fainting spells of *all* the girls in an Egyptian school, the cause of which has never been discovered—interest me because these events are *real*, but this doesn't solve my quandary about writing about my ex-boyfriend's family which I, of course, could do under another name but that would be like turning the author into a fictional character—creating yet another fiction. His fear, of course, is that I will say something derogatory, something he wouldn't want the world to know. Considering the number of readers who may stumble upon this story, however, using the phrase "the world," is laughable. But I think he knows me well enough to imagine that in a certain *smirky* kind of mood I might write something he won't like. Before I met his parents, I had only met the parents of one other boyfriend who wasn't really a boyfriend but a man I hoped would be my boyfriend. I thought, erroneously, that because he'd invited me home for dinner to meet his parents I would soon get my wish. I was in Australia at the time. Later, I was informed that meeting his family was some sort of *Australian* thing. I've never been big on "family" the way my ex-boyfriend is, calling his mother and sisters often and making frequent visits "home," especially now that his father is gone and his mother is alone in the house in the country. Will my ex mind if I say that I dreaded meeting his mother simply because *she was his mother*? I was pleasantly surprised, however, at how easy it was to talk to her, how she laughed a lot, giggled really, and made me feel right at home, which is something I never felt in my own family. Am I on the right trail? A trail my ex will approve? A trail away from forbidden territory. Away from barbed wire. Away from land mines. What if I mention the cobwebs? Will my ex take offense if I say that the first thing I noticed were cobwebs when I entered his parents' house? If I tell you how shocked I was by the cobwebs, will he say that cobwebs are no big deal? And isn't he right? After all, that room, though it was a *large* room (and would have been the living room in someone else's house), was only used for storing old discarded furniture and decades of dusty flea market finds, reminding me (a little) of a man I used to know, a PhD, who spent his entire two million dollar inheritance on board games(!) that he stacked to the ceiling in his Manhattan apartment, leaving him no space to live. He did not have cobwebs, however. At least, I don't recall any. I can feel the *daggers* aimed at me in the eyes of my ex at this point for mentioning, not only the cobwebs, but the clutter in the storage room which, in time, his mother sold in a series of yard sales. To be fair, I should say that several years after that first visit, I moved from the city to the country and now have cobwebs of my own. The other day, in fact, I watched a tiny spider trap a much larger ladybug while the spider dangled on a thread of light. Then, however, I couldn't stop thinking about the cobwebs (which were nowhere else in the house) while his mother kept talking, giggling, about what I don't remember, I only remember her smiling and friendly and nothing like the grim picture I had painted in my mind of a "mother." She said that once she had found a snake in the bathroom, as though it was perfectly natural to find a snake in the house. Would I ever understand her? A mother wearing Bermuda shorts, a tee-shirt, hair cropped short, a mother who mowed the lawn and gardened and taught her son to play ball? A mother who wore sturdy shoes and hiked in the woods with her son and two daughters? A mother called Sally by her children? How about a father they called Ben? Why was it easier to understand a father called Ben? A father asleep in an easy chair in the living room which is the way I drew my own father once when I was twelve. Later, after my father's suicide, my mother and I found a fortune in change that must have fallen out of his pants' pockets over the years and lay buried until we looked beneath the cushion of that chair. Ben's chair was beige. A beige naugahyde chair with wide arms that over time seemed to consume Ben, who had once been tall and husky. He seemed to slowly liquefy into that slick plasticity. Is it wrong to say Ben was sick? Is sickness something to hide? Something to be ashamed of? Maybe I shouldn't have mentioned his illness before saying that I felt instantly connected to him, maybe because he and my ex looked so much alike, and although his father was nearly eighty, I found him as attractive as I found his son, maybe even more so. Will my ex be shocked by this? I liked the slow way his father spoke, carefully considering each word before it left his lips. Ben, my ex-boyfriend's father, who had been an architect, a *thinking* man, who also drew and painted. Ben, whose large sable brush I still use. By the time he was blind, had he forgotten or lost interest in dictating his life story into a tape recorder? A project I had encouraged him to start—while he still could. Music was Ben's last frontier. He played a recorder and sang old songs, accompanied by my ex on guitar. The whole family was musical. Sometimes they would sit in a circle, play instruments, and sing. Now that I've said the word "family" again, can I include my ex boy-friend's sisters without giving away family secrets? Can I say his father's illness was only one family tragedy? Doesn't every family have one or more tragedies? In the framed family portrait hanging in the hall, taken nearly thirty years ago and slight-ly faded by the sun, I think I see a hint of tragedy in their faces. Or is it only be-cause *I know*? Does a tragedy ever end? Once my ex gave a ukulele to one of his sisters. But I no longer remember which one. Was it the sister who, every week, would sit for hours by the kitchen window, slowly, carefully copying with colored markers pictures from Sally's mail order catalogs? Or the secretive one who lives up north in a subzero climate, who cuts her mother's hair when she comes to visit but lets her own hair grow waist-long? For the sake of the story, have I said too little about his sisters? About the tragedy? Or have I already revealed too much? Am I bringing up past pain? Digging my finger in wounds that will never heal? Am I running the risk of damaging—or worse, ruining—my close friendship with my ex? Am I creating yet another tragedy? A tragedy I could easily avoid by respecting his wishes? Is tragedy too strong a word to use? Am I being melodramatic? Isn't tragedy the word we use for something that was *never* supposed to happen? Something that divides life into *before* and *after*? When tragedy strikes, don't we still try to believe it didn't happen? Say it's a dream? A nightmare from which we will escape? When we don't escape, what then? What does my ex do? He plays guitar and sings in a group. He spends an evening a week at a chess club. He dates a poet in Astoria. He walks on a beach in Long Island. He drinks a little vodka before bed. He takes the sister who doesn't get out much to the mall. He helps his mother around the house. His mother prays, goes to church. It helps, she says.

NORMAN LOCK

from Pieces for Small Orchestra

16.

A LACK OF ANIMALS HAS STALLED THE PROGRESS OF OUR ZOO! Elephants, though large, are by themselves inadequate to constitute it with simili- tude. The people will not come for peanuts and pachyderm alone! The Engineer insists he can fabricate a facsimile of any animal, bird, or fish we wish. (He has a box of schematic diagrams, as well as dance steps by Astaire on paper patterns with which he hopes to acquire savoir-faire.) "There must be space inside, however, for a mechanism that can be wound up by a key." He rejects transistors as inelegant. "But the elephants are real!" shouts the Zoologist. "Our menagerie must not be marred by incongruity!" The General is impressed by his intransigence and avers, "Too many have forsaken principles in favor of a life of artifice and sloth." We forgive the General his remark because of the absinthe he is drinking, a habit acquired in a youth misspent on the Con- tinent with poets, rogues, and others living by their wits. The Taxidermist volunteers to stuff the elephants with mattresses. He has already done much in the case of swans with feather-dusters that is admirable. "There will be no offal to pick up," he says, "once they're dead." (As if dung were our only concern!) "What is wanted is monkeys!" rasps the Zoologist brandishing *Introduction to the Primates* by Daris Swindler as if it were a club. We scold him for his savagery as we swivel on our barstools to listen to his discourse: "The shaggy red orangutan, *Pongo pygmaeus* of Sumatra, will give the most delight. Orangutans are arboreal—according to Swindler, who has been among them. So we will have reason to look up once more, now that the sky is no longer with us." "But there are no trees!" grumbles the Prime Minister, who used to punt on a river underneath them when the world was everywhere in leaf and rivers rich with fish. The orchestra wakes long enough to play Brahms' lullaby, which affects us like a soporific, i.e., we fall—each and every one—to sleep, including the Funambulist, who balances on her wire by an instinct stronger than uncon- sciousness. While we doze, a troop of shaggy red orangutans materializes from thin air, or so it seems; and with them is no other than Daris Swindler arrived from Borneo and the Wild Men there. He wears a watch-cap and bell-bottomed sailor's pants because he was one (a sailor, not a pair of pants!) before the study of man's interaction with the simian absorbed him. The Cigarette Girl minces forward with a lacquered tray of smokes. Everything moves so slowly while we are mired in this dream! Daris takes a Camel and dilates on a favorite theme: the venery of *Homo sylvestris*—orangutan, which word is Malay for forest man. "According to seventeenth-century Dutch physician and anatomist Nicholaas Tulp, orangs are as amorous as the Satyrs of the ancient world." So says Daris, quoting the original. Our dreaming selves are polyglot! The General is delighted. "But what," the P.M. asks, "will become of our zoological specimens when we wake and, furthermore, whose dream this time has enthralled us? The answer involves a pin jabbed into the limbs of the musicians one by one until—having reached the Bassoonist—we swim up into consciousness with an appetite for sardine sandwiches. Who can fathom the devious paths of desire? "Look!" the General shouts. "Swindler and his evolutionary gang are gone! Here's a cone of ash that fell from his Camel, and here and here and here is dung!" We retire to the Metaphysicians' Room to debate the (in-)substantiality of figures in a dream (including orangutans)—what weight, if any, they may have; what life for them when they return to where we found them while we slept.

35.

THE PRIME MINISTER'S OPINION is that a Magus is among us—or even two, who (the P.M. cannot help his pedantic nature) must then be called Magi, whose gifts are not always so beneficent as frankincense and myrrh. Might not the General's absence in the photograph of him on the carousel be due to a magician's prank (unless the General is a ghost or vampyr, which the Chanteuse swears he's not)? Perhaps he is a mental episode occurring in the consciousness (or, more likely, un-) of a *jinni* (whose plural form is *jin*). "The Arabian ambassador, whom we often entertained at home when I was in the government, often spoke of them as beings delighting in bedevilment. Might not all of us here be nothing more than toys for one, or two, of those spiteful Mohammedan characters out of Sir Richard Burton?" The Plumber, just returned from unclogging, so to speak, a hotel artery (why not allow the metaphor?), pooh-poohs the idea. "There's no such thing, or things," he says. "My concept of an Over Mind capable of Thought Projection is much more probable." The Taxidermist yawns to hear again this old ground covered. He dreams of a perfect world in which everyone is stuffed and, if motility is desired, equipped with clockwork motors designed by his friend the Engineer. The Telepath happens to read his mind and scoffs: "You propose a universe of robots! Who wants to make love to a girl who winds down?" The General, who is the cause of our current wrangle, enters in his pajamas, saying: "I, for one, would not! I may be old-fashioned, even senile as some claim; but I want a girl to sleep with, not a mattress stuffed with fustian and spare parts!" I regard with envy lipstick traces on the General's face, left there by the Chanteuse. Suddenly, I long for the Funambulist and leave them to debate the issue—P.M., Plumber, Taxidermist, Engineer, and Theologian, who until now has been hiding in the wine cellar. In the Venetian Room I find her on the tightrope, reciting from the Balcony Scene of *Romeo and Juliet*: "Take all myself." "I take thee at thy word," I reply, then continue: "Call me but love, and I'll be new baptized; henceforth I never will be Romeo." She: "What man art thou that thus bescreen'd in night so stumblest on my counsel?" "Your husband." [Silence, then:] "Oh." She seems let down. Suspicious, I quiz her: "Aren't you pleased to see me?" "I am, it's just, I was, you know, thinking of Romeo. You are, though I love you dearly, Norman, not him." I reply that no one is, that Romeo's a fiction, a figment of the Bard's imagination, a Mental Projection of Shakespeare's mind. (There is no escaping these subtleties of existence!) "Wilt thou come finally down, dear wife?" I beg. "Not on your life!" she rudely says. "May I then come up?" Although difficult on the high-wire, love has been possible now and then, for us. "*Nyet!*" I sigh and leave her to her lofty pursuit of Elizabethan love. I feel—how can I explain it?—the *tristesse* following—to speak plainly—copulation. Why this should be, since I have not coupled, is a mystery. In the lobby, among potted palms and bellboys, the Prime Minister, Plumber, Taxidermist, and Engineer are at it still. The Theologian has returned to his Amontillado, of all dry sacks his favorite. The P.M. is, at this moment, proposing a costume ball in which to trap the Magus—may the singular noun be sufficient! "He or she or it will be unable to resist dressing up as one or another omniscient and omnipo-tent archetype like Napoleon, Nostradamus, or the Whore of Babylon." It is agreed, though I am dubious. That night in the grand ballroom copied from the Paris Opera House's, the Plumber masquerades as René Descartes; the Taxidermist, a woolly mammoth; the Engineer, Gustave Eiffel with a model of his Tower; and the Prime Minister as Thomas Cromwell. Hoping to in-gratiate myself with my high-wire wife (sworn never to come to ground again), I arrive, in tights and doublet, as her Romeo. Confounding me for the second time today, she passes grandly overhead as Sputnik! "Can I come to you tonight, my love?" I shout toward the frescoed ceiling. Yet again she answers, "*Nyet!*" Why this obsession with Russian language and technol-ogy, I cannot fathom. The Clarinetist plays, each note a knot within a net of music; but no serpent raises its envenomed head. Nearly all the other guests have come, but none reveals a demoniacal character heretofore dis-sembled—not one has dressed as Machiavelli, Stalin, or a modern sadist. So if there is a Magus or two among us, the case is not proved. Whether I am a unit of information within some antic brain, or all is a product of my own imagining—it matters not at all so long as I am here and my wife is roving over head.

JASON BACASA

from There Was Electricity

Belly Button

ARTHUR TOOK A MARKER TO HIS STOMACH and penned the word *Adriatic*. He held one of his mother's mint-colored pumps between his ribs, turned the bathroom faucet on and closed his eyes.

Arthur couldn't believe the number of televisions at the Kmart. He had never cared much for golf, but seeing twelve swinging men somehow justified the sport. It was if they suddenly had capes on.

He found his mother among the t-shirts.
"Arthur, put that back. We are not getting that."
Arthur swung the five-iron through the collection of draping garments.

As they drove home, Arthur, however muffled, called from the back seat. The car smelled of plastic even more than usual.
"Mom, I'm still not dead yet. Look. Mom?"

She had tried several bleaches and stain removers, but all of Arthur's shirts hung on the clothesline still faintly reading like a best-of the world's greatest bodies of water—Atlantic, Bosphorus, Mississippi, Galilee.

The Dead Sea was a bit unlike the others—a field of red covered the better part of the front of the shirt. On the back, SALT was written as if it were the family name above two large double-zeroes.

It wasn't enough that it was ninety-eight degrees outside. It was as if Arthur was nervous all the time too. His mother had never seen anyone sweat like that.

When Arthur opened his eyes, he thought he was inside the Uni-Mart. Fluorescent lights always had the tendency to make him shiver.

In the cab of the ambulance, Arthur imagined customers shopping, buying loose ends for their one-bedroom apartments. It was one customer in particular—the young girl buying cigarettes—that had saved his life. She breathed into his mouth as if she were preparing for a party (as if it were a valve). Little by little, life began to flow through his arms and legs.

In the few seconds before Arthur's head hit the sink, he tried to determine if it were bath water or sweat on top of the toilet seat. The water began to rise high in the bathroom. There had been a severe blow to the stern of the ship. One by one, the passengers jumped to safety—red life-jackets over their suits and gowns.

Crumbs

ARTHUR MARKED THE CONTENTS. Holy bread. Paperclip. Now & Later. Movie ticket. Moth wings. Not quite sure.

Arthur brought his knees to his chest. His father had to carry him out of the theater.

"There were snakes on the ground eating the popcorn. Shouldn't we tell someone? Dad?"

In the bathroom mirror, Kenny put up his hands to fight the mechanic. The hand dryers made the sound of propellers.

Arthur was only collecting fragments from winter jackets. He put what he had found in various jars, each marked with their names. Kenny's jar contained a book of matches. His mother's, a prescription which was never refilled. At dinner time, he presented them as gifts.

"What were you gonna set on fire, Kenny?"

"What?"

"Dad? Who's Linda?"

There were still fifteen cigarettes left in the pack. She smoked every last one of them, all in one sitting.

Feather Pillow

THERE WAS AN ENTIRE OTHER SKY INSIDE OF THE PILLOW CASE. And various bodies of water. They were even beginning to develop forms of transportation.

Arthur collected every pillow in the house. He created a whole universe from them. Strewn across his bedroom floor were six entities, all of which had a written language of their own.

Arthur opened up one pillow case over another. He listened closely as one language leaked onto the next.

I am realistic that a sphere of influence will exist. But, I should hope that no form of colonialism or imperialism will exist in such a world.

The three paragraph essay was supposed to be on England's expansion into Africa.

Ms. Petruzzo put a *D* at the top of the page and then dialed the phone.

"Not only did I not write the paper, but I'm not even sure that a Eurocentric viewpoint is a fair or appropriate way to approach history."

Arthur's father made funny faces into the phone. Dizzy Gillespie made him laugh the hardest.

Arthur lay in the aisle of JCPenney. He had tried every pillow in the department.

"Harder. It has to be harder, Mom. I can't take the risk that life might exist inside."

The retail associate shrugged her shoulders. Arthur closed his eyes.

Arthur stuck the bread knife inside and pulled down. He gathered the feathers in a pile and set them on fire.

"Stupid civilization. Stupid."

The two boys nearby kept fishing. One of them caught a perch.

"When I put the ashes in your hand, you can say whatever you want, just make sure you say you're sorry."

The boy said he was sorry. Then his brother.

MICHAEL CARLSON

Search Party

It is possible in this old process,
that the student in his notebook
finds the missing girl and sharpens her,
makes her hair like seven flames,
like a gift of old linen or spokes
of meat after an explosion,
but her body is never found.

Rain hits the flat of a spatula.
Cuffs of denim snag on stumps.
The maps we mull, ignored
by roads, declare specific stones
and mention fences. Further south,
in a tall dead grass by the river,
the student sketches gooey bees.

Not one man, but many men,
afraid of owls, of years, of stopping,
need her quiet bones to gleam, though sun
for us is pain. These stones in a row
form the base of a wall, but not
a signal mound or pedestal.
We need a place to start from.

Justice

Bee sounds manipulated by fern shadow
will articulate our final loss
in a song about winter and kites.
There will be no breezes.
What look like cave drawings
on the walls of our mother's womb
will be discovered by airport security
as we try to escape America.

If there is some play of leaves
against a cloudy background, or if
there's wind, its width will animate
the stars and torn and towel-like
set Orion's belt to snapping.
The lost paw of the delirious hound
will bob in a pond water
flustered by bee breath and thunder.

Men will curl and fleck themselves
against the bones of sacred owls,
and other men, who watch them,
speak against idea, against the thought
of wings and who, if anyone,
invented them. Later at the courthouse,
sunrise like a box of blood. The light
acquitting one and killing others.

Chess

What eclectic cleff will signal
the starting point of our apprenticeship
to buoyancy, of shed hours, shot,
shorn in their very own corpses,
of the problem of death reduced
to the talc on a swath of old shale,
the genuine diversion that bullies us
back to the black ice at bottom.

Man must create pursuits in which
his system applies or be killed
throwing apples at swans, knocking
mailboxes over, eating cereal.
The owl has no system. Cold air
collects in the bottom of her nest
and waits there, blank as a witness
destroyed before his testimony.

Does night need, does happiness require
the wilderness of a slogan?
A ghetto with three types of trees?
Not believing in a conscious god,
or men, we heirloom wisdom
in a game that teaches nothing
but time and anger at drowsiness.
Tears are not the shapes we sob in.

Reading the Newspaper

Though the mailman bash our mailbox
with his flute, or children fix
their feet within the filthy feathers
of a broken owl, our nation
must sometime relinquish its echo,
and not to a photograph
of President Haze, or dead words cut
in a tub of stolen moccasins.

There is more to the fire, to be said
of the fire, than a reporter
can thumb in the delicate ash. If we follow
the flame width, we measure in error.
Better the leaf smoke absorbed
in blue sweater, the deer in the lake
that we fear causes cancer,
trees in a faraway weather.

All news is opinion except poetry,
and most poetry, too floppy
to read on the train. The fat facts
withheld from the wind like lead
in a typesetter's lung. Yet strawberries
startle us, seeds cupped in skin. We study
the pores of our nose seventh-heartedly,
confusing the moon with a rooster.

THOMAS KANE

Caligula in the Dormers

The chaste girls sharpen their
teeth. (They are post-
traumatic when they sharpen
their teeth.)

*   *   *   *   *   *

Once separated, the dancer
unloves his shoes. They are,
to him, dust and from dust,
bread. He thinks: The mill is
bread and the mill's rain is
bread also.

*   *   *   *   *   *

And so we do not forget how
(and how!) the chaste girls
cull the animal from the
bone.

*   *   *   *   *   *

As the fish survived the first
bad news but not the age of
sails. How we longed for
their gills. *My parasol for a
gill!* The third perch, a gift
for our mothers. The third set
of scales, a gift for our boots.
To imagine! To imagine the
restraint God once asked of
our hands!

*   *   *   *   *   *

The chaste girls each have a
rock, a taffeta gown to keep
their secrets.

*   *   *   *   *   *

A tender tangle, how we rifle
the pocket of every dying. As
Gericault at the sanitarium:
Byron hated his horse. Byron
also found his horse
irresistible. And yes! A
dinner hat folded into the
pocket. Although a freckle,
imagined resting, imperfect,
in the fold.

*   *   *   *   *   *

The chaste girls are fierce in
their hatred of the wet nurse.
They rush and rush to grow
nearer their finger cut gloves.

*   *   *   *   *   *

If a child came from me, we
would know what of my
father stayed put: Cat gut
pulled to fit around the pegs?
Breath enough to meet a
woman?

*   *   *   *   *   *

And I remember, if a child
came from me, I would be as
Robert Frost would today be
good police. His chin and
blue suit! He takes his lunch
in the penny arcade, among
the fountains in the penny
arcade.

*   *   *   *   *   *

For us, nothing is ruined. The
chaste girls are not fixed.

*   *   *   *   *   *

In a moment, we will give up what about us is mechanical. But for now, we are busy, busy as planets. It is Lent. Everything is our hands. We do not drink the river because we have bled in it.

*   *   *   *   *   *

The chaste girls pry the roof. There is a little princess under the shingles. How they read the book of songs is how she washes in the dark (by a guess whistled by a wren).

*   *   *   *   *   *

Asylum for Shirley Temple! She was found inside her Sunday shoes inside the parade. When she danced, we almost did not notice how badly she needed a new career, a hot water bottle for her tired skin.

*   *   *   *   *   *

The chaste girls are never pleuritic. They are sometimes fed from their mothers' mouths.

from The Threshing Floor

I.

When to ask their forebear:
Were thieves present
only to lick at your wounds?

Will they rummage
our pockets, wear *our* killing
dresses? Because

you, Romulus, would eat
your brother's eyes
for a ruby and for a crow,

will we?—Sleeping,
the collar is undone and kept
far from the mouth.

It is Easter, 1967.
Miniature
are the ways we keep from teething.

Sometimes, it is to imagine
each swan,
perfectly curved. Sometimes

we scold
the shadow for bidding
against the hand.

IV.

The windfall brings
your progeny, brings
the frayed rope left behind

by a stevedore, chewed through
by his part wolf.
What we keep to our pockets

is, itself, a story. At dinner,
it is thumbed,
away from the eyes. On the train,

it is set first in Alaska, set
again in Baltimore. It is what we hate
most in ourselves.

I will never be much good
to the gold miners. I will never
save a part wolf. I can,

but should never, own a knife.
The train's bathroom leaks
our stories to the track. The bridge-

water glows and, somewhere,
a beekeeper glows also, knowing,
to the day,

when his flock will die. He leaves them
a lantern
as apology.

VIII.

The pretty girl cleans in her sluice.
The cripple wears
his Halloween mask. How else

might we be undone by this book?
East of Eden
is Winterhaven, Florida, a boxcar

full of tinsel. Who would
bathe in tinsel over orient dew
but the cripple and the pretty girl?

Where else but here? Until
suddenly, the stonemason delivers on
his angel. The gymnast

does not retard her legs.
The piccolo!
The virgin calf!

We are okay learning everything
again. The baroque! The art
of carving its haunches!

We play children's games
on the beach,
in the cavity on the beach.

LINNEA OGDEN

Girl With Sudden Death Syndrome

The grade I got from a niece of the current
Regime. My sunburned
Nipple, also a variety of Japanese shrubbery.
Did you know the bus is free. Untitled skirts for
Fall. Why didn't you say something.
I didn't want to say anything. Underwater plants wave from
The underwater mirror of the spring. I don't cede
My right to poignancy and have been assured
You did so only recently. Birds ask
And answer *fire where here*
Here here.

New Ears Were Given to the Treetops

our own discarded as a tribe of bluebirds,
sharp as yearning, dispersed. The experience
of letting things transform completely.

More than one hundred thirty wings in the air
as our group was taught to savor
the sound of broken warbling.

I would rather bag my own game
with bullet or eyebeam.
The thrill of notifying another human.

Edward Wilson

My concern is my work. Under that my love for you. That becomes a face
if I wear snow goggles. What are you doing there in England.
Thank you for the gloves. The suspenders. The letters by dogsled.
By horse and ski. This is where I press against things.

I should be sleeping more. I sleep a little. Get up early. Remember the woods
where we courted. Want to kiss the penguin eggs. Want to find a wren's nest
in all this white. Even white beauty. When we won each other for ever. The green
shapes through my mask are too even. I try to sleep more. Put cocaine in my eyes.

There is life for a time. We leave depots along the trail. To come back.
And our trail-breakers leave us things. We trade equipment. I gave up my watch
since none of theirs work. Our two are off by 26 minutes. A grave difference.
We shoot the ponies one by one. Even mine will go tomorrow. We pull from there.

LENI ZUMAS

Leopard Arms

A NEW FAMILY IS TAKING THE PLACE of the woman who choked on a peanut. They arrive in a dented sedan. Their belongings are few. No lamps or sauce-pans, two chairs only, clothes in plastic bags. It's drizzling, so they hurry.

The little girl says, Who's that? and points up at me.

Nobody, says the no-haired mother.

Step lively, morsel! adds the rope-haired father.

My name is not a word; it's a smell. Call me the tang between smoke and scraped bark. Some years ago I fell to Brooklyn, was born as ornament on a block of cheap flats. The man who cut me was jolly and slapdash. His chisel was dull. He made my mouth open as if to growl, snout broad, eyes lashless. I wish I were more frighten-ing. My shoulders, for one, are tiny—they barely protrude from the battlement—and my lips could as easily be laughing as scowling. I look as if I'd been carved with blunt scissors, by an only slightly talented child.

The word you know me by is from *gargouille*, the French for throat. A throat can sing a tune, swallow milk, be sliced wide open. Down throats go slender needles aimed at human hearts.

The family ensconced: parents pouring drinks, girl pacing along each new wall to listen.

A large red charabanc chugs past, its upper-deck riders ponchoed against the rain.

And here on our right, trumpets the guide, we have the apartment where Mel Villiers wrote *Still Life with Gaping Wound.* He waves his microphone at the stack of micro-lofts (formerly a public library) across the street. In the very same building, he continues, is where Polychrest recorded the eight-track demos of *Mumcunt.*

A gust of oohs from the deck.

When're we gonna see where Squinch Babbington's girlfriend overdosed? shouts a passenger. That was in the brochure.

Next block, says the guide.

If Mrs. Megrim had been on her lookout when the bus came by, those tourists would have gotten an earful. *Quit nosing, you nostrils! Why don't you go look at something actually interesting?* Megrim's husband is long dead, her children far flung. She sits on a plastic lawn chair outside the mouth of the building, condemning all who pass.

But today the only person who noticed the bus was the watcher, a young woman on the top floor who stays behind planked-over windows and touches the world through binoculars.

I watch, too: the light dies. Dark water falls. The drinkers and dancers swim out. O kiss me please, o throw me over. Hot rooms stink, are entered and fled. With each small hour the frenzy hardens: *which of these fuckers can I bring back to bed?* Then the night unclenches. Birds' wings begin to itch, stumblers-home pull keys from pants, and the old—already restless—wait on mentholatumed pillows until an acceptable hour to open their eyes. The sun staggers forth. There is only so much it can do, since along these narrow streets the buildings loom and tilt, keeping sidewalks in constant shade.

The edifice I grow from, five storeys of blond stone, is called Leopard Arms. Its dwellers believe I am here to spout rain and to guard them. They're unaware I would make a fine witness for criminal trials. A gargoyle's ears collect sounds from impossible distances, and we don't need eyes to see. A mere adornment, a forgettable decoration, I know everything they do. But they don't do much. They are, in fact, a disappointing lot. I've heard tell of unpleasant posts—the church whose cleric drives tent-pegs into the necks of prairie dogs, or the planetarium whose female staff drink one another's menstrual yield—so I suppose I ought to be grateful; but Leopard Arms is not the most electrifying assignment in Brooklyn. Many of its residents rarely leave the premises. The ones who do don't get far; they return an hour later, bag of provisions on arm, looking exhausted. A few have jobs, but are on the brink of losing them. Because gossip and songs have made the neighborhood popular, it costs far more than its moldy ceilings, anemic trees, and high rates of asthma deserve. I don't know how these people keep coughing up the rent.

We have thrown water from the flat roofs of Egypt, where sacred vessels were rinsed of blood. We have roared as marble lions on the war temples of Greece. From English ramparts we have seen necks swing at the gallows, shoulders run red under the lash. In Paris, a million postcards perch us cutely on Notre Dame. In Freiburg, one of our number defecates upon the cornice of the Munster, his crude pose revenge by a fifteenth-century mason upon the nobleman who refused to pay him.

There is a belief, passed down the centuries, that gargoyles ward off evil. Our monstrous faces must surely be enough to panic the toughest phantom. Churches and ministers, cathedrals, the odd vicarage—we're presumed to defend them from the noxious oils massing round their spires, the midnights waiting to pry with yellow claws their stained vents of glass.

But I am here to tell you: we do not protect.

Our job is not that at all.

You can tell somebody died in here, observes the mother, because it has that shiver feeling.

The father says, Be grateful. It knocked a shit ton off the rent.

People are squeamish, says the mother.

Could we not afford it if she didn't die? asks the daughter.

Jesus, morsel, it's not as if we killed her. The father circles the small rugless room, massaging his bony forearms. This goddamn skin-jacket, I want it off! Why can't I be made of water?

Because you crimed in your last life, says the mother.

Next life we'll be water? asks the daughter.

If you keep on being good. The mother pushes her glass at the girl. Refill my snowbroth, please?

The shame collector lives with his cat, Sophie, who happily does not need to be walked. He has stopped going outside altogether. Food comes on bicycles, and toilet paper is mailed from a recycling company. I twist the dial on his radio: explosion here, pile of dead there. The collector, pinning a hemorrhoid to a sheet of foam-core, listens for a few seconds, then reaches to turn it off.

Into her beloved's room, across the narrow courtyard, the watcher can look with no other hindrance than curtains so flimsy it does not matter whether he draws them. Through her binoculars she sees him wipe his eye, examine the speck, cough.

Look up, she thinks. Look up.

If she had a cat, she would stoop to stroke it. If she had a cat, it would not be a cat but a shark.

The watcher's flat has three windows, two of them boarded. The one in the bathroom is too high and small to nail anything across. She once taped a sheet of construction paper over it, but moisture from her baths made the tape curl off the wall.

A shark, she knows, is not practical as a pet.

Tourists shield upcast eyes from the new-millennium sun, through split fingers see us crouched and leering on parapets, and think: *Such quaint remnants!* We remain, to them, from darker, stupider days. It does not occur to these squinters that no days were ever darker than theirs. One glance at a gargoyle and they think *Medieval superstition how charming* but fail to heed the omens of now: a moron grinning into a microphone, ten-year-old soldiers lined up to march, flags cracking in the desert wind.

In America I have learned the meaning of *head in the sand.*

Under the watcher's binocular gaze, the beloved and his sidekick recline with beers.

How's your new script going? inquires the sidekick.

Crazy.

Yeah?

As in, crazy-awesome!

What's the plot?

It's a porno about Helen Keller.

Huh. Sounds . . .

Awesome?

Is Helen Keller an actual character, or is it more like role-play?

The beloved puffs a palm-kiss at the sidekick. More shall be revealed!

I have not yet heard the young one's name spoken. She is referred to simply as *morsel.* She is the only child in the building. Her stockings are red with white rabbits stitched at the knee. I'm sorry, she says daily, for talking too loud when her parents' heads are killing them. When their heads are not killing them, they debate philosophy—of a sort. Theirs is a rather personal metaphysics. They talk of people who have wronged them, fortunes that have skipped them, the various piques and umbrages scattered in their wake. It seems the world has not dealt them a fair hand.

The father reasons, Assholes are not suddenly—or actually ever—going to vanish from the earth. So the best defense is Hypnos.

Don't forget Morpheus, says the mother.

Since the walls at Leopard Arms are as thick as thick fingernails, shame breeds like a grateful spore.

The collector worries that his snoring will keep the watcher awake. He moved his bed to the far wall, but the room is so narrow not much can be done to impede the travel of his slurpings and honkings and cuh-cuh-*cuchhh*-ings into the adjoining flat. If he sees the watcher in the lobby or hall, he swivels right round. The only mammal who is ever going to sleep next to him, he figures, is Sophie.

Mrs. Megrim, meanwhile, wonders if the flautist hears her crying after short, unsatisfying phone calls with her children. Or if her heavy tread bothers the phantom-faced boy below. Oh, but let him be bothered, she always reminds herself. *Let* him.

The watcher listens to the morsel's parents intercoursing nightly between eleven-fifteen and eleven-thirty, directly under her bed. (The floors are holey.) When softly the tiny sighs begin, the watcher readies herself: face down, toes braced, hips arched, fingers slitted. Sighlets give way to whimpers, a moan or two, then many moans, accelerating. In due course the father joins in with his staccato whinnies. The watcher herself makes no sound.

The tellies switch on by themselves to the news channels. How the fuck, says everybody. The news reveals only a fraction, but that's more than my humans want to hear. Limbs torched, bullets bouncing. Stop looking at that, orders the mother of the morsel, whose eyes are huge at women sobbing round a coffin.

They have no idea I encourage their midnights, rather than frighten them away.

For that, you see, is the gargoyle's way with worry.

We invite.

I am rained on, wind-whipped, scorched. The stone they cut me from was not of high quality, and down the years I have greened and softened. At the academy they drilled us in the history of weather, since we were to live in it. I learned that the ancient Greeks believed truffles were made by thunder: during a storm, the noise would invert itself and sink—newly solid—into fungal soil. The ancient Romans reported that blood and milk poured from the sky, as did iron. And wool. And flesh. Then, of course, cyclones: a notorious peril to seafarers. The nautical remedy was to splash vinegar on the ship before the cyclone's arrival. (Was this effective? The logbooks are unclear.)

My favorite weather is cloud; it reminds me of home. When vapors from the sewage plant waft south to flour the skies, I am, in my way, smiling.

If that child bangs on the wall one more time while my stories are on, I will contact the law.

Oh really? says the mother. And which law would that be?

Mrs. Megrim looks the mother up and down, her mouth a venom bloom. She says, You're so thin it's like a concentration camp happened.

Thank you!

Not a compliment, says Mrs. Megrim.

Actually, says the mother.

The father stops to examine a typed notice affixed to the front door. He is a slow reader. Huh, he says finally, shouldering his sack of bottles.

The new referendum requires all persons over the age of thirty-five to evacuate the neighborhood on or before March 15. Furthermore, per an auxiliary proviso, all persons between eighteen and thirty-five must report to the post office and receive an Appearance Assessment. If deemed inferior for any reason (understyled, overweight, etc.) the person must leave the zip code within sixty days.

Safe for now, says the father, although in a few years we'll be—

Fucked, nods the mother.

The daughter asks, But what if you don't pass the Assessment?

Are you kidding? *Look* at us.

The morsel looks.

The mother says, We're hot, okay?

The only people in the building over thirty-five are Mrs. Megrim and the flautist, who says cheerily, At least they gave us plenty of time to pack!

The referendum can screw, says Mrs. Megrim.

She's been at Leopard Arms since her husband was alive. Together they saw a lot of life pass through these doors. They played rummy here. They bemoaned their children's unwise choices here. They walked across the light-strung bridge after suppers in Manhattan, glad to return to the quiet of here.

I budge not, she declares.

The flautist whispers, They'll come for you eventually.

The watcher's beloved is one of the ones who never go outside. He does his work at home where the sun can't get him. His face is the coldest white, much like those of eighteenth-century women who ate arsenic wafers to bleach their skin. (The arsenic killed the hemoglobin in their blood, and the women grew pale as spiders living on the floor of the sea.)

The beloved reaches the world through his machine. Upon his ashen cheeks, at all hours, jumps blue breath from the screen. He sends reports, receives instructions, unbuckles his belt and digs one hand down to pump while the bodies topple from position to position.

When this latest war started, the academy upped the number of trainees it sent to America. We are sorely needed in the land of the green mermaid. Other places, people are forced to reckon with their midnights because they're standing right in front of them, often holding a rifle. Not so in a country where you can choose, instead of rifles, to think about wrinkle-fighting injections or celebrity custody combat.

During a previous war, slightly to the east of this one, I was fresh-eared at the academy. I couldn't wait to be a dragon on a pagoda, watching gunfire like a cricket match. But my instructor assigned me to the United States.

Shouldn't I go to where the wounded are? I protested.

If you want the blossom to grow, said my instructor, it won't do much good to water the petals. The roots of this suffering are in America. To help the people who are being bombed, you have to go to the nightmare's source.

To his foam display board the collector nails a skinny white leg flecked with golden, girlish hairs.

There are three types of Antarctic penguin, says the morsel.

Is that right, says the father.

King, macaroni, and jackass.

They taught you the word jackass at school?

No, I read it just myself. The king penguin is the size of a goose.

Have you ever *seen* a goose? demands the father. Shit, the fact is, we've never taken you to the zoo. Wife! he hollers at the kitchen.

The macaroni is smaller, continues the morsel, with a white throat.

What about the jackass?

They make a noise like a donkey. And have tiny flippers.

We need to figure out where the zoo is!

The mother stands in the doorway, biting the lip of her glass. But did you see about that kid who got mauled by the Siberian tiger last month? *Through* the bars, she adds. I think he might've died of his injuries.

The biggest midnight sniffing for the mother is fear—which, of course, is every human's midnight, but for her it assumes an age-old guise: fear of the morsel coming to harm because she, the mother, did not take good enough care of her. Tuberculosis, speeding truck, Siberian tiger: so much could happen.

The father is scared of doing nothing they'll remember him for. Not a single footprint—film, book, record, madcap stunt—to prove he was here.

Significant fears to face, I would say; but these two do a bang-up job of not. Their evasion strategy is deftly honed. They sleep half the day, snarled up in each other's arms; the other half they drink snowbroth. Eating is not high on the priority list. Their daughter, in fact, seems to be the only cook in the house. What sauce you want on your eggs, Dad? Hot or plum?

They are practically impervious!

Well, it's my job to thwart their blitheness. To keep drawing the midnights up from the caves, no matter how slippery these two might be.

I'm not sure what my obligation is to the young one. At what age should a person start being visited by eye-opening discomfort? Our instructors didn't teach us a great deal about children. I think I will leave her alone for now. She already has her parents to cope with, after all.

The watcher and her beloved happen to cross the lobby at the same moment.

She emits a gurgling scream.

He says uneasily, Whut up?

Oh!

Huh?

Hi, she corrects herself.

He nods and hurries out the door. She stands still for several minutes, listening to his voice—three dazzling syllables—play back, play back.

As the sun drops behind the scaffolds of a half-built high-rise, the mother returns from a rare day out. Mrs. Megrim, sitting guard, sees her spit gum onto the sidewalk.

Pick it up! she yells.

The mother walks faster.

Megrim stands with difficulty and arranges her bulk against the door, blocking entry.

Are you kidding? says the mother, adjusting her sunglasses.

I kid not.

Look, I need to get upstairs. I've had this tampon in since 7 A.M.

Pick it up off the ground! says Megrim.

It's not *on* the ground, it's in my cunny, growing lethal bacteria.

You want somebody to slip on that? Pick it up, dirty!

I had two job interviews today. Move out of my effing way.

Not until you fetch your effing garbage and stop expecting the world to be cleaned for you.

Not strong enough to shove her aside, the mother stomps back to retrieve the wad.

The shame collector's grandmother has taken to ringing several times a day. When he answers, she does nothing except breathe and fidget; then, before hanging up, she whispers: Poop.

He imagines her in the assisted-living facility, next to a jar of plastic flowers, fretting fruit-bar wrappers in her speckled hands. So he picks up every time, even though the sight of the Florida area code sends a blade into his lung.

How you doing, Nanna? he murmurs, pinning to his board a lame joke he told at the Halloween party.

The flautist departs well before the deadline. A great excuse to travel, she remarks to Mrs. Megrim. I'm going on a singles cruise!

Decent, nods Megrim. But you're still a weakling.

A shark would not be practical, knows the watcher. The tank alone would take up the whole flat, even if she could find someone willing to install it.

He stirs milk on a low flame. According to her logbook, he likes milk to be hot and weather to be cold. He likes cereal to have marshmallows and women to be drunk. Ten-thirty is his preferred hour to rise.

Look up, she whispers. Look up.

Look up because here I am.

There is a lot about the beloved that the watcher can't know. Such as that he spikes that milk with mock absinthe. Such as that he doesn't even own a mattress, and sleeps on a sleeping bag full of twigs and dirt. This girl is really getting the short end of it—in love with deadly marine beasts and writers of smut! I ache to expose him. But that would be solving her pain for her. We are not trained to give them shortcuts.

Agape at his screen, he squeals into the phone: Smoke these subject headings, chap! *Kaela gets laid by her horses. Jalisa sucks off her cows.* It's more or less poetry! *Average moms open their legs for you.*

You don't have a junk-mail filter? demands his sidekick.

I don't *want* one, because this poetry's going straight into Helen Keller.

Sunlight enters the body through the eyes, so the residents of Leopard Arms, dark-glassèd whenever they step out, do not get enough vitamin D. Even the morsel is forced to wear red plastic contraptions that make her look like a miniature-golf docent.

A lack of D causes rickets in the young, osteomalacia in the older. Is the morsel walking knock-kneed? When she came home from school yesterday, I noticed a hint of a limp. Could her bones be turning to jam?

At the academy, where we train before manifesting as architecture, they are very firm on one point: *Do not sympathize.* You will think these humans are hapless, indeed pathetic. Do not give in! They must tackle some truths. Confront a few facts. If you let them lead lives of carefree denial, of callous fun-seeking, the race will self-destruct even sooner than it's scheduled to.

Although, chuckled one of my instructors, scratching the horn that left his right eye in shadow, that wouldn't be such a bad thing, now would it?

We baby gargoyles tucked behind our desks giggled too, but nervously. The job seemed massive—beyond our gift.

The girl taps on 5-C, palms flat on the sticky door to keep from falling. She is wearing her new skates, smuggled out of the lost-and-found by a teacher who took pity.

The collector answers, holding a box of adhesive strips worn across the bridge of the nose to reduce snoring. They have just come in the post and he wants to practice before night. Yes?

Will you please come watch me skate because I'm not allowed to alone?

Wull . . .

Because I could get hit by a car or abducted or also killed.

Can't you ask your mom?

She's still asleep.

What about—

He is too.

The collector looks at his watch, raises an eyebrow. Sophie throbs at his ankles.

So can you?

Wull . . . He is nauseous at the prospect of showing his face in public.

Please? Her rabbity knees are twitching.

He sighs. No, I can't.

The morsel nods.

I'm sorry, I just—

That's okay, she says.

At dawn on March 15, the old emerge from their homes. Some are whisked into the cars of impatient relatives; others lurch by themselves into taxis. Once the sun is quivering above, the rest of the banished start making their way. They pile crates and boxes, picture-frames and cacti, into borrowed vans. They push laden shopping carts toward the bridge. They glance wistfully at the new coffee-shop/handmade jeans boutique/gym but cry, Fuck this neighborhood anyway. Asthma's not on my Christmas list!

Mrs. Megrim watches the exodus from behind her curtains, shaking her unusually large head.

The morsel has been hurting at the back of her mouth.

You probably just drank something too hot, says the mother.

I was scalded?

Yes you were. Get a piece of ice.

The almonds of her throat are aflame. If anyone were to look, they'd see a raw red swelling. Nobody looks.

A Complete Guide to Hazardous Marine Life contains a photograph of the shark she pines for: not a big shark, only a few feet, but fierce and beautiful. Brave. She has peered into its tiny eye a thousand times, even pressed her binoculars up to the page, trying to see to its heart. A shark would defend the watcher from the loneliness I have called upon her. Loneliness, according to our instructors, is among the worst of midnights. It is not a flashy problem like crack, nor easily sympathized for, like cancer. Instead it works slowly up your spine, taking sips of the fluid.

The tour guide exclaims, As you may have guessed from the cute foot traffic, this area has finally been cleared of erstwhilers. Local representatives have been trying to pass an age-and-beauty law for several years and were at last triumphant, making the neighborhood the most enviable address in the entire—

Too bad *you* cannot live here, observes a tourist.

Excuse me?

Well, you are no spring turkey.

The guide's eyelids flutter, but he contains himself. Now then, if you will crane your necks to the left . . .

On the third day of tonsillitis, the morsel requests a visit to the doctor and is told, Do you think *insurance* suddenly fell from the ceiling?

Pocketing house key and pink wallet, she strides off toward the high street. Returns with a lemon, a radish, and a thick yogurt made in Iceland. She squats over a patch of dirt from which climbs a spindly tree, digging until she finds her quarry.

I'm sorry, she whispers, and chops off the earthworm's head with her key.

Please do not eat that.

If only I had a voice she could hear!

Where is Megrim? Watching her stories, of course. Dammit, Mrs., you are needed.

The tonsil-poultice, pestled in a plastic cup from a hamburger restaurant, is one part radish, two parts worm, and three parts polar curd. Delicious, she whispers staunchly. The parents, heads on fire in the next room, can't hear.

The watcher scratches on the wall above her bed, in black pen: Love is when a thin flame flies under your skin.

Two floors below, across the courtyard, the beloved halts in mid-pump. He is wincing, not in carnal pleasure but in ordinary pain.

Fuck my back kills!

One can only hope that the twines and tissues of his lumbar are disintegrating, thanks to insufficient vitamin D, a little more each day.

I learned a new thing at recess, croaks the morsel. Want to see?

Stupid with snowbroth, they nod.

She laces her fingers and clamps her fists together. Here is the church, here is the steeple, open the doors and unload clips into the people.

Ha! says the mother.

Do it again, says the father.

In America I have learned the meaning of *last straw.*

Do not try to save them, warned the instructors. One may only teach lessons—never rescue.

But I've been in this country long enough to know that you can do anything if you just try hard enough and don't ask the government for enfeebling handouts.

I hereby climb out from under the wet blankets of the British Empire, and pledge: I *will* rescue.

Not yet sure exactly how.

Oh-em-gee, chap, were you aware that *Pete's mom is ready for hardcore action after some beers?* Or that *crazy farm women are screwing in the barn?* A lot goes on in agricultural settings.

Helen Keller didn't live on a farm, did she?

Sure she did, says the beloved. A farm of the mind.

Nanna, says the collector, did you know that my transformation into a shut-in reeking of cat pee is almost complete?

Breathing.

I haven't left the apartment in a month, he says.

Rustling.

Literally, he adds.

Poop, she says.

Across the water from their horned wisdom, I am betraying my instructors. Merely to entertain the *idea* of rescue is in flagrant defiance of the gargoyle's mission. We are to nudge humans out of their nests, not weave new ones for them.

I can't think of a way to reach her. Not directly. I must act by proxy, entrust the salvage to a go-between.

Hoarse and feverish, the morsel decides to keep herself home from school. The sight of her alarms the parents when they rise at noon.

What the eff? says the mother. It's not the weekend! And what's that smell?

I can't talk, writes the morsel on a take-out menu, *so I am making some cookies.*

Right ho, says the bewildered father.

My powers are limited, but they are powers.

A grain, a grain, a grain.

(I haven't concentrated this hard since my leaving exams at the academy.)

From these grains, be gone all sweetness!

(My stone eyes ache.)

From this cupful, leach all music, expunge all hue, until the cup is sand.

Charity's legs are spread on the ranch! shrieks the beloved, hunched pantless at his screen.

The watcher can see he is excited, and wishes she knew what his words were; she imagines them as little flowers of anguish. *If I had a shark, I could ride it across the yard and through his window and then—*

Oh dear girl, you couldn't.

A knock. Soft, insistent. The beloved debates whether to answer, then—because he's bored—steps into his corduroys. The watcher loses sight of him when he moves for the door.

What are you selling these for?

Only five mere dollars, she whispers.

No, I mean, what organization?

The morsel shrugs.

I'm not paying if I don't know. You could be raising funds for the U.S. Army.

It's for my dad and my mom, squeaks the morsel.

They're making you hawk baked goods for personal gain?

They're not making me. I thought of it just myself. They need some money.

But you can't—I mean, that's just *not done*.

I'm doing it, the morsel points out.

Would you like to buy some delicious cookies?

She dangles the ziplock with its freight of charred lumps.

What flavor?

Oatmeal, the morsel whispers. Just five dollars only. You can try one for free.

The collector munches contemplatively. This is far from delicious, he says.

The morsel blinks.

In fact it tastes like crap.

He bends to feed the other half to Sophie.

The morsel stares at her thumb.

Did you follow the recipe? he asks, nearly kindly.

She nods.

I suspect that *sugar* is an ingredient you overlooked.

No, I'm pretty sure.

I advise you to whip up a new batch before you go on peddling your wares.

The morsel blinks faster.

Here it is. The moment. Please let it succeed, my stratagem, my dicey ploy! I don't pray, because who to? but I concentrate my very hardest.

The old woman reaches into the ziplock, brings a black chunk to her mouth. *What will she say?*

This is nastiness. I wouldn't pay a dime, much less five dollars.

I'm sorry, mouths the morsel.

Never apologize, says Megrim briskly. Just make more.

I don't have more ingredients.

Megrim crunches her mouth into an almost-smile. Well guess who does?

I am embarrassed to feel so wildly relieved. It hardly befits a creature of my station. But her swollen little almonds—and the steeple—and the bloody broth—it simply would not answer.

Mrs. Megrim hands the morsel a wedge of butter wrapped in paper towel. Grease away!

The assiduous child sets to her pans while Megrim beats the dough. The heating oven (seldom cleaned) fills the kitchen with ghosts of ancient suppers, pork loin and bread pudding and broiled cod and plum pie.

They sent a needle down his throat, explains Megrim, to find out what ailed his ticker. But while they were doing it, he died. Right on the goddamn table. The needle must've hit something else.

That's so bad, says the morsel.

Yeah, it was. It was the worst thing of all.

I wish that didn't happen.

Well, thank you, says Megrim.

Mature ladies showing nasty tricks, mutters the beloved.

Mrs. Megrim has donned her best dress, a blue silk her husband gave her. Too big for it now, she has slashed vents in the back and sides, through which surge rolls of petticoat'd flesh. In the bathroom mirror she dabs on lipstick. The morsel admires its color, the lit-up brown of raisins. She asks can she have some too and is told to dream on.

My nephew is a doctor in the Bronx, states Megrim, and we're paying him a visit. He'll tell us whether those tonsils need to come out. Here, put on your rag.

My pretty coat, corrects the morsel.

I'm sorry, but that hardly adds up to a coat. Wrap this around your neck.

What is it?

My people call it a scarf, says Megrim.

Do you think my mom is beautiful?

Well, ha, well, I—just look at you! Could a child so handsome have come from a non-beautiful mother?

What is your favorite place on Earth you've been to in real life?

The Bering Strait. On my honeymoon.

What was your favorite thing to make your kids for dinner?

Hot dogs. They had low standards.

And what is the leopard's name?

Henh?

Our leopard.

You mean that fellow above the door?

Yeah him.

My name is

Search me.

But my name is

Doesn't have one, concludes the girl.

Are we done with this interrogation or what?

The morsel hesitates. The question she wants most to ask is not polite. But her worry that Mrs. Megrim is going to leave—a new black dot on her heart—eclipses all else.

Aren't you scared, she blurts, of getting arrested for being not young and then have to move away?

Megrim cackles. No, hon, they won't catch me. I know the tunnels.

I can smuggle food into a tunnel, says the morsel.

That'd be decent.

I'll bring you eggs! And also sandwiches!

Quit shouting, or a rawhead will come for you in the night.

What does one look like?

So hideous, says Megrim, it can't be described.

The crone may know the tunnels, but *I* know what the Evacuation Enforcement Inspectors look like. And upon them I shall invite amnesia, whenever they approach.

The bus is passing once again. I have the spiel, of course, by heart. But today the tour guide strays from his script—he points the microphone at me.

Me?

Has it dawned on them, perchance? Am I about to receive, for the first time, some credit for my work on humans' behalves? I don't need applause (we were trained to expect none) but I wouldn't kick a bit of acknowledgment out of bed. The watcher, for instance, could have thanked me for whisking her out of Leopard Arms and thereby away from the most futile infatuation on record. All it took was a gentle prodding of the Enforcement Inspectors. She had never gone to the post office for her Appearance Assessment, and when they knocked on her door, they found that all was not garden-fresh in Denmark. The girl's skin puts one in mind of stucco, and her hair hasn't felt a grooming product since before the war.

While she waited for the moving van, clutching her stuffed great white, she might have raised her eyes and smiled. She did not.

The shame collector's gratitude did not exactly runneth over, either, despite the lengths I went for him. I got word of the animal clinic, did I not, in one of my brothers' buildings, wherein works a lovely deaf veterinarian? And I tempted the feline ague upon Sophie, did I not? And the collector now has an ice-cream date for next weekend. But there has been no appreciative wink for me, only his jaw at his knees.

In that urine-colored building, announces the guide, is where Brosef Killick wrote the screenplay for *Mount Saint Helen*, which has recently been wowing special-interest audiences across the country. According to my sources, he still lives here, though one might reasonably ask: why not relocate to Tinseltown, Brosef?

You mean he's in there right now? coo the passengers.

Quite possibly so.

Fuckin *'ell*! An evident fan stands up and waves frantically. Hey, Killy! Down 'ere! Show us some dingle!

Please take your seat, says the guide.

The voice, whose lost aitches spark in me a blurred nostalgia for home, gets worse. Look out yer window, you tosser!

A window opens and Mrs. Megrim's enormous head pokes forth. Shut that pie-hole!

You shut it, granny.

She withdraws, only to return with a rose-lidded bowl. I'll show you shut it! she screams, hurling the bowl. She's brawny for a woman of her years: the pottery soars all the way to the bus (narrowly missing the Killick enthusiast) and shatters on the linoleum deck. A little beach of sugar unfurls at their feet.

Nice throw, says the morsel. Elbows propped on the sill, she leans her head against the formidable bicep. Her cheeks are cherrier, thanks to the protein and vegetables she has been ingesting regularly at Megrim's kitchen table.

The tour guide gawks up, shocked to see such an over-age human loose in the neighborhood. Jesus, he murmurs, I thought they got rid of them all.

KARLA KELSEY

Consequence and Garner Run Through

But if the grove of candlewood emits the cadence of a small plane overhead and the frozen summerpool, then this sopped-over vitality

becomes a mode of moving through wind through what renders us as near, the icon useful in its gold and the how of its eyes. The image was painted centuries before you were born

and so this recognition, but those eyes are not to be argued with. More importantly, the sound of air forced through a pinhole.

* *

And so gone to camera, gone to clutching in the gallery because what had been said had been recorded and then

inlaid in the scene. Our lips not matching the dialogue as the improbable rises behind. As the sky uplifts in sound composing as fallen from the nest I had never felt so.

* *

What the silent said within that corner of warm and such companionship. The city left behind in alternate memory

blistered from the outside. You are another character now that your defenses have been relinquished or at least this is what we call a softening of light

and the lines around my eyes show less, or at least I feel them less, am less, myself, of an etching. These are simple things dampered and bodying.

* *

What are we but prediction based on pinks ringing out nightfall as speech settles in the pit of my throat. Cloves seep into your eyes

at last the look fixed across centuries but this still doesn't warrant such rivers tendered as storm. As listening into the recording,

a texture of yolk emitted to sky but of course with dappling with what the linden says.

Consequent

And the words carve this, anchoring it in as in a boat, as in a coursing meant unto the calf's down, the blood in the dust and no longer. There is no melancholy like that built out of heat and rusted metal, what spills creating gesture, my hand damp and limp and I am afraid there was nothing much else to have been spoken.

The Voyeur

She doesn't gaze at her subjects, she induces them to gaze at her; she selects them for their confidence, their potential to become under-stuffed. Not for what she is but for her regular feat of vanishing, I know her: the cut-and-glued life-size mockup, the unpeopled place, the pellucid mirror that parses *interior*. It is hard to be good when there are so many fabulous faces to admire, such a menagerie of loss. Fabulously, they enact familiar bedroom dramas, the kind scratched in crayon and littered with the terribly usual, hand-picked and perishable—a bowl of fruit, a crate of disposable diapers, a headless crucifix with pearls of water pouring from the nipples. I look, and the paunchy self-as-clown holds balloons. I urinate in suggestive arcs, brandish severed heads on pikes, or am broken into parts and stacked—a painted and compiled lost tribe. Everywhere: the smoothed ridges of the brow, the rough dabs that dimple the spine, the cupped back of the knee, the gestural marks. And here: up the well-worn stairs, the low-lit guest-room, the whole lived whorl beneath blades of a ceiling fan. Strangely, I never see you there.

The Pioneers

We were odd candidates for grandeur, though we embellished everything, let little go to waste. Our lean-to constructions of pocket-lint materials—ticket stubs, rope, the occasional twig and soda pop top—limply resisted beauty, evoking instead a kind of match-struck causality. When things worked, they did as if in a puff of smoke. When things didn't work, we'd grow that much more weary. We slept above the bones of enemies killed in battle, dreaming the dream and nightmare of encyclopedic knowledge. Specimens collected: grinning spiders, raven-eyes blinking in starry skies, scavenging insects beset by monstrous shadows. How did these animals move through their world? In trysts with hustlers, games of strip poker, encounters on the street; sitting ass-flat at the three-way crossroads of boredom, buffoonery and something imminently dire. Waking, we'd find crude analog mechanisms standing in for us, enacting our all-too-human feelings. When we'd fall sleep once again, a microphone pointed at our head, a nearby un-pressed record on a phonograph would be poised to play back our dreams. That old curiosity shop, a crackpot's studio jammed with junk. Peeping through the windows, seeing the midden of plastic prairie dogs and how-to books, miniature tractors plowing rust, metal hobby planes landing on piles of rosaries. What confronted us eye-to-eye like a knowing sibling, like unsettling road signs? It's all coming back again—at break-neck speed, in a procession of empty black galoshes.

JUSTIN MARKS

Sonnet IV

The bizarre sound of my own
name repeating and people
praying
My hair getting
unwieldy in a world filled
with an abundance that approaches
formlessness Strangeness
and beauty Truth
is a melody like a leech
or the aftermath of the disaster
there is no trace of A killer
sunset going down
When you open your eyes
someone familiar may be waiting

Sonnet V

Dreaming in the driver's seat
and an acute fear
of buttoning my jacket The rest
on the cutting room floor
Just say what to do and it will be
summer Wondrous
Soft and fuzzy I don't mean
to make no fuss
Truth is a traffic accident
in which bones break
the skin Procrastination
in a foreign language
Betrayal of one's best instinct
I saw a femur once

PETER JAY SHIPPY

After

After sewing his heart
Into his throat

We swathed my son
In mosquito netting

And used the Renaults
To pull his body out

On the floe as skaters
Danced the starlight waltz

Around his corpse until
Their blades cut him free

To constellate
In the whirl of symptoms

Uncle

She found the body
Hanging off a pear tree

When I came across Gram
She had already cinched

Her own belt around
Her own brown neck

And was shimmying
Out on the limb

To join her son
As was our custom if

The tree had been a Bosc
But this was a Bartlett

When I pointed that out
We both laughed

And took a pull
From my flask then spit

Vodka on the trunk
And set the tree on fire

Also our way and
As we walked home

She mumbled *son*
Of a bitch son of a bitch

And we both laughed
Also our way

MICHAEL ZEISS

Notes Toward a Supreme Action Movie

The Pitch

THE SOUL OF THE INDIAN who sold Manhattan to the Dutch possesses the
creaking copper body of the Statue of Liberty and rampages through New
York City. A young man attempts to save the city by transferring said Indian's
spirit from the statue into his own body. It's *Godzilla* meets *Frankenstein* meets
Ghostbusters meets *Dances with Wolves*.

——Will the hero be a scientist type?

——Yes. In the first scene we see him playing chess with an old man in
Central Park.

The studio execs analyze the grosses of movies that feature the destruction of
New York. A slight dip in the line was supposed to begin an age of entertainment
without destruction or irony, but this age did not occur, in fact the line streaks like a
missile to the chart's upper corner. The execs are sold. The movie is to be made.

We Meet the Hero Playing Chess

In the original script the hero's name was Jim Stalker, but the director was
not satisfied with that. The hero needs to be more than a Frank Dux, Dutch
Schaeffer, Martin Riggs, Gabe Walker, John Matrix, Frank Martin, Jack Hall,
Jack Bauer, John McClane—so the director chooses Kelvin for its scientific ring
and Barrow for a darker Tolkien-Viking feel.

Kelvin Barrow, then, is twenty-six years old, pursuing a Ph.D. in physics
from Columbia University. We first meet him in Central Park, playing chess
against an old man. Kelvin thinks simultaneously about the game going on
before him and his thesis on victims of multiple lightning strikes. The old man
sips from a silver flask.

Kelvin has poked and prodded his subjects, put them through CAT scans
and measured their electrical fields with painful prongs attached to every part
of their bodies. He has found that multiple-lightning-strike victims hum along
at an increased level of electrochemical activity that provides a perfect ground-
ing spot for any lightning fork flailing about in the sky. Glenn Ford from Akron,

Ohio, is one of these unfortunates: struck by lightning fourteen times while working as a farmhand these past ten years, he has now changed careers to a less itinerant gig as Kelvin's lab rat. He lives off his stipend of fifteen dollars a day, sells his blood plasma when he needs cigarettes, and stays at a shelter for home-less men in Queens.

Tonight a vicious storm system is headed up the Eastern seaboard. Glenn is to meet Kelvin at Battery Park. Kelvin will watch from a safe distance while Glenn, beneath a specially constructed dome of lightning rods, tempts fate by study-ing a laminated sheet of word problems, thus increasing his brain activity and amplifying his electrical signature. While doing this it is important that he stands very, very still.

Kelvin glances at his watch—four o' clock! There is no time to waste. He moves his piece one last time, knocks down the opposing king, and salutes his opponent with a bow. Then he is off on his mountain bike northwest through the park.

The old man smiles wistfully as Kelvin rides away—he was just like that young man once, a real whippersnapper, full of vigor and vim. Now his mouth is dry and dusty. Like I'm already in the grave, he thinks, and takes another sip of whiskey.

An Island Is Destroyed to a Catchy Tune

Oh, to be young in the grandest city of all, riding a mountain bike through its un-natural preserve! A catchy tune follows Kelvin, featuring mandolins and wood-winds, African thumb piano and bass viol in counterpoint to wailing electric guitar and the sound of a muezzin moaning on his minaret. Kelvin weaves his way through joggers and rollerbladers by the dozens, all fit and happy, the young rollerblading women in skimpy clothing, the older women with their husbands, frumpy but cute. Kelvin rides on, paying them no mind: in his head he stud-ies equations for cloud charging, formulas for the average number of negatively charged leaders trailing down from a storm, the number of positively charged streamers likely to rise up to meet them. Maybe for a moment he studies the outrageous breasts of the woman who just passed wearing a thong (an extra im-ported from Venice Beach), but only for a moment. The sun shines, the citizenry is exultant and partially nude, but a storm is coming and there is work to do.

A stray cloud obscures the sun, and the catchy tune shifts. We hear, in the bridge, the low moan of a wooden flute. As the cloud's shadow falls over the park, the rollerbladers and joggers and dog walkers fade and the surrounding skyscrapers melt into fat taffy-tufts of mist.

For we have ordered up from the virtual set department a complete and exact rendering of the isle of Manhattan, circa 1626, every last tree, bit of moss, branch, rock, hill, and stream. Outcrops that were leveled rise groaning back; springs and rivulets once stagnant and brown rush by swift and clear; and a dull roar heralds the rippling green rebirth of ten million trees up and down the isle. The city disappears. Kelvin now rides alone, a dim figure through the phantom past.

We pan north, and zoom in again, down to the island's topmost tip. We make out two figures, at first dim but growing clearer. One figure is fat and white, out in a grassy clearing, the other young, slim and brown. What's that—a handshake? An exchange of goods? Some beads? A bolt of cloth?

After the deal goes down, the young Indian heads south. We see his figure flit below the forest canopy, and follow his progress by the deep crimson color of the cloth he carries and the glint of beaded glass. Soon he reaches the eastern shore of the island and uses a small boat to paddle to Sewanhacky's shore.

The pale Dutchman leaves the clearing and walks west through the forest, down to the Hudson where a ship waits to take him south to the island's tip, where there's already a settlement, but now one with enough legitimacy to keep the other European powers at bay.

We see the young man on the larger island now, huffing as he hurdles low branches, bead and blanket and trinket slung over arms and shoulders. Guitars thrum. The flute wows and screeches. He reaches home, a seasonal camp on the shore. He extends a bead chain to an old sachem and throws his red cloth down. The wrinkly-eyed, wise-looking chief stares at him. Storm clouds pile up above the unbroken green glade, mists congeal into a thick wall of fog. Fat water drops fall, striking dirt and pine needles.

The old sachem has a vision, he raises his arm and tells it to the young man, and as he tells it, we see it, in a wide shot of the entire land as it shifts, groans, buckles, and rumbles. From underneath its skin come streets, steel spikes, water-tower tops, cut cornices of granite, marble, and brick all exploding apart the forest floor. The waters of the rivers boil and from beneath rise bridges like the skeletons of leviathan, fanning wiry fins and cables to the sky. From that one little ship and that tiny southern fort flabby forms spill out like grubs, pupate wildly in every form and color, and start buzzing incessantly in all the languages of the earth.

The young man is stunned. We read in yellow subtitles:

— I hope by showing me this vision, old man, you do not imply that I am responsible for these things that will come to pass.

The flute screeches in the upper octaves now, guitars and bass below it thrash to a frenzy. The old sachem calls on the power of the Great Spirit; he clenches his fist and a great fork of lightning breaks from the clouds and sucks the young boy's soul screaming into the night sky. In the dirt a burning bolt of cloth and dollops of molten glass are all that remain.

And then quiet: before us, the city entire, lights winking in the night, a beacon on the hill, the golden door beneath the lifted lamp. It has settled on top of what-once-was, crushing it all with the quiet weight of time's passage. The only sounds we hear from this height are the distant bleats of car horns and the deep timpani of purple thunderheads cruising monstrous through the sky.

In one of those buildings, by one of those lighted windows, Kelvin's pensive face peers out. He hopes the storm has not done its worst; he needs more rain, more forked fire blasting to the earth in crooked streams.

Liberty Comes Alive

A soul has been flitting and flopping from airwall to airwall and gust to gust above the lapping green waters of the harbor. We see its dim outline against a gray thunderhead, with Liberty's spiked crown below. Then a white flash splits the shadowy figure, contorting it in a gruesome gesture of pain, as the bright bolt impales it through the chest and streaks down to the statue's copper head. The figure curls inward, into its heart where the white bolt is blasting, then curls further, bending into the crackling stream, and all at once is sucked through. The fork bottoms out on Liberty's solemn head, illuminating it like a flaming crown.

Rage lights the eyes of the statue and howls through the empty stairway from the head down to the back of the left leg. The statue turns its head, this way, that way, and then lowers down the lifted lamp, Liberty's beacon. Huge plates groan—rivets pop—undergirders buckle—beams bend. The statue steps off the pedestal, strides in four steps to the edge of the island, and slips quietly into the sea. The lamp is lifted again cresting the waves and shooting white sparks, moving like a ghost ship as the statue's feet stride the seafloor toward the bottom tip of Manhattan.

—You see that?

Kelvin and Glenn have been at the tip of Battery Park these past few hours, Glenn beneath his tent of lightning rods, studying his laminated sheet of word problems, Kelvin with his video camera and electrical instruments ready to capture and measure the first strike that comes.

Glenn looks at Kelvin.

— See what?

Kelvin had seen the statue start to move, he had seen it walk off the island into the water. He keeps filming. Glenn turns and sees first the torch, now the upraised arm, before the crown surfaces in a foaming flood and the terrible face emerges. Glenn runs as fast as his pointed cowboy boots will carry him to the South Ferry subway station.

The statue now steps on land, a girlish Godzilla. Kelvin films as Liberty walks to the park's northeast corner, where a flagpole rises from the bronze plaque at its base. The statue reaches down, uproots the pole, tosses it aside, and with one huge foot (still trailing its broken shackles) crushes the pedestal and plaque. Though the statue cannot roar, though it is not equipped with anything like vocal chords, Kelvin watches through the viewfinder as the tilting head rocks back and opens its mouth—the sound of metal groaning and plates straining under immense stress rushes from inside, filling the night air with sharp and dissonant vibrations that pummel Kelvin's eardrums.

The statue looks up the long stretch of Broadway, takes two massive steps, and with a backhand blow of the torch swats Wall Street's great bull, sending it spinning end over end into the harbor. It is now in the labyrinth of glass it flew above for so long, aching to touch, break, smash, shatter. Liberty raises its torch high like a dagger, poised to stab and slash.

Years Hence

Who else is Kelvin's girlfriend but a stylish, petite young blonde who works as a perky television reporter on the late-night news and has a collection of snappy scarves? How could it be otherwise?

Kelvin has followed the statue uptown, but now he stops filming and rushes to the offices of Channel 26 news, where he knows he will hand to his girl, sweet Shelly, footage for the year's most sensational story.

Years hence, we find her sitting on her porch swing in a nondescript subdivision of a nondescript suburb of a normal, wholesome American city. Behold a five-bedroom house, with a two-car garage. The children have left it now, are off to college perhaps or even beginning their careers, and she has time to remember the night when Liberty got loose.

— They gave me the story that night. It was all because of Kelvin. He had the footage. That was my big break. Then I got the co-anchor position and went national a few years after that. He was soaked through with rain. He came into the office and plopped the tape down on my desk. By that time we had sent a camera crew out, but to have that first footage. It meant my whole career.

— Later that evening? Yes, I was there. I know they say he had a backpack with wires and everything but I don't believe he was going to do what they said he was going to do. He was trying to help. I think he was going to deactivate it. And then I—I—I'm sorry. Can you turn the camera off for a minute?

In the Situation Room

After Kelvin leaves the newsroom two men in dark suits and sunglasses stop him on the street and rush him into a waiting limousine. They take him to a situation room at an undisclosed location.

As the disciples must have been both pleased and envious to see Jesus ascend to heaven, so the sight of some regular guy being whisked away in a limousine to the center of earthly power stirs these feelings in us. It may be rooted in the need to know that somewhere out there is a center of control, a secret senate that pulls the levers and spins the wheels of the world-machine. And if *we* were asked to join it—if it somehow needed *us*?

Kelvin is taken to a nondescript building, past a gray doorway, offered a seat on a comfy couch, given coffee and pastries. A general comes to meet him, gives him a hard-assed, squinty-eyed look.

— Liberty is loose in the streets. Barrow, you witnessed this thing's coming to life. We need you, son. Come with me.

We hardly need to go into the look and feel of the situation room; the room is always the same. The aides are there, they have very few lines; they shuffle papers, take notes, and if they wear glasses, they take them off and chew on the ends of the frames. The chief of police is a competent fellow, but he would rather not butt heads with the DHS or the Pentagon. The camera focuses on the buzz-cut, square-jawed general of the New York National Guard, jabbing at people with a thick finger and barking out orders. By looking at him one assumes the existence of three or four less fortunate siblings, who were left in their infancy on an exposed hillside to wail, wither, and die. He is a veteran not only of the first and second Gulf Wars but also of Vietnam, and so broad-shouldered, bold, and pleasing a form he has, that we almost don't notice—until the camera pans in for a close-up—his fake leg. It is gunmetal blue, with a combat boot on the foot. May God bless him, and may God bless America.

The general addresses the team assembled at the long, polished table.

—What does she want from us? Why *Liberty*—of all things on this goddamn earth that we have prepared for, why *her*? Why one of *ours*? NSA, CIA, are you sure you have no clandestine statue animation programs?

— None, sir. At least none we know that we can recall being aware of.

— Sir, the military potential of this development is huge, I mean, it's just in the wrong place now, but imagine letting a few of these ladies loose in Tehran . . .

There is a brief silence, and then Kelvin speaks:

— I saw it rip apart the flagpole that commemorates the sale of Manhattan.

— Who's that boy?

— I had him picked up, the general says. He was an eyewitness to its coming-to-life. Figured he knew something.

— Now, the general says, what does the flagpole have to do with all of this?

— I first made the connection, Kelvin answers, between the rampaging statue, Lady Liberty, and the Manhattan island bead-deal when I saw the statue stop and rip this flagpole and pedestal, known as the Netherlands Monument, from the ground. It heaved a howl through its steel ribs—a strange, sad, melancholy groan, like the creak and crank a rusty tanker ship must make on the high seas.

But, gentlemen, let me take you back a year or so. My girlfriend and I had always wished to make love in a library. It was at a public branch, in the evening time, when we went to prosecute this secret desire in the far, obscure stacks of old dusty history books—you know, the kind of books you may find in a garage sale, that for some reason have swastikas on them. Reaching to unclasp her bra, my hand hit a stack of books, and one fell open to the floor. We hit the ground, too, and later I read the open page, which my head lay flat on, my nose stuck in the open crease by the spine, a dew-drop of love-sweat hanging from the end, about to fall.

I read that the West India Company's director, Minuit, after being sacked by the Dutch, started working for the Swedes, founding a new settlement farther south, by the Delaware River. In 1638, on his way back to Sweden, he stopped in the Caribbean to pick up a load of tobacco. There Minuit's ship was swallowed up in a hurricane and he and all hands perished. But then I gazed cross-eyed down to read these italicized lines that sprung roughly from the part of my face between my nose and upper lip out to the edge of the page:

There is a legend that the young native who sold the island to Minuit for a handful of beads was damned by the Great Spirit to fly ghostly above the island for all time; and twelve years after the deal, was so angered by the trenches running with the piss and waste of New Amsterdam, that he filled up his ghostly lungs with the cool Atlantic Air, blew it out as a great spirit-bellows, warming the air and the currents and sending them south, to form a great hurricane where his enemy now sailed, and it fell upon him, dashing and splintering the ship and all of the men therein to pieces even the sea-worms could not nibble upon, being so small, and not tasty besides. Many say this spirit still hovers above the island of Manhatto, biding its time until it may take further revenge—

Gentlemen, I propose to you that it is this same vengeful spirit that stalks our streets tonight in the guise of Liberty!

Barrow Off the Case

Usually we would show the reactions of the people in the situation room to Kelvin's speech so the audience knows what to think. Who would let them judge for themselves, when they're sitting in a multiplex in a part of town zoned only for airports and discount malls, having just come from a meal at the quaint gas-lit French bakery that sits in the middle of a field of home improvement stores and parking lots? We should not trust them too much to figure things out. We need some close-ups of a few military men saying, upon Kelvin's revelation that one of the isle's original inhabitants is behind the current mayhem, "That boy is good," or, "I think he's onto something," or even, "He's right, and may God help us all." It is better this way, for all of us. This way no one gets confused. (Oh life! Oh America!)

But instead, the general says:

— Bullshit. Get him out of here.

For these movies are not any good unless the hero is *taken off the case,* but keeps on it anyway. If Kelvin has to shoot his way, he will do it; his aim will be true for twenty minutes, and those who spray bullets at him will always miss; if he has to build a machine (he will build a machine), he will build one that two large research foundations and a hundred brilliant scientists could never discover the physics of; if bumbling officials warn him of the dangers ahead, he will go into those dangers willingly, and he will say smartass things to the bumbling officials. Order, government, and society are useless; it is these white men with percussive names who are our only protection, though researchers funded by conservative think tanks have told us of distantly related but nonetheless similar thoughts found in the blown-open brains of angry postmen, high-school shooters, mad dictators, disgruntled lovers, and suicide bombers. The threads of society snap and fall, and from the loose, frayed pile spring madmen and action heroes, finally, fictively, dangerously alone.

The Death of Ms. Swan

Liberty is closing in on the former Plaza Hotel, and beyond the Plaza, the unbroken green of Central Park. She has just put her foot through a fashionable boutique and crushed Monique Swan, twenty-four, a shapely, miniskirted retailer with a navel ring glinting below the tight fabric of her cropped top, with high cheeks, bright green eyes, nice lips, a good smile, in a word, a beauty, radiant and pure: a beauty the shop's older, richer, better-kept women envy with every swipe of their gold cards, who has just been sent, well, let's not mince words, screaming by the filmmakers to a horrible and bloody action movie death.

The director instructs his cinematographer to use a special lens, one that will reveal invisible spectra of anguish and pain, and tells him to slowly pan the camera down the long avenue using a crane shot that as it zooms also rises above the destruction this twisted spirit has wrought, yet when the producers ask later about this footage, because they think this would be a perfect place to use Barber's Adagio for Strings, the director mumbles and pretends to answer his cell phone, and Vittorio the cinematographer pretends not to understand, for the footage was too unbearable to watch. Everything was made of darkness, but differentiated in banded hues and thicknesses, a kind of cosmic background radiation of suffering that would never leave until the last human expired. Superimposed on this darkness were sphered hatreds the color of dried blood; vicious green spirals of fear squeezing people's skulls; grief, in mists of light-eating black that hissed in jets from vacant gazes; physical pain dribbling like mercury from stunned mouths and slackened jaws; and mental anguish that geysered through wormholes puckering space itself. In the foreground, Monique's absence formed a ragged gash around which the spirits of everyone who now thought or would ever think of her dimmed inconsolably, and something like a thorn-covered vine reached out from that absence across time to grab Monique's mother by the ankle, pulling her down puffy-eyed and still in her robe, though it is now a late afternoon six years after she had first heard Monique was dead, dragging her inexorably into the darkness that this taking of her daughter has created, into which she disappears, first up to her waist as she begins to slacken, the despair comfortable but sickening, like an overdose, her head now disappearing, until there is only her hand, which drops a coffee mug with a picture of Monique on it when she was eight and dressed as Tinkerbell for Halloween, and then the hand too is pulled into darkness. The mug, as if demonstrating the persistence not of grief but of love and memory, does not shatter but lands on the asphalt with a clink and wobbles to a stop.

The Machine

In the meantime, Kelvin has built his machine.

We have chosen not to show the machine-making scene; it has been done before, and parodied before, and done again with the parody in mind. All we must know is that the machine exists, and that Kelvin has constructed it.

We do not see too much of it—just some wires, cables, and gauges—before Kelvin puts it in his backpack. He cinches an old leather aviator's cap on his head, and strings wires from the cap down to the pack. Then he lifts a pair of gloves from his worktable, each glove also wired to the pack, the thumbs and pinkies of each poking out to allow two very large crab-like banana clips to protrude, and he puts on each glove and he practices squeezing the clips together, scuttling back and forth across his living room. He turns on his television to get the latest location of the statue—it is now just entering Central Park—and then he leaves his apartment. He takes a cab to the Museum of Natural History, then jogs across Central Park West, under arches of branch and bough, down a dark path into deeper shadow, where purple fluorescence spills from black lampposts and pools on the pavement. Across the park a green foot carrying the weight of

450,000 pounds of copper and steel steps west to meet him.

Kelvin has been so focused on the coming fight that he has not noticed the two men in dark glasses following him at a distance, who have actually been tailing him since his eviction from the situation room. The men are extremely agitated, receiving instructions and frantic questions in their earpieces, their pistols drawn since Kelvin left his apartment. In the cab behind his they debated whether or not to shoot out the tires, but now they lose him in the shadows and radio ahead to keep clear, *any sudden movement could set this guy off.* These days it is not a good idea to walk around wearing a big backpack with wires sticking out of it, you're liable to start a panic, or get yourself killed.

Forces Against Liberty Arrayed

The general and the police chief have decided that the Great Lawn is to be the place for the showdown. The tourists and joggers and corporate softball teams and trust-fund hippies playing ultimate Frisbee have been evacuated, and now as Venus rises in the new fallen night snipers shift on the battlements of Belvedere castle, and in the center of the lawn sixteen tanks take aim at an imaginary point one hundred feet in the air.

Liberty passes southwest of the Metropolitan Museum, sees Cleopatra's Needle rearing its pyramid-top to the evening sky and then the horde gathered to meet it on the wide expanse beyond. The statue steps across the trees and walkways into the field.

— Steady boys, steady, the general whispers into the radio.

The whole construction of the statue is in revolt under the tremendous pressure of the walking, rivets pop from the copper sheets, some dangle and fall, but the statue stays intact, supported not by a spine but by the staircase that has been built from its base up through one of its arms.

— I've got it in my sights, general, the tank captain says.

He aims right above the tablet, still clutched in the statue's left arm, at the heart that would be there under the thick robe instead of a pocket of empty air swathed in metal sheeting. The captain has told the other tanks to aim at the joints, the head, and the torch. Just one word from the general and the scream-ing shells will burrow into their target and explode it to pieces.

Liberty steps into the field. Searchlights raze its body with cutting white cones. Her mouth creaks open and blares out a groaning, hollow bellow.

— Ready, the general says.

The statue takes another step.

— Aiiiimmmm, the general says.

The police chief holds a cheap Statue of Liberty postcard in his hand, two for a dollar, six for two dollars, twenty for five. His eyes are swollen as he says, "May God help us all."

And then the FBI comes in on the radio:

— Sir, we have someone coming through the perimeter, it's that boy, he's wired with explosives, our snipers have a clear shot, just say the word.

— Put him on the radio! the general says.

— He has no radio, sir.

—Well give him one!

A tank hatch opens. A corporal jumps out and approaches Kelvin with his arms out and slowly, carefully puts a walkie-talkie on the ground.

—Take this, he says.

The corporal runs back to the tank. The walkie-talkie squawks.

— You are in the middle of a top-secret military operation, the general growls. You must clear the area immediately.

— General, Kelvin says, you must listen to me. That is not Liberty, you must believe me, an impostor has taken over its hallowed form. I can save her, just keep your guns aimed and ready to fire if anything goes wrong. I need five minutes.

On the other end, silence.

— General? Kelvin asks.

The statue is very near, its footsteps boom and the shrieks of its grinding plates pierce Kelvin's ears.

— OK, the general replies, you have five minutes.

The Hero Triumphs?

Hey! Down here! Put down the torch and lift me up. Do what I say or these guys will blow you back to 1626.

Why should I do what you say?

If you put the torch down I will give you a different body. But first I really need you to put down the torch.

All right, all right, the torch is down.

Now put your hand on the ground. I'm going to step onto it. After I step onto it, raise me to your mouth.

Now here we are, little strange man, face to face. Ouch! What is that?

Some clamps. Do they hurt?

A bit.

Do you know how you came here?

In the storm.

I am going to start another one to help you leave.

Where will I go?

Into my body. You will have to get to know me. I love a girl. I study science.

And if I refuse?

Then you will be killed!

Little man, first let me tell you some things that I have seen, and then you can tell me what I should do. Not long after your ancestors first settled here, they started a dishonorable war on the flimsiest of pretexts. Some Dutchman was killed by a Wickquasgeck, it is true, but that native's whole hunting band had been set upon by Europeans some years before and slaughtered, and he was the only one to survive. He waited a long time for his revenge and he took it honorably, even though that one death did not make up for the deaths of twelve of his people. Yet because of this your ancestors attacked. They came without warning in the middle of the night. The men were cut down. Infants were thrown into the river to drown. Their mothers were raped and slaughtered. Even after being set upon, many made their way to the fort, they were confused, not sure who attacked them, they thought they might be protected there, some of them carried their entrails in their hands, some of them carried their own hacked off limbs. They found no protection, they were left to die or if they happened to live they were taken captive, some of them were tortured and mutilated, one was castrated and his own privates were stuffed in his mouth, then he was laid on a stone and his head was beaten until it fell off. A Raritan sachem was tortured in the genitals with a split piece of wood, until he agreed to betray his people and give up his land. And the craziest thing about your people was that they walked among us after that as if nothing had happened, as if they had done nothing wrong. From the sky I watched the fires of the people's summer camps and gathering grounds wink out one by one, until in just a few years I needed only my two hands to count them, and these were people who had once been as numberless as the oysters in the water.

At this point the general cuts in on the walkie-talkie:

— Barrow, it has been four minutes. It appears that you are negotiating, and you need to understand that we do not negotiate. The only way to not get killed is to kill those who would kill you.

And the statue says to Kelvin:

— Little man, I agree with your general.

But then it will never stop.

And the last thing Kelvin hears in his life on this earth is the statue:

—What makes you think it *can?*

And the general:

—What in all human time disposition history or memory?

With a quick snap the statue closes its hand, and the general fires his guns.

The Movie Ends, the Lights Come Up, the People Go Home

Shelly, Kelvin's girl, is there with her camera crew and sees the strange form on the statue's hand, wait, zoom in, she says, and then, my God, it's Kelvin, and just seconds later the statue's fist closes and its body is bathed in sheets of flame. People scream, the tank shells are so powerful the statue doesn't even seem to fall, it just disintegrates in the air, and people start running, but Shelly's knees go out and she hits the ground.

Among the swarms of people running stand the studio execs, looking for the director. One of them stops the actress who plays Shelly and shouts:

—You aren't even pregnant, are you? We can't even have a scene years later, with you in the country, where we clearly recognize Kelvin's features in a butterfly-catching three-year-old?

— No, Shelly says, I'm not. I don't think that will ever happen.

The cops in the park are moving the perimeter back, the lights of approaching squad cars are flashing red and blue. A policewoman sees Shelly on the ground, she takes off her windbreaker, wraps it around Shelly's shoulders.

— Come on girl, let's get you on home, it's not safe here, it's still not safe.

from Bob, or Man on Boat

WHEN BOB FISHES THE RIVER, fishing for fish, he is fishing for more than fish.

There are some fishermen and fisherwomen in town who fish so that they can talk about fishing for fish.

These fisherpeople fish so that one of these days they'll be able to tell you a fish story about the big fish that got away.

Bob does not fish so that Bob can tell that kind of a story.

Sometimes, though, what I do think is this.

That Bob is fishing for the fish that, when Bob fishes this fish up and out of the river, this will be the one fish that will teach Bob something other than how to fish.

I do not know, for Bob, what that something other than how to fish could be.

I can't imagine Bob doing anything besides fishing for his fish.

The river, without Bob out on it, in Bob's boat, fishing for fish, the river, it wouldn't be the same river.

It wouldn't be the same river that it is when Bob is out on this river fishing for his fish.

The river, without Bob on it, fishing in his boat, the river, it wouldn't even be a river.

Now that I am imagining this, the river, this is what I believe would happen to it.

The river, if Bob was not out on it, it would turn, first to mud, then to dirt.

And the fish in the river?

The fish would turn to stone.

*

But that's not gonna happen.

Not to this river.

Not to Bob.

Not to the fish that Bob is fishing this river for.

Bob, when one day Bob finds and fishes out of the river that one fish that will teach him and tell him what to do next, what this fish is going to tell Bob, at least the way that I imagine it happening, is this fish is going to tell Bob to keep on fishing for fish.

And this fish, for saying this, for telling Bob to keep on fishing for fish, the river, it will kiss this fish.

This river, it will throw this fish back.

Back into the river.

Go fish.

*

Oh, if you teach a man to fish.

The river becomes his home.

Bob is sitting on his boat.

Bob's baits are not in the river's water.

Bob is, at the moment, just sitting there staring out across the river at what I do not know.

Maybe this is Bob thinking.

What is Bob thinking about?

Fish.

His fish.

What if Bob never finds the fish that he is fishing for?

Is this what Bob is thinking?

Or is Bob thinking this?

That the fish that Bob is fishing for, it is somewhere in the river waiting for Bob to find it.

Bob is an optimist.

If you teach a man how to fish, Bob knows, that man will fish forever.

He will never go hungry again.

Such a man is Bob.

Bob is only hungry for one fish.

The fish that is the fish.

There are fish in the river that are considered eaters.

This fish is not that kind of a fish.

And there are other fish in this river that are the kind of fish that you throw back when you fish them up and into your boat.

Come back when you're older is what we say to these kinds of fish.

And then there are the fish like the fish that Bob is fishing for.

This kind of fish, I'm not sure what you're supposed to do with this kind of fish.

To fish this kind of fish up and out of the river, I can only imagine that this might be like coming up to the man who is your father and hearing this father call you his son.

What do you do at a moment like this?

You hold onto it is what you do.

You hold that man in your arms.

You hold your hands onto that fish.

*

But how long can you hold a fish out of water before this fish starts gasping for breath?

You only get one fish like this.

You only get one father who is your father.

You only get one son if one son is all you've got.

There comes a time when you've got to let go.

There comes a time when you've got to look this fish straight in the eye and then that's it.

It's over.

And the river keeps flowing and flowing.

*

And so Bob goes home.

Bob goes home to his boat that floats on the flowing river.

Bob goes home to the river.

Where Bob fishes for fish.

*

I go home too.

To be with my son.

I am a father.

My son is a fish.

*

I like to tell my son stories.

My son likes to hear me tell him these stories.

In each story, there is always some kind of a fish.

In each story, there is a man in the story who is fishing for this fish.

This man, I always call him Bob.

The story always ends the same way, with Bob living happily ever after.

After Bob catches his fish.

*

What my son always says to this is, What happens next?

What does Bob do after he catches the fish?

That's the part of the story, I tell my son, that I don't know what happens next.

*

What do you think happens to Bob next?

Sometimes I ask my son this.

My son says that he thinks that Bob, after he catches the fish, Bob gets eaten by the fish.

Bob gets eaten by the fish? I say.

I say to my son, Is that a happy ending?

My son reminds me that this is what fish do.

Fish eat, he tells me.

Fish eat other fish.

*

So in my son's version of this Bob gets eaten by the fish that he's been fishing for.

That fish must be a pretty big fish, I say to my son.

It is, he says.

It's this big, he says, and he stretches his arms out as far as he can get them to stretch.

It's as big as the river is, he says.

He says that this fish, it's as big as from where our house is and it goes up all the way to the moon.

That sounds like it's bigger than a whale is, is what I say to this.

It is, he says.

It's a moon-fish.

This fish, my son tells me, it swam all the way down from where the moon is.

That's some fish, I tell him.

I say, That's some story.

It gets even better, my son says.

Tell me, I say.

What happens next?

*

What happens next is this.

This fish, this big moon-fish, it has swum down all the way from where the moon is to eat up all the fish.

To eat up all the fishermen.

It won't stop, it won't swim back to the moon, until there's nothing left for this fish to eat.

*

So maybe I should stay away from the river, I say, if this fish is gonna eat up all of the fish.

It won't be safe to be fishing the river if this fish is gonna eat all of us fishing men up.

And what my son then says to this is that he thinks that might not be such a bad idea.

*

Three days later, I go out on the river.

Out on the river that night, I see Bob's boat tied up to its dock, but I don't see Bob sitting up in Bob's boat.

I do not, at first, think that something's gone wrong.

I think to myself that maybe Bob has gone into town to pick up some gas to gas up his boat.

But the river, without Bob sitting on it, there's something big missing from this picture.

That night, I fish more fish out of the river than I have ever fished out of it before.

And I know why.

I know that the fish that I am fishing out of the river are the fish that would be Bob's.

But because Bob is not fishing the river, I catch more fish that night—there are so many fish piled up on the bottom of my boat—that it's hard for me to keep count.

That night, I'm up half the night cleaning fish.

The guts, that night, I don't bury the guts the way I usually do out back in our backyard garden.

I put the guts into two buckets.

In the morning, I go with these two buckets of guts, down to the river, and I throw the guts in.

I think about Bob and how Bob believes that the guts of the fish, when Bob gives them back to the river, the guts turn back into fish.

I think about my son's story about the moon-fish that is eating up all of the river's fish.

I think about the river and what would happen, one day, if the river ran out of fish.

I think about Bob again and what would Bob do if the river one day ran out of fish before Bob fished from the river that one fish that he has for so long been fishing for.

I think about Bob's boat and the way that it looked last night without Bob in it.

It looked just like the dead man's boat must have looked when those two boys in Ohio first saw it sitting there in the mud on their river's muddy banks.

So I get in my boat.

I go in my boat down the river to where Bob's boat is.

Bob's boat is sitting there, rocking in the wake made by my boat as I motor up to it, to see if there is any sign of Bob.

There is no Bob sitting there in Bob's boat.

Bob's boat is just a boat.

What I think now, what I know now, is that there is more than just something big missing from this picture.

There is something wrong with this picture.

The river, it is missing Bob.

The river's not the same without Bob out on it.

There's something wrong with this river without Bob fishing for the fish that live down in it.

So I go back upriver, I go into town, and I start asking whoever I see if any of them have seen Bob.

Nope.

Not since last week.

It's been a while.

I bought some fish from him last Friday but I haven't seen him since.

This is what the townspeople who know Bob have to tell me about not seeing Bob.

When I go back out onto the river, to ask some of the fisherman and fisherwomen if any of them have seen Bob, they all say the same thing: nope, not since last week, it's been a while since Bob's been out on the river.

But let me tell you this, they also tell me.

The fishing around here, it's never been better.

I got more fish than I can eat, they say.

I hate to say it, one fisherman says this to me, but this river is a better place without Bob on it.

I give this fishing man a look.

I want to take one of my fishing hooks and hook it through his lip.

I want to take an anchor to this man's head.

I make a fist.

Fish on, this man hollers.

I watch this man set his hooks into the lip of a fish.

This fish, I think, it could be the fish.

It could be Bob's fish.

I pull away before I get a look at the fish that is about to be fished up into this boat that is not Bob's.

That night, I can't sleep.

All night long, I keep picturing Bob, walking along the bottom of the river, looking for this fish.

*

It's true that the big fish who live in the river like to be big fish in the river alone.

It is also true that the littler fish who live in the river like to swim together in the river along with other little fish.

This is true, too, about the people who fish for these fish.

There are people who fish the river who like to fish close to where there are other boats fishing for fish.

It's believed that where there are fishing boats fishing for fish that beneath those boats there must be fish to be fished out of the river and fished up into these boats.

Sometimes, this is true.

But Bob, you will never see Bob's boat anywhere near any of these bunched up boats.

Bob is like a big fish out on the river fishing for the fish that, like Bob, this fish likes to be a fish alone.

Bob fishes the parts of the river that other fishermen and other fisherwomen believe are dead.

Bob knows that no part of the river is dead.

In Bob's eyes, the river, every last piece of the river, it is alive.

It is alive with fish.

It is alive because of fish.

Bob is the fish that I am fishing for.

Is there a bigger fish for a man to fish for than the fish that is his father?

I can think of only one fish that is bigger than the fish that is the father.

The fish that is the son.

*

The fish that is the son is a fish that wants to be fished up from the bottom of the river.

*

I am a fish.

I am a fish.

*

When I fish, I fish for Bob.

When I go out onto the river, in my boat, I am not just a fishing man.

I am a fish waiting to be caught.

*

The river is a bridge to Bob.

In my boat, I float and I drift and I motor on by Bob with the hope that one of these days Bob is going to look up.

One of these days, when Bob looks up, he will see a light that he is looking to see.

One of these days, when Bob listens up close, he will hear a sound that he is listening to hear.

This light, this sound, it is not coming from the inside of a fish.

This light, and the song behind it, it is coming from a boat.

Not just any old boat.

It is coming from this man's boat.

And I am the captain, I am the fish steering and standing in the back of this boat.

*

One of these days, I am going to holler out, to Bob, Bob, take a look at this fish.

I will stand with my arms spread apart as far as I can stretch them, to say to Bob that this fish that I am talking about, it is a big fish, it is a fish so big it is too big to fit inside this boat.

Will Bob even look up?

Will Bob lift up his head?

If Bob knows anything, it is this.

The fish that's already been fished up out of the river, that fish isn't the fish that he is fishing for.

It's not the fish that you can see.

It's the fish that you can't see.

The fish that hasn't yet been caught.

The fish that hasn't yet been named.

When Bob reaches his hands into the river, there is no telling what he might fish up.

*

And then, one day, up from the river, it is the sun that rises up.

And then, like this, in the light of this light, I see the man that I call Bob.

Bob, I say, when I see that it's him, but Bob doesn't see me.

I am the son that Bob does not know.

I am the fish at the bottom of the river waiting to be fished up.

*

Bob fishes.

Bob is fishing.

Bob was fishing.

Bob fished last night.

Bob will fish again later tonight.

By day, Bob sleeps.

When Bob is sleeping, Bob is dreaming about fish.

When Bob sleeps, Bob dreams about fishing.

Bob dreamed today, as he was sleeping, about fishing for that fish.

That fish, in Bob's dreams, it leaped up out of the river.

Bob dreamed that he woke up on the river.

In Bob's dream, Bob dreamed that the river was his bed.

Bob dreamed that when he woke up from his dreaming, the fish was sleeping next to him in this bed.

Bob reached over across this bed and put his hand on this fish's fin.

Bob shook this fish's fin to try and wake this fish up from its sleeping.

But this fish did not wake up from this sleeping.

This fish was not sleeping.

This fish, it was dead.

*

It's true.

Fish in this river die.

It happens all the time.

Sometimes, fish stop breathing.

Sometimes, fish stop swimming.

Sometimes, these fish float up to the river's top.

Sometimes, these fish float on past Bob and Bob's boat.

Sometimes, Bob will fish these floating by fish up out of the river, and Bob will fish these fish up into his boat.

Bob does not fish these dead fish up out of the river and fish these fish up into his boat so that he can sell them.

Bob does not fish these dead fish up out of the river and fish these fish up into his boat so that he can eat them.

What Bob does do to these dead fish that he fishes up out of the river is, Bob guts the guts out of these fish.

The guts of these dead fish, Bob throws the guts back into the river.

Bob throws the guts of these dead fish back into the river so that the guts of these dead fish can turn back into fish.

ROB SCHLEGEL

Lives of Tree

The northern saga eyes forest
In seeds. Timbers

Spinning water, the pond's surface
And oil. The hill is dark

With crickets
Glass bottles keep

When soil emits ink
And axle and thunder stalls

The harvest; mutes the summer
And violets. Down

The tree's creased bark
Lightning starts a seam of heat

Until curtains of flame fabric
The branches as flames and

The sound of flames shape the trees
Burning their first farewell.

Lives of Animal

See the slaughter and
Blink once. Stab

The dark with shanks,
Pretty metals, dripping

Stars. Custody in the air;
In the body cavity

Of the animal arrange
Thirty lit candles.

Twice, frost
Sharpened winter's shears,

Smoke of flesh—its profit
And umber ruin.

Film in Place of a Legal Document

Where the green pump calls for wonderful arms
to bring up water in iron gulps

pan left: to distant fluctuations, to hooves freaking
insects out of grass.

The soundtrack said: *You think your thirst*
arcs from the waterspout
when in fact it arcs from the ground.

Sinister, like a ventriloquist draining a glass of water
while making
a whole statuary sing.

To the left of the linden in June, to the left of the graveyard's
human quiet

a neighbor worked a pneumatic hammer.

It was left to the ocean to matchstick the hull,
left to the darkroom to develop the trees.

Sending Owls to Athens

Redundancy redundancy.

                                     Moon of my collarbone long ago broken.

Moon overlapping my look at the vascular. A dog-eared page says

Neptune green. A fourth type of song

                                            is performed upon

a cricket's invasion of territory. Broken in

the place of broken. Or nothing would argue my nervous system: grays

in the grays of nephogram, ash tree's flourish

where the library steps.

                                      Wind in the color—

there is no such thing. No color to color the color.

Thicket Play

I asked the sun to stay outside.

                I called its effort *disentangled.* I put the body

there as marker, held up as if

                    in place of. Or else

a thing stooped down upon, and snapped.

                    Pictured then

as clasped inside. Claw paw hand: I made the body as mainly

its branches.

          One branch

I called the *childhood coffer.*

Inside it were

the many reasons.

JULIA COHEN

I Carry a Basket for the Fingers That Fall

The nests outside swing wider
than my house   my hilltop
the crest on the mantel calling   for veins

When I fork this light two bodies
        blend into the face you held
Jumbled letters   glisten on the backs
of flowers

In the frozen garden I feel
fetching   how I met you   how sleep
        mists our daily envies

so the ovals upturn & open

* * *

Small breaths penny   the floor
into soft nooks & wetness
        descends down the chimney

When I take my gloves
off the water is   wetter
        tastes like the day I learned

to run with a basket of sheets

* * *

Don't back away from
the face's missing fingers   I'll be at the altar
of your sleepcoat   an emaciated tree

with my offer of nametags
        & a broken dinner plate

I've never moved slower

No oily necklace   no bicycle seats offer
        to cut the sheet into smaller sections

* * *

I could saw the trees into a bed
        to angle your sleep

But you would still be sleeping
        Yelps from the chimney
are the victors

JENNIFER HAYASHIDA

On Tourism

Port cities capture vigor, relevance rendered by gravity, asserted in the hull of a tanker square with cargo to/from Hong Kong, Nassau, Gothenburg. Transnational stencils are lessons in resource distribution—concentric spheres of the tropical, the factory, the market, the middleman.

Each port hole a moon socket, the poem a lazy eye cast upon capitols of industry and import/export, the canal a phenomenon of necessity, tectonic interventions prompted by the ideal line between *Here* and *There*.

In Marseilles, swastikas along the waterfront, semiotic injunctions against touristic pleasures, the rain also a memory, as sky or as window frame, the train otherwise without grammar, the day otherwise without reminders.

Tourism spiked the economy as the bartender spiked this drink and you went home with a stranger to another shore, this one flecked with cigarette butts and bottle caps—the ground an experiment in working class leisure. For each cap another degree of relief, like pissing by the side of the road, like giving the dog up for dead.

Mulen Suburb

grow filthimmel mischief breeze
unseemly rain-swim dugg in luften
prickiga and kalla pinpricks meet naked
lilytight forest mat   jordig starmark
birches resist, become loja spjärnar again
we "stretch our benen" och hoppas for storm
irresponsible excuseweather
längtan for Alfapet, kaffe, videofilm
wallpapered tv-realities
even testbilden stimulerar senses
and we smallsleep med covers in soffan

nedhukad in the heather   snabbkiss
afraid för rumpants   barr in underpants
cityshod skogsamateurs som kick svamp
och mossa from jorden, forget fröken's cautions (ca.1984):
"It tar hundratals of years for mossa att grow."
ofrivilliga forestfoxes saknar sense of pastorala
promenader pick single lingon
en fist of rosiga bär forgotten i bilen rotten
inklämda in the backseat tillsammans med small change
och a petrified gummisnodd

COREY FROST

Système de Montréal—Montreal System

THE NIGHT OF THE STORM I AM ALONE IN MY APARTMENT. The plastic I bought at Canadian Tire is beginning to peel off the windows and I have decided not to go home for Christmas. When the power goes out, I say, I'm thinking of a person—you tell me who the person is. It's like those games you've played where people take turns asking, *Are you an animal? Are you a movie star? Are you alive?* and you answer, *Yes I am, No I am not, Yes I am.*

C'est une question un peu bizarre, peut-être, mais . . . um . . . I'd like to know . . . the voice on the system, the answering service . . . who is it?
Pardon? C'est qui?
Oui, c'est qui, cette voix? Who is it?

I am a real person. I am alive. I'm not famous. I woke up at 2:00 P.M. one day and had an experience that upset my daily routine, so subtly and yet so powerfully that I was forced to re-examine what I had until then regarded as my life. Although it began suddenly, the experience took a year to unfold completely, and by the end I was left wondering, How did I get here? Where do I go from here? and also, What will I leave behind when I go? By the end, I (that is, the person I'm thinking of) was also thinking of a person, because a mystery is often solved by another mystery.

C'est qui? Mais, je ne sais pas vraiment. C'est . . . je suppose que c'est une actrice. C'est une voix enregistrée, vous savez. Ou bien quelqu'un qui travail ici.
Oui, je suppose, okay, mais . . . I wanted to find out the name of that person, or . . . to find out if I could maybe talk to her . . .

The experience began while I was checking the messages on my telephone. This is a service provided by the phone company that obviates the need for an answering machine, which had itself obviated the need to answer the phone. The telephone I'm thinking of is located in an apartment that has two wrought-iron balconies, hardwood floors, high ceilings, and electric baseboard heaters that are pitiably insufficient in the winter months. On that day it was particularly cold in the apartment, and when the phone rang repeatedly I stayed in bed. The bed is a well-worn futon with mismatched quilts. A ringing telephone can be a difficult stimulus to resist, but I'm indifferent to it and it's the city I'm thinking of that fosters that indifference. When I did get up, I found there was no more coffee.

Mais, elle n'est pas ici! Je ne sais meme pas son nom, et si je le savais je ne pourrais pas vous le donner, pas de question!
Why? Pourquoi?
Pourquoi? Parce-que si je vous le donne, il faudrait le donner à tout le monde, à toute la ville . . .

Perhaps many people had called that morning, or maybe the same person had called over and over, but there was only one message, and all it said was, "Where *are* you?" What caught my attention and caused my *bouleversement* was not the message, though, not the content of the message, but the answering service itself. The voice that tells me how many messages there are, usually as familiar and unnoticed as my own, had been changed. Before, the voice had been professional almost to the point of condescension, and slightly robotic. But the new voice was real and nuanced. It used exactly the same words, with exactly the same rhythm and intonation, but the difference was unmistakable.

C'est une question un peu bizarre, peut-être, mais . . . c'est qui? [Basically, the speaker wants to know the identity of the person on the voice-mail system. French is not the speaker's first language.]
Pardon? C'est qui? [Casual bewilderment. The *téléphoniste* has a stressful job. She's probably been told to give a false name if anyone asks for it—in fact she has one all picked out. *Giselle.* She can't tell what is being asked, and maybe she hasn't decided whether or not this is harassment.]

I had stopped hearing what the voice said. Once you know the routine—listen, press 1; delete, press 7—there's no point in listening to the words. So when I heard a different voice speaking them, it was as if I could see through the words, directly to the personality. They became transparent, not because their meaning was readily apparent, but in the opposite sense: the words had no meaning, they were simply the substance of a mysterious identity, located not even at the other end of the line, but somewhere between this end and the other end.

The new voice, with its new identity, acknowledged the meaninglessness of "Listen, press 1." The voice was saying to me, "You and I understand one another. We both know what's going on, and it's more than a simple phone message."

Oui, c'est qui, cette voix? [Here, a touch of defensiveness. The speaker may be unsure whether the confusion is due to the question itself or the imperfect French in which it was rendered.]

Mais, je ne sais pas vraiment. [She doesn't know who it is. Really. Pause.] *C'est . . . je suppose . . .* [She supposes it must be an actress, or someone who works here.]

But something else caught my attention. This new voice was familiar, so familiar that at first I hadn't noticed how easily it fell into place in my mind. Could it be that I knew this new voice, knew her as a real, embodied person?

Oui, je suppose, mais . . . [Can I talk with her, the caller wants to know?]

Mais, elle n'est pas ici! [She is not here! The *téléphoniste* hints, through metalinguistic cues, that the person calling is a lunatic.]

Perhaps it was only that I'd heard the voice before—perhaps the same person had recorded the voice mail system at the place where I used to work, or maybe it was the same voice that says "Watch your step" at the airport. A few days later, when it was too cold to go out, I spent most of the afternoon phoning the electronic systems I knew—the university, the library, the train station—but none of them answered me in the same voice, and I couldn't remember where I'd heard it before. Gradually I became convinced that it was someone I knew, or had once known. Over the next few weeks, as the city thawed and I went about my meager business again, my conviction wavered like a mirage, but finally it solidified in front of me and blocked my path.

Pourquoi? [Why?]

Pourquoi? [Why?]

C'est juste que je pense que c'est quelqu'un que je connais . . . et j'aimerais savoir comment la rejoindre . . . [The caller confesses that he thinks the voice may belong to an old friend, whom he would like to find. The caller would like to say more, but is beginning to feel the futility of the task.]

I imagined how I might contact her. The question seemed absurd, since every time I picked up the phone, she was there. Every time I wanted to contact someone else or someone else wanted to contact me, she was the messenger. But I couldn't send a message to her. She had no name, no number.

Mais c'est impossible.

The first few times I called the phone company I was completely rebuffed, but finally I convinced someone to take my name and number and to pass a message on to her. By this time, I was uncertain if I really knew her, or if it was just the voice I knew. My connection to the voice was somewhat obsessive, I suppose, but it wasn't delusional. I wasn't one of those frustrated individuals who fall in love with celebrities and then try to get their attention by killing other celebrities. It was simply that this voice, with its confident pronouncements and its reassuring cadences, made me feel better about my life as a non-celebrity.

Je ne peux pas vous promettre qu'elle va vous appeller. [The sympathetic *téléphoniste* says that she can make no promises.]
Je sais. Je vous remercie. [I know. Thank you.]

About a month later, I got a message. I'd been home all day, and the phone hadn't rung. It had been dark for hours when I realized that I'd eaten nothing that day except a bagel with cream cheese, so I picked up the phone to order food. I was surprised to find it beeping. A message had been sent directly to my voice mail, as if it had emanated not from a distant telephone but from somewhere within the system itself. It was definitely the same voice, but the effect of hearing her speak spontaneously disoriented me. She left no name, no number. And no indication that she recognized me from her past.

Bonjour. C'était une des téléphonistes qui m'a donné ce numero. She told me that you believe you used to know me. But well, I must tell you, c'est une période très difficile pour moi. I have tried to . . . sever . . . all contact . . . avec mon ancienne vie. J'éspère que ça ne te fait pas trop de misère. I hope you will not be offended. If things go well, maybe I will phone you. But I can't promise. Please, je ne veux pas que tu essaye de me trouver. Goodbye.

And that was the last thing I heard her say to me. Which is untrue, of course, in at least two ways, since I continued to hear her voice every day on the answering service, and since even this message was not actually her, but only another recording. It was, in a way, more "real" than the recording I normally heard, and maybe it was the only thing I ever really heard her say. But this "real" voice also seemed to come from another world entirely, and in a way I felt that the real voice was the one that told me, "You have no new messages." One voice was natural and the other supernatural, but I couldn't tell which was which.

I played it over and over, paying attention to how the nuances of the voice corresponded to those on the system. It had a distinct vocal signature—certain vowels pronounced certain ways, certain words liaised—just like a written signature, or the marks made by a particular typewriter. But the voice also diverged at times from its little rituals, and in those hesitations or sudden changes of direction between languages, there was a momentary escape from the persona on the system. In those moments, when the language blew open like a curtain in a window, I thought I saw a glimpse of a person I used to know. I couldn't see a face, only a familiar outline—perhaps even intimately familiar. It was not just an acquaintance, I realized, but someone I had, in some way or another, loved: a boy, a very peculiar boy I had met one summer, not here, but somewhere I couldn't recall. I remembered his skinny frame and the soft short hair at the back of his neck, but when I tried to picture his face the curtain blew closed again. Neither could I put a name to the shape, or any words we had shared, except a murmured phrase, an exclamation that was half laughter. The voice, though, was unmistakable and clung tenaciously to memory. The pitch was different; it was now a woman's voice, and older, but I heard in it the same boyish laugh.

To me they were the same person, the woman and the fragmented boy. The voice was female, certainly, but like the words she spoke, the gender seemed arbitrary, a part of the user-friendly interface. It was not accidental that the voice was female, I realized: voice-mail systems are always inhabited by women. Maybe the voice on the phone had been digitally altered. Or maybe the boy I had once loved was only a boy in my memory. The more uncertain I became, the more I wanted to meet this person—but not because I wanted the mystery to be resolved.

But she didn't call again. The summer came rather unexpectedly for me, as it does every year. I puzzled over her identity and found a place for it in my mind, but did not put it away. Every day I listened to her voice, and when I picked up the phone I felt an instant sense of well-being. No matter how often I listened, even though it said the same few phrases over and over again, for me the voice was always saying something different and intriguing.

I started to indulge in a kind of dream-like, quasi-sexual meditation while listening to her instructions. It wasn't hard to imagine that a real person was talking to me on the other end of the line. I would turn on the speaker-phone and wander through the menus. If I waited too long before choosing an option, as inevitably happened, she would gently remind me of her presence by asking, "Are you still there?" And if I still neglected to press anything, she would tell me she was sorry I was having problems and ask me to try again later. This was a new kind of intimacy, I thought. It seemed historically significant.

Once, after I had pressed 4 and was fiddling with my "personal options," I was suddenly startled by a male voice, which referred to the answering service itself, this world in which I was living, as "*Système de Montréal*—Montreal System." I hung up the phone, but later that night while I was riding the metro, thinking about my telephonic existence, it occurred to me that the city itself is a system. As with language, the individual elements—the words or the people—have no meaning without the system of which they are a part. The Montreal System is a meaning mill, processing bits and pieces of languages and lives and churning out a city. Now that system seemed directly linked to my own nervous system, my body, my voice. And what meaning would I have, I found myself wondering, without this system of desires I had built around myself?

The end of the experience, near the end of the year, also came through voice mail. I woke up one day to find I was out of coffee again, went out to find some, and spent an hour on the mountain taking photos of the sunset. I'd missed the daylight entirely the day before, so I wanted to preserve some of the fading purple light in case I ran out later on. I hid a paper bag of warm bagels inside my jacket and walked home in the dark, wading through knee-deep drifts of snow along Avenue du Parc. I had one new message.

Hello. You don't know me, but I'm calling on behalf of Kathy Tremblay. It's very important that you call me.

The caller had repeated this in French and had left a phone number. I didn't know the man's voice, and I didn't know who Kathy Tremblay was, but I called back right away and the same man answered. He asked me if I was a friend of Kathy's, and I said that I hadn't seen her in a long time. He said my number had been in Kathy's address book, and he was trying to contact all her friends because, well, Kathy had died. The cancer had finally won, he said. He asked me if by any chance I was a relation, and I said no. So far he had been unable to locate any of Kathy's family. "I don't think that she was really in contact with her family," I said.

"Yes, so it seems," he said, and then he told me that the funeral was happening on Sunday. I took down the details and thanked him, and then as he was about to say goodbye I asked if he had known Kathy well himself. He explained that he'd been hired as the executor; he had never met Kathy, although he had once talked to her, over the phone.

After hanging up, and even during the conversation, I felt detached. Kathy was a name I didn't know and didn't even particularly like. Death is a physical effect, and in this case the physical body had never really existed for me. In fact, only now did it have a real presence, lying on a table in a mortuary somewhere, soon to be in a casket surrounded by flowers. Then it would be buried in the cemetery on the mountain, where I could visit if I wanted to, on Sunday after-noons. But the voice was not with the body and never had been. When I lifted the telephone receiver again the same familiar voice greeted me and assured me there were no new messages. For almost a year the voice had been repeating these words to me, to everyone in the city. It was possible that the telephone company didn't even know that the original voice, the true voice, was dead. But was the person on the phone the same person who had died a few days ago of cancer? On one hand it seemed that fame had made her immortal, but on the other hand, perhaps fame is a kind of death, that steals you away from yourself and fixes you in eternal, inaccessible space. Maybe, from the moment her voice was recorded, she was already dead.

The funeral home was only a few blocks from my apartment, a massive pres-ence occupying a corner I passed almost daily. I had always been obliquely aware of its function, but the thought of entering the building made me see the corner in a different way, and changed something in my relationship to the whole city.

The exterior walls were stucco and seemed incongruous behind the snowbanks, while inside, the carpeted lobby with its tinted-glass light fixtures, waxy plants and raffia-wrapped chairs felt vaguely like a somber Greek restaurant. It was the first time I'd ever been to a funeral in this city. I didn't associate the city with death, even though living here was a constant process of mourning something or other: someone leaving town, some job falling through, some restaurant closing. But now, in this space that was so intimate with actual death and reminded me of family, I suddenly felt completely foreign, an outsider again.

Opposite the front entrance, on an easel next to a pair of doors, was a black letterboard whose white push-in letters read *Tremblay*. Inside, about thirty people were sitting on metal chairs facing a lectern and a daïs where the coffin floated amidst a cloud of flowers. Across one of the larger bouquets was a banner that read, simply, *Goodbye*. The coffin was open, but I couldn't see the face inside, only a pair of hands holding a lily. The service had already begun, so I sat down in the back row. A white-haired man stood next to the lectern, saying something to the effect that it was a tragedy to see a young life cut short so abruptly. He confided, nevertheless, that he was able to find meaning in the mystery of death by speaking with God, and he was confident enough to assure us that we too would find solace if we listened for His voice. The audience was mostly women, dressed in somber grays and cream-coloured silk blouses. They clung together in small groups near the front, and I had the impression they all knew one another. Some of them seemed to be in a state of shock. I was so absorbed in observing the audience that at first I didn't notice that the white-haired man, who was one of only a few men in the room, had stopped speaking. His head was bowed, and he was absently pulling at the sleeves of his suit jacket, as if he thought they were too short. It was quiet, and I became intensely aware of small sounds: the creaking of chairs, the zipper of someone's purse, the traffic outside. In the front row someone was softly weeping.

After what seemed like a long time, the white-haired man lifted his head and spoke again. "Before she died, Kathy wanted to record a farewell to her friends, and she asked that the recording be played for everyone who gathered in her memory. So at this point I ask you to listen to this final message from Kathy, so we may all remember, cherish, and inwardly respond to her words in our own individual ways." Then he nodded to someone standing near the back, and there was the low airy sound of speakers being turned on, and a moment of anticipation before her voice suddenly filled the room. I closed my eyes when I heard it and tried to imagine, with the static from the speakers, that I was hearing the message on the phone, speaking to me from the other world. But the voice was fuller, richer, in stereo, and it resonated across the quiet, carpeted room, taking on a nearly omnipresent quality. I was not certain, after all, that this was a voice I knew, and not even certain that it was the voice from the message system. I became confused, again and on a new level, about who this person was. Unable to pay attention to what the voice was saying, I focused entirely on its pitch, timbre, tone. For a moment, I thought I glimpsed a familiar shape in the sounds, but just then her voice began to choke, as if tiny pieces were missing from it, and then I heard her say a final goodbye.

I would have talked to the other people present, but I felt that the questions I wanted to ask were somehow inappropriate, immodest. It was obvious that my desire to connect this woman to my past could not be satisfied by talking to anyone there. After the room had mostly emptied out, I finally gravitated to the front. She was wearing a high-collared, emphatically feminine dress the color of a tropical lagoon. Her hair, auburn with streaks of blond, curled in wisps around her ears. She seemed to be in her thirties. It was hard to see her complexion through the makeup, but it seemed that she had spent some time in tanning salons. I didn't recognize her face. There was no face in my memory for comparison, though, so I wasn't convinced that this person was not the boy I had once loved. A familiar amalgam of curiosity and desire made me want to look beneath the lid of the coffin, and under the aquamarine dress. Are you a real person? Are you a movie star? Are you alive? From the face, with its cosmetic surface and its lips sewn shut, I couldn't tell anything about the rest of the body or the body's history. The system of signs that might have told me had collapsed, along with the circulatory system, the nervous system—all the systems. But I was not obsessed to the point of breaking all social and legal taboos; I had not gone that far. So I sat for a moment in a chair, and then I signed the guestbook. I felt compelled, for some reason, to leave a false name. Then I went home.

C'est juste que je pense que c'est quelqu'un que je connais . . . et j'aimerais savoir comment la rejoindre . . .

Mais, elle n'est pas ici!

For two weeks her voice continued to reassure me every day, and I made my own recording of it to be sure I'd be able to hear it whenever I wanted. Then it was replaced. I don't know how many times I called during those two weeks. I would sit and wait for her to ask me, Are you still there? And then I'd press a button and wait again for her to ask one more time. Are you still there?

The night of the storm I am alone in my apartment. I am thinking of a person. Who am I? I am not the "I" of the previous story, but I'm not "me" either. I am not famous, but I am alive. My science fair project is a homemade computer. I made a grid of wires, and connected tiny red light-emitting diodes at all the intersections and connected the ends to little switches so that turning the switch for 2 and the switch for 3 would light up the light for 5, but it doesn't work, because I don't know anything about electronics or computers except how to write a program in Basic that will print my name over and over again until I stop it. When they come to my table I tell the judges that the batteries died, and I still win second place because I have good posters. My computer has a shoebox keyboard, and if you turn it over it just looks like a jumble of wires, but all you have to do is connect this one to this one here, and connect this to the nine-volt battery, and all the LEDs glow. Then you can imagine it looks like a small, complicated, underground city.

from The Mothering Coven

X

LEAVES USED TO PILE ON ONE SIDE OF THE HOUSE, and now they pile on the other. The wind has changed direction. And who is subscribing to all these magazines?

Agnes closes the kitchen window. She checks the herring. No bubbles.

"The oven isn't even on," says Agnes.

"It must be a Bismarck," says Mrs. Borage. "You never cook a Bismarck."

Mrs. Borage has a logical mind. She sits in her rocking chair, snipping pictures from *The Helsinki Winki*. The pictures are better than the articles. Mrs. Borage wonders if it is the Finnish language that she finds objectionable.

"Or else I don't have the patience for very long words anymore," thinks Mrs. Borage. Mrs. Borage stands up.

"I caught a herring once," announces Mrs. Borage, "in Lake Chargoggagogg-manchauggagoggchaubunagungamaugg." Mrs. Borage sits down.

"That felt wonderful," says Mrs. Borage. It's settled then; she objects to the Finnish language.

Mrs. Borage picks up her scissors. She is snipping pictures of the Finnish National Hockey Team. Mrs. Borage does not object to Finnish hockey players. Mrs. Borage is about to turn one hundred, but she can still appreciate a Schatzilein.

[∴]

Agnes folds the laundry—Bertrand's crimson gambeson—she's washed it again. Laces, broken. Stuffing coming out. Is that mildew? Agnes looks closer. Death caps have sprouted along the quilting. Pale green diamonds on a crimson field. The sickly yellow fringe, that's honey tuft, and the leather collar, trompette de morts. Agnes heaves the gambeson back into the dryer drum.

"The tenth, or tithe, is often given to the Imperium," says Agnes, to no one in particular.

"But we weren't ten," says Bryce.

"Agnes, Bertrand, Bryce, Fiona, Dorcas, Hildegard, and Ozark" says Dorcas. "Mrs. Borage, eight."

Besides, is Europe still the Imperium? There are so many abandoned castles, so many unemployed knights, entire orders in desuetude. The Esoteric Order of Night-Blooming Phlox. The Order of Brücken. The Noble Order of Girdle. The Order of Pussywillow. The Order of Radish.

[:]

Bryce has taped Bertrand's postcards to the refrigerator door, to the microwave door, to the television screen. Now she is coating them with polyurethane. She adds a bit of moss to Lake Nero, to simulate an algal bloom. Over here—silica flakes! They give a badly needed glimmer to the deserts of Poland.

Bryce imagines Bertrand in the deserts of Poland. Will Bertrand see the white and gold Polish eagle? Will she see Queen Wanda the Drowned?

The moss absorbs a good deal of polyurethane. Bryce has a terrible headache. Headaches are always the danger with the plastic arts.

[:]

The telephone on the mantel is tiled with mirrors, sunflower seeds, golden nuggets of bee pollen, and, of course, the delicate skins of glue Bryce peels from her fingers, nine whorls and a pollex loop, repeating. Agnes has a sudden urge to pick it up.

"Hello?" says Agnes.

"ZZZZZZZZZ!" says a collective voice. Agnes hangs up, puzzled.

"A dial-tone?" asks Agnes. As far as Agnes knows, the phone has never been connected.

X

Mrs. Borage is in the yard, raking leaves into enormous piles. The wind keeps carrying the leaves away. They fly back and forth past the dining room window.

"Should we help her?" asks Bryce.

"Her movements are so regular," says Fiona. "It must be a form of raking meditation."

Now Mrs. Borage is carrying rocks from the garden, rocks and cabbage heads and dried pumpkin vines and red lettuce hearts, big armfuls.

"She's weighing down the piles," says Dorcas. "That's very clever."

Mrs. Borage goes back and forth, back and forth, from the piles to the garden.

"It looks fun," says Ozark. Bryce is putting on her green mackintosh. She's been meaning to make leaf lapel-pins for quite awhile now, and maybe a catkin sash.

"I'll get the wheelbarrow," cries Dorcas. Fiona blocks the doorway. We look at her.

"No sudden moves," says Fiona. "We can't interfere with the Theta-brain."

"The Theta-brain," says Dorcas. "Of course." We cluster again at the dining room window. We try to peer less obtrusively. This involves curtains.

"Achoo," sneezes Ozark. Fiona glares. We glare. We peer between the curtains.

If Mrs. Borage is jolted from her trance too soon, she could be trapped: her soul on a shamanic journey, her body piling cabbage heads on oak leaves, back and forth, back and forth, for all of time.

[:]

Suddenly, Mrs. Borage stops, her arms filled with bottle gourds. She realizes that she has built eight cairns on the front lawn. They give the property a somber aspect. This is not at all what she intended.

"Fiddlesticks," curses Mrs. Borage. Mr. Henderson comes out of the Colonial next door, covered in clay. He is a potter and very fond of Mrs. Borage.

"Hello, Mrs. Borage," says Mr. Henderson. He regards the compost heaps, towers of harvest vegetables, rotting. He has a feeling that death is near.

Mr. Henderson thinks about death a great deal, alone in his garage, spinning and spinning his bowls until they're so thin he can see his hands through the walls, like the bowls are made of glass. He pulls the walls up, higher and higher, narrow shafts that hold for an instant, tall and translucent—glass reeds, glass flutes—before collapsing again, into mud.

The smell of wood-smoke is in the air. Of course, Mr. Henderson sees the faces of the dead in the wrinkles of the cabbage heads. We all do.

"I don't," says Mrs. Borage, stubbornly. She still sees with her Theta-brain, which gives her a distant perspective, as though she is flying above the surface of the Earth. Mrs. Borage sees topological formations, for example, the shallows of Lake Chargoggagoggmanchauggagoggchaubunagungamaugg.

There is Mrs. Borage, far below, casting for herring, casting into a cold wind, wearing squirrel fur. The hook lands behind her in the fanwort.

Mrs. Borage shivers.

The ground is whitening between the cairns. Deep within the non-Euclidian curvature of the lettuce hearts, tiny ice crystals are forming.

Mr. Henderson is a large, shy man who knows nothing about Euclid. He knows that he would like to mold a piece of clay into a lettuce heart and give it to Mrs. Borage. He's so excited to get started he almost runs back to his house without saying goodbye, but he remembers just in time.

"Goodbye, Mrs. Borage," says Mr. Henderson, shyly, but Mrs. Borage is still gazing into a lettuce heart.

"Does this look like the physical universe?" asks Mrs. Borage. Mr. Henderson takes the lettuce heart. He had always thought the physical universe had no shape at all, just a multi-directional nothingness with deep space objects floating around at varying speeds. He realizes that he has been ridiculous. All these dark folded places, opening everywhere at once—of course, that's what the physical universe looks like.

Mr. Henderson can't make a lettuce heart now. It's far too daunting. He leaves Mrs. Borage to her compost heaps and goes inside his drafty Colonial. He makes tomato soup on the utility stove. He drinks tomato soup, alone in the dark, big house. His eyes hold no expression. They are big and blank, like the eyes of the blue-back herring, like the eyes of Abraham Lincoln, like the holes in a glass flute, shattering.

X

We sit in a circle on the carpet, eating cinnamon toast from a large platter. The cinnamon toast is very hard and brown, with clear butter dripping. Everyone is chewing cinnamon toast. Mrs. Borage listens to the reports of cinnamon toast. The burnt cinnamon smells oddly like gunpowder.

"Taken orally, and at low velocity, gunpowder extends the life expectancy," remembers Mrs. Borage. Bryce jumps to her feet.

"Fireworks!" shouts Bryce.

In the rubble of the Security Spray Complex, Ozark has found the remnants of a Gypsy encampment. It is a snow-covered flannel backpack. The rest of the encampment has vanished without a trace. Ozark is suddenly afraid that her inventory is suffering from logocentrism. Shouldn't there be more untraceable encampments? More vanishings?

She unzips the flannel backpack. It is filled with delights, beers and spray paints, cigarettes, a Jacob's ladder of prophylactics, all kinds of sparklers, bombs, and rockets. Luckily, there is a pink lighter in the front compartment. Ozark never carries a lighter, or loose change for that matter, or tissues. Something has always worked out.

Mrs. Borage sees a woman climb onto the battlements. She is hurling flares into the sky. Do the flares make an eight-pointed star?

Yes, the lesser conjunctions of Venus shower down, glowworms and ashes.

[:]

Everyone looks at the platter on the carpet. It is empty.

"Do you remember eating anything?" asks Dorcas.

The parlor is a mess. The wingback chairs have been tipped over; the card table is broken; the tank has shattered, and the clownfish! They lie dry and dead on the carpet. Bryce flips over the nearest card. It is from the pinochle deck. A young man, with a feather in his hat, and a mustache. He doesn't look healthy. The love disease.

"Am I disgraced in fortune?" wonders Bryce. She opens up the daily paper.

"Align with the syzygy," reads Bryce. What kind of horoscope is that?

"I just wrote it because I like the word 'syzygy,' " remembers Bryce.

What did she write for Mrs. Borage?

"This one is inspiring," says Bryce.

"You shall rend the veil of the phenomenal world," reads Bryce. She looks at Mrs. Borage expectantly.

"Inspiring," nods Mrs. Borage. Which veil is Bryce referring to?

"She must mean the vale of tears," thinks Mrs. Borage. "They always mean the vale of tears unless specified."

[:]

Agnes comes back with cinnamon toast. It is terrifically burnt.

"Thank you!" says Dorcas.

"Thank you," says Fiona. Dorcas has started thinking about witches, how they can turn into cats and regain themselves eight times, but the ninth time they stay cats forever.

"What about shamans?" thinks Dorcas. She crunches her cinnamon toast.
"Thank you!" says Dorcas.

[:]

Mrs. Borage's teeth have never given her a moment's trouble. Agnes's teeth are square, but serviceable. Bryce's teeth are tiny and resplendent. Dorcas feels oral shame: her peg laterals, her crooked bicuspids. Fiona's caries do not enter into her psychic register. Behind Ozark's shy smile: an inner ring of milk teeth, weaker and smaller, but tenacious, like shade plants.

No cinnamon toast for the foreign student Hildegard. She's still sleeping in the room beneath the stairs. Agnes is beginning to wonder if she mustn't be enchanted.

"Adolescents do need large amounts of sleep," says Agnes. Are they all enchanted? At least a little bit.

When Hildegard was awake, she listened to her small silver headphones at the dining room table and she emptied pixie sticks into her yogurt.

"Pink tastes best," said Hildegard.

"It's some kind of synaesthesia," said Dorcas. Mrs. Borage closed her eyes.

"Pink," murmured Mrs. Borage. "Yes, it tastes like salmon."

Agnes watched Hildegard eat the pink yogurt. Hildegard sang to herself, eating.

"Can't you hear my love buzz? Can't you hear my love buzz? Can't you hear my love buzz?"

She wouldn't like it if Agnes answered. Agnes learned not to answer the questions someone is singing from Bertrand.

"Can I try the salmon yogurt?" asked Mrs. Borage. She took a spoonful.

"Oh yes," said Mrs. Borage. "It is delicious."

[:]

Dorcas cracks her slice of cinnamon toast; Fiona cracks her slice of cinnamon toast; Agnes, crack; Ozark, crack.

Crack! Cinnamon toast between the interminable teeth of Mrs. Borage.

Bryce hangs her cinnamon toast from the hat-stand. It is terrifically burnt. She will call the hat-stand, "After the Tunguska Fireball," in honor of all the catastrophists born beneath the burning sky in Siberia.

[:]

"Mmmm," sighs Mrs. Borage. She pops open a bottle of cranberry mead, and she holds the bottle in the crook of her arm. The mead is cold in her mouth and hot in her chest, as though the mead starts at Axel Heiberg, and flows south, Crane Creek, Horse Creek, Turkey Creek, converging at last in the Indian River.

"It would make sense if humans had several esophagi," thinks Mrs. Borage. "On the principle of tributaries."

Why don't they?

"That might be where evolution went wrong," thinks Mrs. Borage. "Unless it was elsewhere."

STEPHANIE ANDERSON

Damn Your Calomel, Pills, Opium, and Blisters

The wide road with grassy margin
Stole quietly into the lake
          Cool drink has preserved me
Caulked each fall with clay
Like an eagle's eyrie
          He has passed his life in worse than solitude
Servility despised
Even a dead wildcat
          Hence despotic habits
Crowded with piles
A strong one-horse waggon
          With an occasional hen
High clay ramparts of shore swept
An immense curve
          Girt with a belt of forest
Of homespun blankets and bolts of cloth
Blue ground with the sprig
          Well bedizined with Roses and Gambage
The Colonel's Creek till
His will no appeal
          Very type of an aristocrat
The old man ere he returned

We Poor Dancing Bears

From my residence I only see stars
This spartan existence a perfect hospital now

The tinselled mantle
The leaden-colored waters

Beset with rocks and quicksands
Cold as if butter would not melt within our mouths

These dolesome times like compositions
On wretched hurdy gurdies

Musicianers pulling up thistles
I cut them for ever

You will at all events be as well off anywhere
A sad impostor contented with trial

Figura

From synthetic crash of sea; sea's admonishment
presaged on the newly sheer slip of shore

(grow me a face
where she is buried)

I in my half-shaded bode, shadow

of contiguity, event
sundered to a simple limb, history
cloaked and needful

ask how many
simultaneous woods are she
hooded through

or what bespeaks the tender
auto, its mad patience
to begin being—

JESSICA BARON

Balance

We need a place to start from. As follows:

INNER : INSTRUMENT :: PSYCHIC : LIFE

AUXILIARY : ROLE :: BODILY : APPARATUS

A VIRTUOSO : TO PLAY :: A MASTER : TO FEEL

ATTENTION : A REFLECTOR :: SILENCE : A FLIMSY AFFAIR

The following statement:

CHORDS : HARMONIZE :: WE : EVOLVE

That depends:

A CONCEPTION : FORTHCOMING :: A REASONED FORM : ARISING

To be more exact:

THIS LIFE : SUMMED UP :: THINGS : BEGAN TO HUM

Quite right. How could it be otherwise? How should I
know? What is it? How should I know? Who is it? Believe
in what? What shall I imagine?

G.C. WALDREP

What Is a Cittern

Body of rose lie down at daybreak, ebony shadow, duplication of breathe. My voice is not essential. When a rotary covenant is unavailable the incarceration cinches, garment as from the late woolen centers of the deciduous plain.

(A group of INMATES sandblasts the east exterior wall of the Shrine to Music.)

Figuration of the neck, three heads—two human—armigerous. As for fray, for vitrine. What issues. An identity: a Maltese cross, a game of chess.

In a high place many men in rough tunics lie bleeding. Runnel of flagstone, litmus: legend. We pretend indifference. The ivory hairpin, the secreted cameo—all govern. *Step onto the mixolydian scale.*

As carved from a single block of wood. Head, neck, soundboard.

Open scrollwork: hieroglyphic of a nervous recompense. If one could stop one's ears. And *see*, simply. As bolt from blow. The hand in its "cheerful" pantomime: blood-fat, like a sausage. Touching here & (now) here. We surmise. Imbrication of chalcedony.

Still the wave seeks, beneath muslin, through closed doors. If a hand strikes a chord and no lover hears it, does the forest advance?

For no sedimentary pleasure. Deeply worn frets.

One always suspects the forest but the forest is not always there. Cowslip & nettle: (breeding place for): wyvern, broken consort. As though *come shrieking down from the night sky, twig of thyme left rustling—*

(The INMATES collect their tools, turn the corner of the building. They are laughing lightly, comfortably as they walk away.)

What Is a Canzone

Geneva as a system: of stoppages, exquisite needlework, of the catalogue of the Prinzhorn Collection. A venerable casuistry. Yet dwells there. May line its nest with stray objects / some shiny, some soft. In the nature of lay.

East of Mishawaka the country opens into itself like snowfall. Thumb-check & broomstraw, baby's breath, lily of the valley. Prayer comes to seem like just another bleak exercise in consensual harbor abuse.

FORTRAN as a provisional malady, neoclassical representations of the ideal city. In exile the clouds seem larger, more outlandish.

There is another story, the story of Science and of the fierce breath of Science. The pocket drone, the soul cured of its grey animal.

Aside from mitosis no one's getting any younger here. Cab Seven to Base: "Should I pick up the blood then?" Base: "Yes." Cab Seven: "So call ahead. You know I hate to wait." Base: "You know you always have to wait."

MATHIAS SVALINA

from Above the Fold

The war light
shines thief in the machine,

always ending
in a hanging.

Dock the cotton
in war night.

The zoo is dire:
it hurts
the light.

Was one Susan
the wharf?

Was the sister
nearby, silent?

The shriek startles
the boulders, sunning

the ferns
& summit.

When diesel stains ether,
the viral lease,
the verses we hear

are nevers. A hump of days
wound round the altar,

the inseam of a scarecrow.
Behave, weary,

chiseled & white.

Discard the skin
your parents
left dangling
from your throat,

their Buick,
the smell
of a watch spring.

The farmer
founds a hospital
of blades

& all the patients
bury themselves
in mulch.

The priest
stands over the crowd
of unblessed waters,

the light
the stained glass windows
refracts into whispers.

Learn a trade
in suffering.

Speak the tongue
of the snake's tongue.

Be strong
& choose your strength
in the parasite.

LILY HOANG

from The Evolutionary Revolution

Water World

A LONG TIME AGO, long before man walked, this planet was filled with
water. Its center did not derive of a core so hot that it melted itself;
rather, the earth was a sphere of solid liquid. Above, the atmosphere exists
as it does today, only cleaner, much cleaner. The surface of the water did not
splash waves because there was nothing for the water to collide with except
air. A long time ago, the water was so clear that man flying in the air could see
directly through the water, straight to the other side of the planet, except back
then, man had horrible vision. Only the rare, exceptional man could see the
surface of the water. As such, man was forced to rely on her other senses, such
as memory, kindness, and dream interpretation.

There was, in fact, a fairly extensive period of time, approximately an era
or two before the Evolutionary Revolution, when man could hardly open her
eyelids out of sensitivity to hydrogen. The moment she opened her eyes, they
would sear with such ferocity that as a sub-species, man decided to never use
her eyes again. As such, man would flap her little red wings to stay as stationary
as possible as friends used strands of hair and mucous to seal their eyes shut.

It is said that man started using her eyes again when a young girl named Emily
heard the song of a merman twinkling from the surface of the water. She'd never
dreamt of him before, she had no memory of his voice, but his song contained
such sadness that out of kindness, she pried her eyes open with the tips of her
talons, using all the force she could, and it is said that the tears from the tearing of
flesh melted the cemented spit enough for her to open her eyes, and from those
eyes, she saw deep into the ocean, deep into the most tortured song.

Opened Eyes

Emily's eyes, being unaccustomed to the hydrogen, crackled, but she was
unafraid. Her eyes, being unaccustomed to wind and height, automatically
barricaded themselves behind moist lids, behind darkness, but she, being the
bravest of men, was determined to maintain strength.

It is said the merman's song seeped its melody deep into her liver, where all impurities are filtered and the contamination of her body by his song made her pry her eyes open with her toes, and when her eyes opened and she could finally see, she fell deep into the merman's song. It is said she was the first to fall, but this cannot be substantiated. Although she is the first recorded man to be lured by a merman's song, oral stories offer many more examples of men who have ripped cement from their eyes, begging other men to bite off the seal, so that they could finally see what kind of being could create melodies of such penetrating sadness.

It is said mermen dream in shadow and light, and sound is muted so that only semblances of noise can be heard. It is said mermen actively chose to dream this way. Mermen were particularly divisive and because they knew that man above the water could not see but relied solely on her other senses, mermen created dreams man above water could not navigate. It was a strategic move.

The day Emily divided the atmosphere, falling freely, hydrogen cutting her freshly opened eyes, she was unafraid. She somehow knew she would survive, that in the water, her eyes would no longer hurt, that his song would always be near, and even though she, our young heroine, wasn't frightened, we know better. We know that even though she's strong and unafraid, she most certainly ought to be. Yes, she would have known better, and even now, even now as she's sinking lower than man has sunk since they lived under water, she should know better than to think she can still be a heroine, but she doesn't.

The Extinction of the Poets & Philosophers

There was a time when all men lived in the water. Back then, there were more than ten species of human, some of whom have survived, such as men, mermen, and arguably, prophets and storytellers. There are many who have gone extinct. Poets and philosophers were the first to die off, their lungs unable to withstand the gravitational weight when they emerged from the deep ocean. They were delicate creatures and not particularly smart. They were much akin to goats or sheep. They would follow each other, without a clear leader, huddling in packs, pushing each other forward. It was the force of that push that allowed any movement at all. If a poet was pushed westward, the whole pack would follow, and it was quite common for these species of man to be particularly vulnerable to bruises and skin breaks. Often, a poet or philosopher would cut his own skin and let his blood lead the pack, and they, faithful followers, would shimmy their loose bodies around the water, meandering behind the blood, until the blood, being thicker than water, floated upwards and upwards, until the poets and philosophers felt their small bodies expand and contract, but they could not discern this as pain. They continued their mission, pursuing the strand of blood until their bodies started to retreat into themselves. First, their skin sunk into the muscles, diving deeply into their own pores. Then, the muscles dissolved into the bones until even the bones had nowhere left to go. As the bones floated away, the surviving poets and philosophers would follow and follow until nothing remained of them but a large number of free floating bones.

It is said, however, that the souls of these poets and philosophers still reside in those bones, that they have managed to reincarnate themselves, but this is merely speculation, a rumor we can neither prove nor deny.

Prophets

As a species, prophets were much like storytellers. They didn't have a specific body type to distinguish them from other species, but unlike storytellers, who were photocopies or clones of other existing bodies, prophets would find a body they liked and imagine death until life is removed and they would shimmy into the vacated carcass. Much like storytellers, it is assumed that prophets have been extinct for many centuries and eons, but this cannot be substantiated because they move from body to body without much effort.

According to the rumors of man, prophets were very cruel. He would kill another body before he has even made himself comfortable in the body just acquired. To maintain strength and ensure there would be no questions or strings, it was typical for prophets to eat the newly abandoned body. Depending on the species he chose to live in, it could be quite difficult to consume another body. Man, for instance, is only accustomed to moon vegetation; flesh of any kind could make her quite ill, but the prophet doesn't care. He imagines the body can chew through bone and the body does.

Prophets are a frightening sub-species. Long before they went extinct, all the other species had petitioned the Extinction Sub-Committee of the Evolution Council to ask that prophets, as a species, be removed from earth. Prophets, upon hearing this rumor through their man-spies, began to concentrate on extinguishing the Extinction Sub-Committee, and that was the end of the Extinction Sub-Committee. Unfortunately, they had forgotten to destroy the petition itself, and the remaining Evolution Council, upset at the great loss of their fellow council members, quickly signed off on it.

It's unclear if any prophets survived this cleansing, but it would not be at all surprising if many of them simply disguised themselves, making their prophetic nature invisible for only long enough to survive. It wouldn't be the first time prophets were forced into extinction.

Before the last, or seemingly last, prophet was killed, he was said to have said that there would be a great revolution based on evolution, that the councils will be to blame, if only in part, but there would be a clash of species, and many would die. He gave the revolution a time, far into the future, so far away that many ignored his words, but they did see the way he crunched his eyelids down so hard that there appeared a small crack on the ridge of his nose. Those who were there claimed that he cemented the future right there, right before his death, this last prophet decided to destroy the earth, just like that.

The Spreading of the Word

Word spread quickly that she had fallen into the water. Man by nature enjoys juicy news, and she did not hesitate to elaborate fantasies as to how it happened. The story of her fall became so distorted that the merman was no longer a character. One man's version of the story went like this:

Emily was flying around as she was always flying around, you know, kind of crooked because she was a crooked kind of girl, and then a whole herd of rhinoceroses came charging at her and punctured one of her wings.

One man interjected, What the hell is a rhinoceros?

The storytelling man said, It's a large bird with a horn the size of your arm.

The storytelling man said, Emily was so scared, flying with one of her wings hurt that she thought maybe she could take refuge on the surface of the water, poor girl. Without her eyes to tell her that the water wasn't solid, she couldn't know. How could she know? Poor girl.

The storytelling man was old enough to remember the day when man had eyes. She rarely mentioned it, but this was a desperate time. A man had just gone missing. For all she knew, the girl could be dead. For all she hoped, the girl was probably hurt pretty bad, probably would never fly again so she may as well be dead, but she hoped for the hurt. It made for much better stories.

Every man's story was slightly different. In another version, some man was jealous of another man so she gouged out her eyes and tore part of her wing, only to realize the man damaged was Emily, which was not the man she'd intended to harm. In another version, Emily picked a fight with a small pack of birds, thinking they were bees. She'd been craving honey, being pregnant and all. The birds pecked ferociously, creating holes in her skin and planting mites. The mites ate at her bone until she had no more bone. Luckily, the mites had damaged her nerves so she couldn't even feel the heights from which she fell.

Either way, the story of Emily's fall became renowned, and in every version, there was some mistake by some man because of their lack of eyes.

Within days of Emily's disappearance, the Imperial Council held a public forum to discuss the future of man. Men were becoming increasingly fearful. This was the first disappearance in a century. Men were most frightened because they'd heard stories about the men who lived in the water, how vicious they were, how they ate the carcasses of decomposed men from above the water, how they could both see and sing. The Imperial Council met and discussed the options of how to attain better vision. Days later, the Council had not come up with a decision. Months later, they were still deadlocked. Years later, when men had forgotten all about Emily, the Imperial Council decided that they should stay exactly as they were. They should not open their eyes, they should not look for Emily, for after all, it had been years, and almost everyone had already forgotten her. The Imperial Council itself, after such a long deliberation, had forgotten why they had even started discussing using their cemented eyes again.

Of course, news of their decision spread quickly around the skies of the earth.

EVELYN HAMPTON

Discomfort

WHILE I AM TALKING WITH HIM I AM ALSO WALKING, and I've lost track of where I am by the time our conversation pauses. Curtains get in the way, obstructing light as clutter obstructs movement. He is not someone I have ever been comfortable with—I can't recall his name—so I am more aware of my body while I'm walking and intonation while I'm talking than I am when with a familiar person, whose ways of judging me won't surprise me. It doesn't help that he's a back-patter and an arm-grabber, likes to touch while conversing. The wind, when it lifted and filled the curtains my mother hung in my bedroom, caused the curtains to take on the proportions of a body. When I am with him I take on his mood and bearing, which I don't generally do with anyone anymore, not since I was a child and an excellent mimic because shy and easily frightened. He tells me that we should see the exhibit he's so excited to see and has been talking about while we've been walking away from the building where I should have turned right, gone three blocks, and entered my apartment building. I like to eat meals alone and know I will be hungry at the exhibit because hunger, for me, is what happens when concentration lapses and becomes boredom. He will not yet be hungry because absorbed in his surroundings, so I will pretend not to be hungry.

I have finally arranged my apartment in a way that I like—sun on uncluttered surfaces, and blinds, no curtains. After I threw out all the things my mother had in storage, I bought the sort of table I've long admired but never purchased. Now I have the sort of table I admire, purchased from a furniture store near the printing shop where my father worked until his early death. The shop is still there, but it is owned by different people, not the two brothers who were identical in their rough treatment of me, so that they seemed to be the same person. I feared their language and mannerisms but not their bodies, whose names I could never remember, so I couldn't loathe them, because I might call one by the name of the one who was absent and thus not treating me in a way—patting my back, lifting me over his head, twirling me in circles and setting me down when I was dizzy—that made me nervous and uncertain. I rarely saw them together, so I came to think of them as one person. Of course I realized it was the wind and not really a person, but the likeness was uncanny, wind being an excellent mimic, in sound and movement, of human distress. Though I once pretended to be near-sighted, groping my way along blindly, I now wear glasses. The table is used, but the wood has been treated well, and its surface glows when sun fans across it through the blinds I keep open should something beautiful or unexpected happen outside my window, which looks out on the brick wall of the neighboring building—should the brick wall crumble, that I might see it.

The exhibit doesn't pertain to my interests, but I agree to go. Then I anticipate trying to find my way back to my building, where I look forward to eating a meal alone, facing the window and the brick wall beyond it, a meal that I purchased to celebrate something that is probably important to no one but me, so I don't mention it to the man after we agree to see the exhibit, and then our conversation pauses while we continue walking. I want him to part from me so that I can turn around and go back to my apartment. I liked the way my dresses belled out from my body when I was spun, but I hated having to stumble in circles, watched and laughed at, after. I'm too uncomfortable with him to mention that we've passed my turn, and I'm beginning to hope he doesn't ask me where I'm living. Telling him where I'm living would be like admitting that I've let him lead me away from my turn, that I've given him this power, and that now I will have to do more work to get where I am going than he will to get where he is going. I like to eat alone, though this can be difficult in practice. As a child I was often reminded that one cannot exist in a vacuum. Feeling my way along blindly, I wanted to find an unexpected doorway the size of my body. But then I realize I don't know where he's going, and I don't know where he lives.

Perhaps he was lost before we met on the street outside the market where I purchased the meal I anticipate eating alone, and he approached me because I am familiar, having a place in the structure of his memory. Like a body, only less reliably constant in proportion. The dampness had caused many of the boxes to become sodden, their contents mildewed, pages of books and letters and other handwritten documents illegible. Sorting through all of my mother's belongings took me weeks. Working alone in her dingy basement where light was scarce and dampness pervasive, I often became confused about where I was in the process, about which items I had decided to discard and about which I was uncertain. Stumbling, wanting badly to grab onto the first solid shape I came to for support. Clumsily, I shuffled together papers, photos and files, and as if a strong wind had blown across everything, any order that may have been there, and which may have told me something I didn't know about my mother, such as how she ordered her memories, was lost. I became lost easily as a child, losing myself in places I knew well, like the hallways of the elementary school building, when anything about the places—light, wall decorations, crowdedness—changed, and in conversations. For this reason and probably others, I resisted change as if it were death. But while one order was lost, a new one was created, one that might have told me more about myself, had I looked at it with discernment. Once I grabbed a man who I thought was my father and was roughly shaken off, as if being given a lesson.

I'm not sure why I waited until after my mother's death to purchase the table. I remember I felt certain that he was my father—the proportions were right—but rightness is a matter of conviction, which is often based on misunderstanding or at least near-sighted apprehension. As I walked to the furniture store to choose the table, I felt that today is the day, and now I will do it, buy the thing I've long wanted but deny myself because I feel my stay here is temporary, of insubstantial time. The doorway was the fantasy of a child, but I still look for it when I am lost or lonely, and sometimes I misapprehend a structure or shadow and for a moment believe that I have found it, that I will enter, that I will become something different. A curtain shifting before closed windows. My mother preferred curtains, but when arranging my apartment I have chosen blinds because I never liked curtains. As a child I felt they were concealing bodies in their folds, the bodies of judgmental people who would follow me without retreat until I was old, and who one day would carry me away like wind carries away leaves of paper. Finally my father would pick me up and carry me away from discomfort. A conversation in which I'm ill at ease and lost finally pauses.

Finding the doorway made to fit only my body, I would enter and thereby escape the present situation. In a situation over which I have no control, I try to fit my preferences to those of others, and so will always be in many ways a child who is often lost and hungry. He likes to talk about his work, now I remember this about him. The exhibit will include something by him, he says, and though he is critical of some of the work that will appear near his, overall, he says, he thinks it will be a good show, well-organized, a good opportunity to network. I didn't like being the center of their attention and wished to hide behind a curtain. I feel the food I've purchased for my anticipated solitary meal losing heat, and this loss seems to come from my body. The exhibit, he begins his every sentence, the exhibit is . . . . If not a child, then a receptacle for others' thoughts and emotions.

Frustrated, I threw away all of the damp boxes. It has begun to rain, and I fear the food I've purchased will be soggy by the time I finally find my way to my apartment. One box contained a ceramic sculpture I made as a child of my head. My mother kept it though it was not good, showed no talent, and made my face look too large and irregular where in life it isn't. Perhaps she enjoyed that about it, how exaggeration of the familiar can cause pleasant discomfort, such as laughter. I threw it out with the rest of her things, and afterward felt light, as if some weight had been lifted from my shoulders. I don't remember much about my childhood besides moments of discomfort.

I would get up to close the window and find it was closed and locked tight as a vacuum. The trails of ink along the walls of our house came from my father's hands between his arrival home from work and when he went to the sink in the basement, a pause mediated by distance and usually silence. He didn't operate the printing machines, the machines were operated by men whose faces were always red and thrown back in laughter at jokes my mother called off-color. The machines were loud, with many tubes and wires, and many dials and buttons, none of which, when I examined them, were clearly labeled. So I came to think of them as one person. Sometimes my father would have to touch them, and his hands would be stained. My mother and father were rarely in the same room together, even while sleeping. I'm not sure I ever saw them touch one another on purpose. Our walls were off-white and absorbent, showing paths my father's hands had taken, which distressed my mother because the ink was so apparent, and what would it say about us, and so on.

She kept saying that one day she would paint the walls a deep crimson or purple, perhaps aubergine. My mother was a librarian and had stories about the words and stains she would find in margins of returned books. She said she found an odd note, written in looping handwriting, in a book about a condition that causes those afflicted to read and write letters and words backwards. If I can claim that a sense of direction is like the ability to read, then I will say that I have written my path through this city in a way that I cannot now decipher. Or perhaps it is a problem of memory. Once I entered the door, I would not be able to pass back through it. Partial entry was not permitted. No backpedaling. After

I threw away all my mother's belongings, I considered that because she was a librarian, she had likely put them in a specific order, possibly one that would be unique and telling.

I have certain preferences pertaining to ink: I don't like it to smear or run or bleed through the paper. Finally the pause is interrupted when he asks me to write my telephone number on a small card he hands me so that he can call me about going to the exhibit. It is his calling card, and I see that his address is the building we're standing outside of, the doorway large and overarching. My understanding of such doorways is that they're meant to be intimidating, suggesting the smallness of the one entering compared with the largesse of the overall structure. I am both relieved and aggravated that he has not invited me in, and as I'm writing my phone number, the rain causes the ink to run though we're standing beneath an awning—the rain is running off my hand and onto the letters I'm writing—the ink being the kind that bleeds and runs away. My handwriting is often difficult to decipher, and sometimes I make it difficult on purpose, to hide or obstruct the information contained there. You cannot always be alone, aren't you lonely, and other questions asked of me by my mother. She didn't want the walls to look like a bruise, she eventually decided, so she didn't paint them.

Because I was unable to carry the table to my apartment, a man at the furniture store strapped it to the bed of his truck and drove both me and the table the twelve or so blocks to my apartment. With furniture, it's just the surface you have to be careful of, but with people, unless it's a dead person's body, in which case it's more like furniture, there are all these invisible little things that can set them off, the little things related to bigger things, the big things like filters or warped glasses through which people perceive themselves and their surroundings. This, though not exactly, is what the man told me as we were driving, and while I thought the comparison between furniture and people was simple, I understood what he meant, that a person's past experience alters how she perceives her present surroundings, whereas the experience of furniture is recorded primarily on its surface. Along the way, the man got lost while telling me about how much he enjoyed the job at the furniture shop after working for so many years as a driver, first of a limo, then of a hearse. I did consider and fear when choosing it that its structure was compromised in ways that would only be apparent later, when I wasn't expecting it, though this has not happened yet as far as I am aware.

As I am writing my phone number and watching the just-inked numbers blur, he calls the work of another sculptor superficial, which is a word I don't like, because who's to say that what's below a surface is not another surface, that one is better than another? I liked to trace the ink marks on the off-white walls with my finger the way I liked to trace my parents' signatures, mimicking the loops and folds of their thoughts as they were writing, as if what's written is any indication of what the writer was thinking. When I knew him best was when I was in school, studying painting, and he was an assistant professor who let it be known that painting, while often subtle, is inferior to sculpture because it lacks a dimension, but I never knew him well, and didn't want to. This seemed like such a simple criticism, yet one he held to with conviction, and it became part of his reputation, which surrounded him like a vacuum. Other words that are similar to *simple*, and which I know I've used, perhaps unfairly: *facile, surface, superficial.*

Finally we part, he going into his building, me turning in a circle before setting out in a direction. Realizing that I was being watched and possibly mocked, I would press my skirt down though the feeling of baring my legs was alluring. I look into doorways for the comfort of seeing someone in the midst of entering or exiting, the door opening, the air of inside and outside exchanging, a mouth slightly open as if awaiting an answer or arriving at the beginning or end of a sentence, and I suppose I do this because I would like to be where they are, in their thoughts for a moment. I tipped the man and thanked him for moving my table, which I could not have done alone, and he said something that concluded what he'd started to say earlier but left hanging—pink faded gum in the corner of his mouth—while he negotiated parking in a too-small space by pulling forward and backward, over and over, pivoting the steering wheel about his palm, motions that make me think of the tortuous movement—false starts, circling, and backpedaling—that goes on in me while I negotiate difficult conversations, and often while I'm writing, which is like having a conversation with one's memory.

People want to give you directions, said the man helping me with my table, They want you to listen to their problems and do for them what they can't do for themselves, which is different for everyone, we all have different strengths and weaknesses, you might be able to do something I can't, but I can do something your neighbor can't, so power among people is constantly shifting, and I can't understand how any one person ever gets to a place of importance, though ignorance is rampant, and—

I make my way back to my apartment by asking for directions at every corner, a practice I would probably not like in another person, but now that I am lost and in need of direction so that I can go to my apartment and eat the meal that by now is cold and probably hardened where it isn't soggy, I forget about what I dislike in other people, so I feel like a stranger to myself. The bag of food has become heavy because sodden with rain water, but probably most of the heaviness comes from fatigue in my muscles. I can't now remember all of what the man said while he drove me and my table to my apartment, or how he said it, but it was something about nobody being alone, or all of us having to work together, the sort of thing I would not say aloud because I fear it would sound facile, though sometimes I think it and say it to myself, as if I'm trying to persuade a multitude that traces circles in dirt with its toes while it listens.

The doorway to my building is stuck open, as it always is, by a doorjamb fashioned out of a folded and faded cigarette box. Inside my apartment, I strip off my sodden clothing. My style of clothing might be called makeshift. Same with my style of decorating, except for the table, a concession to a growing sense that I am stuck corporeally—I don't believe in a soul or afterlife or the supernatural—moving in one direction, my past decisions providing unseen momentum that will eventually carry me away from everything familiar. The curtains that billowed across my closed window were likely moved by the air vent in the ceiling above them, or some other reasonable explanation. The next thing I do is I take containers of food out of the bag that is now falling apart, disintegrating in strips and pieces, and I set the containers out on the table, seeing that the mark the clerk made on each container as to its contents has bled and faded, thinking of my mother, who was very difficult to get along with in old age because she thought I was someone else, a person she called by different names, sometimes the name of someone she loathed, sometimes my name, which marks me as someone. On an uncluttered surface, I set out my meal. I do all of this while naked.

DAVID WIRTHLIN

from Houndstooth

A MOLOTOV COCKTAIL FLIES through the air, rotating end over end as it moves forward, graceful in its slow motion revolutions. It stops mid-air, suspended. A drum beat plays lightly in the background. Boom boom pop, ba boom boom pop, boom boom pop, ba boom boom pop. Like that. The bottle, the gasoline inside, the air surrounding it, almost everything is motionless. Only the flame still burns, still continues to devour the rag. The bottle is clear glass, and the sky behind it is cloudless.

The fire peters out.

The Molotov cocktail surges forward, ripping through the air until it slams into the target with a thud and lands on the ground. Music stops. The target is a cardboard outline of a generic car. It resembles a car in overall shape, but has no characteristic features. There are no wheels, windows, doors, mirrors, fenders, nothing. Where the driver's window should be is a hand drawn target. The bottle lies on the ground near the tail end; the rag has come loose and gasoline is spilling out.

Iggo rushes to the bottle and picks it up. Gasoline spills on his houndstooth pants as he turns the bottle upright. He kicks dirt over the spilled gasoline and walks to a row of bottles fifteen yards away from the cardboard car. Adjacent to the bottles, a gasoline canister and a neat pile of rags. The drums pick up again: boom boom pop, louder now.

Iggo picks up a bottle and fills it halfway with gasoline. He picks up a rag, stuffing it into the bottle until only a couple inches are dangling out the top. Iggo flicks the lighter and the rag is on fire.

He throws the Molotov cocktail toward the cutout. It sails two feet over the top of the car, shattering against a cluster of rocks. They ignite. Iggo rushes to the fire. The music fades to silent. He throws a thick wool blanket on the fire. Everything is silent and motionless. Smoke sneaks out from the edges of the blanket.

Iggo walks to the cutout, head down. He kicks it, knocks it down, bends it, it breaks. He stands next to the broken car, unmoving. From up in the sky, Iggo is only a small dot.

A beat up station wagon drives down a suburban street. Look close at the driver, it's Iggo. He pulls into a strip mall parking lot and parks in front of a bookstore. Iggo steps out of the car, walks to the store entrance, opens the door and enters.

He wanders around the store aimlessly, occasionally glancing at a blonde girl behind the checkout counter. He has a couple of books under his arm: *A Contemporary Guide to High Tech Explosives* and *The IRA Cause*. Alikki the blond is busy talking to a customer, and several are lined up behind for help. She catches an Iggo glance and smiles.

Iggo continues to wander until Alikki is alone at the counter; then he approaches her, places the books on the counter.

— Some interesting choices, eh Iggo?

—Yeah, pretty cool.

Alikki scans the books, the bar code reader beeps.

—That'll be thirty-six seventy-eight, she says. Then with a smile, After your discount of course.

— Of course.

He smiles and hands her two twenty dollar bills. She smiles as she puts the books in a plastic bag.

—Thanks, Iggo says.

— Come back soon.

— I always do.

Alikki brushes her hair back with her hands and puts it behind her ears.

— I mean real soon, she says.

— How soon is real soon?

—That's up to you, Alikki says.

Iggo sits at a kitchen table with his two books in front of him; *The IRA Cause* is open. The kitchen is starkly white, with only a few silver accents, and spotless. There are no loose papers, nothing on the refrigerator doors, and the sink is free from dish build up. Doris enters the kitchen with a bag of groceries. She sets them on the table and sits down next to Iggo.

— Can you explain your infatuation with the IRA to me again?

Doris picks up the book and looks at its contents. She closes the book and hands it to Iggo.

—We've covered this Mom, he says. We're Irish . . . and Catholic.

—We're one-eighth Irish, and we're not Catholic.

— Grandma's Catholic. That makes us Catholic.

—That's not how it works.

— That is how it works.

— See? Doris says, If we were Catholic I would know that.

— Mom, are you being unsupportive?

— I'm just trying to understand what I'm supporting.

Doris stands up and starts removing the groceries from the bag. She removes each item and places them carefully in a cupboard. She makes her way back and forth between the table and various parts of the kitchen.

— Sounds unsupportive to me.

— I'm always supportive Iggo.

Doris pulls a carton of milk out of the bag and carries it to the refrigerator. She opens the fridge—it is stocked full of food. Juices, meats, breads, leftovers, dairy, all neatly arranged by category.

—When's Dad gonna be home?

— Any minute now. Why?

Iggo smiles and stands up. He walks toward the door and, just before leaving the room, turns to his mom, and says,

— I want to talk to someone supportive.

She laughs and throws a loaf of bread at him, but Iggo is already out of the room. The bread bounces silently off the door as it closes. The plastic bag opens upon impact, slices of bread litter the white tile floor.

Iggo sits on the brown leather couch in the living room. The room follows a brown on different shade of brown color scheme. Dark woods and tan accents compliment the chocolate carpet.

Iggo draws a picture of a car exploding. The people inside the car are wearing oxygen masks and protective suits. The car itself hovers above a cloud of smoke and fire. Miniature Molotov cocktails form a border on the edge of the paper.

Bill walks in and says, *Hola Iggo.*

— Hey Dad.

— *Iggo, por fin. ¡Que elegante!*

— How's the spanish coming along, Dad?

— *Bueno. Muy bien.*

—Your accent keeps sounding better.

— *Gracias*, Bill says. He sits down next to Iggo on the couch, Yeah I think I'm almost ready to start my book.

— I'm excited for you. It's gonna be great.

— I'm super pumped. Literature in the Spanish language is just so much better than our English trash. Bill looks at the picture Iggo has drawn, Not bad, he says.

— Thanks Dad.

— How's the explosives coming in real life?

— Slow.

— How's the IRA thing?

— I'm over it. It wasn't what I thought.

— Don't get discouraged. You think I learned Spanish overnight?

Iggo folds up the drawing into a one inch by one inch square and stuffs it into his pocket.

— I just wish I could blow stuff up right now.

— You just wait, Bill says. He puts his arm around Iggo and pulls him close, You'll be the best damn bomb builder this family has ever seen.

— Thanks Dad.

Bill looks at his watch and says, Where's your brother?

— I haven't seen him since the day before yesterday.

— Really? Bill says. He cups his hands around his mouth and yells, Honey? Have you seen Ian?

From somewhere else in the house, Doris says, Not for a day or two.

— He'll be fine Dad.

— I guess if your Mom isn't worried, *entonces yo no preocupo tampoco.*

Iggo drives up to his house in his station wagon and parks directly across the street. The neighborhood is well kept, with deep green lawns and new roofs. The only exception is the house directly across the street, a run down version of the other houses on the street. Faded gray paint and a moldy shingle roof create the exterior facade. The lawn is overrun with crabgrass and dandelions; the flowers are infested with white flies and aphids.

Iggo gets out of his car and walks across the street to his house. His brother, Ian, lies on the front lawn, face up. He stares up at the blue sky, in a trance, and does not notice Iggo's arrival.

— Ian?

—

— Ian?

——

—— Ian?

——

—— Hello?   Where have you been?

Ian slowly raises his head to look at Iggo.

—— I'm going back, ya know, Ian says.

—— Going back where, Ian?

—— It was so much better there, says Ian, laying his head back on the ground.

——Where?

—— It was amazing. I want to go back so bad.

—— Fine, Iggo says, Don't tell me.

—— I can tell you later.

——Well, good luck sliding this one past Mom.

—— Mom? says Ian.

——You haven't been home for three days.

Ian gazes at the sky. A cloud drifts by.

—— Oh no, I haven't been gone for three days. Three hours maybe, but not three days.

——Ask Mom how long you've been gone.

—— But Iggo, everyone was getting along. I didn't care I was fat. People were nice and happy. All the girls were beautiful, and they didn't care I was fat either.

—— Ian! Stop saying you're fat.

—— Okay. If I was though, they wouldn't care.

A rusty pickup truck drives up the street and stops next to Iggo's car. A drum beat starts to play. Ba boom boom pop, ba boom boom pop tsss.

—— He better not hit my car again, Iggo says.

—— It just didn't matter what I looked like.

The truck parallel parks behind the station wagon. A leather skinned old man steps out of the truck. He walks up to the passenger side of Iggo's car and spits on the window.

A bass line joins the drum beat. Dumm dumm. Dumm dumm. Dum de dum de dum. They both increase in volume.

—— Hey! Thanks for spitting on my car bro!

The old man looks up at Iggo, startled. He gives Iggo a menacing look and walks away.

— Don't walk away from me, bitter old man, Iggo says. Why are you so bitter?

The leather face disappears around the side of the faded gray house. Iggo glares at the old man's truck.

A distorted guitar riff jumps in line with the bass and drums. Chukka chukka chink. Chukka chukka chink. Chukka chink chukka chink. Chukka chukka chunk chunk.

Iggo looks at the truck and the old man is sitting in it. He hurls a Molotov cocktail at the truck and makes it through the open side window. The interior is engulfed in flames. The old man tries to extinguish the fire by spitting on it.

Iggo picks up a small missile launcher off the ground, hoists it over his shoulder, and points it at the truck. The music gets louder. He takes aim and pulls the trigger.

The missile speeds toward the truck. The old man stops spitting and screams.

And then silence. Everything moves in slow motion. The missile is almost to the truck. It reaches the truck, enters through the open window, and hits the old man directly in the face. His head implodes on impact. The music picks up again, louder than before, as movement returns to normal time. The truck explodes, shooting twenty feet into the air. The explosion repeats from the front, side, back and top views, in rapid succession. When the truck reaches its peak, it disappears and the music stops.

Iggo's eyes search the old man's yard for movement. The truck is parked behind Iggo's station wagon, with no signs of any explosion. Iggo crosses the street, approaches his car, and sees the enormous amount of spit dripping down the side. He walks past the truck, staring at the gray house for several seconds.

Iggo returns back to his front yard. Ian lies on his back, staring at the sky.

— I even farted in front of the girls and they didn't mind, Ian says.

— Did you see that? I hate him. He's gonna be sorry he messed with me.

— And if I ever did anything wrong, I didn't have to apologize cuz they forgave me right away.

— Hello? Ian?

— Oh   hey Iggo.

— Did you see that?

—What?

ANDREW GRACE

Wild Dogs

I used to wake early and watch the sheep lift their heads in fear.
Once, a wild dog took shape out of the wood-frost,
slicking its blue tongue, its coat itself a polluted ice,
then hard lunge, gloss of rent muscle, red rash inwound

on the boneyard, no sound, everything disfigured
in mist, everything with its skeleton mask on.
I thought the sheep were meant for hunger, the way
our hunger is meant to become its own guide to call to.

This mist, here, years after, devolves into a mouthful of wool.
I used to want to witness loss, to have my shoeprint in the sheep's
blood be a seal to mark the act as closed. But it is not necessary.
The proof is obliterated by darkening shifts of grass.

I used to wake early and watch a blurred face that came
to be mine flare up in the mirror. Now, in the fallen night,
I can see what is not meant for hunger—throb of stars,
your cool, unwashed skin: trademarks of what rises.

Divisible

Concussions of light.

River, bridge, abandoned mattress.

As if out of need, it is late in the year.

Wolves' bivouac for flense and birth.

Tremble of backwater imperceptible, as when a fever returns.

Too far for me to lay a hand there once or lightly.

Poverty of linden.

All of my errors have been of omission.

I cannot bring a world quite round

Blacksnake armada.

Or is it moccasin.

I cannot bring a word down for the room I left behind.

Poverty of mission.

And other maimed unities.

The room a group of voices has left.

Asphyxiations of wind.

Crawfish odyssey.

A group of voices: myself, brother, mother and

Omissions, stopped waves.

We will meet at the river.

A wolf placenta stains the abandoned mattress.

Our hour will never come.

from Sancta

I have lost the plot of the story you are telling; the flat clear nouns you release into the air dissipate like fleet herds between us. You say something about using the sleight-of-eye an onion makes for sadness to your advantage. Then a young storm, gone too quickly to believe in. Rain-cooled brimstone seeps up as today's dusk. Like me, the last light feints focus. Thus we are liars.

———————

This is the Chapter in which everything changes. You are gone. A cab's double script unspools down the dirt. I remember driving you somewhere. Snow purged an obscure thirst of a parched, white sky. We talked about the life after our deaths. Unwashed in an abandoned land. Houses on fire, or else, the escort of fire. A march forthcoming. We would walk upright, salt wandering to salt. Late and far.

———————

Dead farmers praise millennia dust and the white blood of weeds. Someone's dead daughter praises in great sheets across the flimsy shields of ginko. The dead lovers press black hands all over our faces, but come up short of praise. We are unredemptive to them, as are their pasts. The dead pilgrims, lost in blue pines, have stopped praising and forgotten how. They step from us and are not missed.

EMILY GROPP

THE SEA WHERE IT WAS, it was arduous. I imagined a
superterranean line from you to me. What I saw in
the sea made me not ravenous. Some children like to
wallflower. While supper shook onto the floor from the
constant shelling, potatoes and peas stuck to my spoon.
I sat the bear down in my recurring dream and begged
it be good. Over a number of lines you're no more
related to me than birds who flock at the close of day,
some here, some there. Corner is to hide, and open
plain is to see what's coming. I hold my breath between
seconds as if there's anything but between.

THE STATUE ON THE WHERE is a word with here inside
it as planes herd us to the next hilltop: when you look
at it what happens to a pyramid of cannonballs: living
inland from slave castles queen mothers forbid the elderly
couple to mention they're there: there is a word with
here inside it: when Jules said MY RELATIVES LEFT BY BOAT
the question was IN THE FIRST PLACE WHY DID THEY LEAVE:
each day we reach one destination to see what a binocular
look-out is:

WE CAMPED IN A YELLOW DOLLHOUSE Sunday to Sunday
tired, blacking out in stories, a heart monitor taped to
my breasts, I lugged my last plum, into doctor's offices
cluster, bombs in dreamfields wreck, cause célèbre and
effect, I tried to say any loud gasp, any bump and I was
on your time, shock didn't want to, be aftershock, itself
so you pulled its hair out, didn't want to lose me, don't
you think, I didn't want you to see, what tape left on my
breasts, shape of a country, I let become, a country on a
map, a country in a dreamfield to retrospect,

DAN HOY

I Am Full of Blood and Biofuel

Eight weeks and $3 billion
and what I want is tucked away in the small of your back
like a tapeworm. I would give my firstborn
for a tool calibrated to waste
no energy and no measurable amount of time. The needle
will sedate them first, if you're scared.
My experiments save lives.

Thanks to Your Binding Spell

I spend lunch w/ the chemos and wake up
dreaming of me excreting my feelings
all over your chest. I hate Cleveland
but this is the world so I might as well
lay my faces on the table. Next time
leave me and the Tetragrammaton out of it.
O resplendent Angel Gabriel, I'm sure it was
technically the opposite of black magick
but come on. Like my most sensitive areas
you're like my extremities, but worse.

Counter Clockwise

I don't mean to interfere
w/ all the diagrams of this extraordinary head, breasts and groin.
I just want to differentiate the menstrual blood/blood/urine combo
from what is ethical and what is equal. If
first you have to figure out what they mean by sucking the hind teat
so you can not do that
then do that. Then go about your average, everyday events.

ANDREI SEN-SENKOV

Circus Freaks

circus freaks are floats
trembling on the waves of the sea
like sawdust
searching endlessly
for some lost family
at the misty bottom of the earth

Max & Mimi : Conjoined Twins

twenty years ago
siamese twins
were carefully removed from a woman
and became a jar
of human yogurt

everything glows inside itself
a spoon is the size of god

Gunther : Man-Fish

his skin is covered with scales
like outdated yellow pages
with old phone numbers
used to call places
that no longer exist
except the yellow pages
aren't waterproof

Steven : Tattooed Man

the bird on his chest
is in a cage

and when he breaths
it wants out

Translated from the Russian by Zachary Schomburg

EUGENE MARTEN

from Rat of the World

THE MOTEL STOOD AT THE EDGE OF THE CITY CENTER, near the foot of the West Hills. During the day the manager was an old guy with a white mustache who told them that summer would be hot but not as hot as they were used to, and dry. He told them about the rain. He told them where the zoo was, and Chinatown, and to stay out of Old Town, which was right next to Chinatown. At night it was a college kid who sat over an open textbook, the phone pressed to his ear.

The room was on the second floor. Two doubles. There was no pool but they had cable and air. They were new to cable and spent most of the first day watching MTV and public access, the road still moving under them like a treadmill. There were no movie channels, you had to pay extra for a movie. Miss D giggled at a Korean soap opera.

Jelonnek looked in the phone book, but if he had one it wasn't listed.

"If I could call long distance," Littlebit said.

"Are we still in the United States?" Miss D asked.

You could see the mountain from the bathroom. There was a small square window in there and when you sat on the toilet you could see the top half of the mountain, its white peak against the blue sky, and nothing else.

At night a man went past their window carrying a red and white lunch pail. He was small and walked as though one side of his body were dead weight. He had a room on the second floor.

In the morning Jelonnek went to the office and paid for another day. They had a weekly rate but Jelonnek declined; they weren't going to be here that long. You just had to lay low for a while, till things blew over.

He went to Dunkin Donuts across the street and bought a dozen, glazed. Miss D ate four of them and watched cartoons. Somebody knocked and said in a Russian accent, "Room to clean." They sent her away and left before she came back, drove around town getting no more lost than they already were. Miss D asked the question that had by default become the slogan of their situation, which was such that Jelonnek was almost beyond annoyance.

"Maybe tomorrow," he said, partly because he'd never been there himself, but it already seemed they'd reached the end of the line; what else was left but to drive off the edge?

They wound up in a vast park on the other side of the hills. The zoo was there, and so were a Vietnam veterans memorial and tennis courts and twenty miles of trails. There was a rose garden with five hundred kinds of roses and a Japanese garden with tiny waterfalls and bridges and a pond of big orange fish that went for anything you dropped in the water. Miss D watched them eat her spit. The trail was shady and cool and they made way for joggers wearing bright chemical colors. The trees had small placards nailed to their bark. On the placards were the names of the trees, in English, and below that was Latin or Greek. Miss D moved ahead like an advance scout, tree to tree, reading off the names with no little difficulty, and anything that wasn't fir or pine was news to Jelonnek. There was one she couldn't read at all. Its bark was ringed with black and white stripes and Miss D said, "I'ma call that a zebrawood," and Jelonnek had to admit it was a good name, and wondered what he might have named it had he been in Adam's skin.

Littlebit strolled behind, taking her time and muttering.

The trail led to a clearing on top of a hill where there was an old carousel and an ice cream cart. A friendly kid with a shaved head and pierced ears operated both. Jelonnek wouldn't buy Miss D a popsicle, then changed his mind, and then they each got on a horse. Littlebit sat on a bench. Miss D invited her to join them and Littlebit said, "Is you mad? Feel like I just got off one."

The kid turned the carousel by pumping a long wooden lever. The buildings of the city and the mountain spun by, then Littlebit on the bench. Jelonnek kept expecting the bench to go by empty on the next pass, but it didn't happen.

After the park they bought fast food and took it back to the motel and paid for a movie. You called the office and they added it to your bill. They sat and lay on the beds with the lights off and the air conditioning on, while before them played out the story of an evil android from the future who comes to the present to kill the boy who will otherwise grow up to . . . . Jelonnek wished he'd thought of that, too, though it was a sequel whose plot was identical to its predecessor. He thought about *Armageddon Zero*, still locked in the trunk of the car. He thought about money, how he could feel them running out of it. It seemed to be something that was always happening, even just sitting there, like a slow leak, a meter running somewhere.

He went to the office and the kid glanced up from an histology manual. Jelonnek asked if there were any copies of yesterday's paper lying around. All that was left was the entertainment section but that was what he wanted. He took it back to the room and Littlebit was on the phone.

"You got the best hand," she said to someone. "What time it is over there?"

"I wanna call somebody," Miss D said. Jelonnek looked at her. He'd thought about making a call of his own.

"You ain't never lied," Littlebit said. "Yuppies, Japs and dykes. They bums dress better than we do."

Jelonnek opened the paper and poured over the music listings the way he had the White Pages.

"Did he . . . hell, no."

Miss D whispered in her mother's ear.

"Be easy then," Littlebit said. "Miss D wanna bother you." Jelonnek reached over and pressed the cradle button before she could, and Littlebit almost slammed the receiver down on his finger.

"Goddamn you tight," she said.

"Is you tight, Jelonny?" Miss D said.

"Yeah he is," Littlebit said. "He too cheap to sweat."

Then she said she didn't mean it. She said she was playing.

Jelonnek sat by the window. "Find anything out?"

She hadn't found out her cousin's phone number or address, but whoever she'd spoken with had told her something about Sunday night. If it was true. If it was true, maybe it was just as well they could no longer afford to go back.

Later the man with the red and white lunch pail limped past the window. Jelonnek peeked through the curtain. One arm was short and had fleshy nubs at the end like rudimentary fingers.

Littlebit had trouble sleeping, Jelonnek could hear it. Early in the morning he found her sprawled on the bathroom floor because the tiles were cold.

"Don't feel good?" he said.

"I sure damn don't."

"What's the matter?"

"I need twenty dollars."

"Make it ten," Jelonnek said. "I'm cheap. I'm cheap and this is the last time," he said.

He remembered why the day manager had told them not to go into Old Town, so they told Miss D they'd be back with breakfast and hung the sign on the door. They drove through the gate to Chinatown. The gate had five roofs and marble columns and was guarded by two lions, one male and one female. There were restaurants and red lampposts, cherry trees, the street signs in two languages. Then Old Town, which was what it said it was. Buildings that looked like they should have had horses tied out front, and some of these had been converted into galleries, shops, or office space. One was being demolished and only the facade was left, like a set in a Hollywood western.

They drove around blocks. The streets were in alphabetical order and some people crossed them slowly, without looking. Jelonnek beeped at one of them, a white-haired woman in a baseball cap, who stopped and turned and looked at them, a bag in each hand.

"She'll suck your dick for ten cents," she said, and spat on the windshield.

"I'll do better than that," Littlebit said. Jelonnek ran the wipers.

A shelter, train depot, comedy club, a bar where everybody was on their feet with a man standing outside, looking at pedestrians and drivers in a certain solicitous way.

"Him?" Jelonnek said.

"Look for a white one," Littlebit said.

They saw him on a block where one whole side had been razed, pacing before mounds of rubble. Jelonnek pulled over, looking around. The guy came near and leaned in Littlebit's window. Jelonnek didn't look at him; he could barely hear what they said. He passed the bill across the seat. The guy took it and opened his mouth and something dropped from it into Littlebit's lap. Jelonnek drove carefully away listening for sirens. He told Littlebit after that she was done.

"Sure damn am," she said.

"This was the last one."

"I mean."

They passed a laundromat and he said they should wash clothes soon.

"I'm sayin," she said.

They took the sheet from one of the beds. Filled the trash can with store brand soda and cheap beer and ice, then covered it with the plastic the ice came in. They bought fried chicken and biscuits on the way.

Heading west there were more tree-covered mountains and sometimes they had strange-looking bald patches where the trees had been cleared away. Miss D asked which were mountains and which were hills, and she asked about the chicken. She wore her bathing suit for the first time since Nebraska. When the grades got steep Jelonnek drove in low gear as he had the night before they got into town, and if there was only one lane traffic would stack up behind him like he was leading a pilgrimage. Once he pulled onto the shoulder and let them pass, and they read the license plates. Out here people expressed themselves through their license plates.

After two hours or so they saw a sign and turned off the highway. A narrow road twisted through a rain forest so dense Jelonnek turned on the lights. Ferns brushed the car. The road led to a parking lot on top of a cliff. Shorebirds cried overhead and when they got out of the car it was rock and trees and then just water and sky. Miss D forgot about the chicken. A trail zigzagged down the face of the cliff and she forgot to be afraid of heights. When they got to the bottom she ran to the water's edge and waited for them, Jelonnek with the trash can and the sheet folded over his shoulder, Littlebit carrying the food. The waves kept chasing Miss D back toward them.

They took off their shoes and held down the corners of the sheet with them. The sand was soft and not too hot, then damp and smooth and firm as a floor where the waves came in. Up close the blue was almost gray. Littlebit stayed just out of reach, wearing a dark sleeveless dress that dropped off her shoulders like it was still on the hanger. Rumble-rush of the breakers, the water so cold it made the bones of your feet and ankles ache, and Miss D screamed in pain and joy. Your feet sank in mud and the surf rushed back out as hard as it came in, wanting to pull your legs out from under you. Jelonnek threw out his arms. Miss D screamed. The ocean withdrew in layers, hissing white foam subsiding to cloudy brown, and then sheet upon sheet upon clear sheet shedding each other in as many directions. The sand smoothed to a shiny unbroken slickness in which for a moment everything was reflected.

"Jelonny we standin on the sky!" Miss D yelled.

They got as used to it as they were going to get, and still you couldn't do anything but wade. No one was in deeper than waist-high except the dogs, and even the guys with surfboards wore wetsuits. Miss D remembered she was hungry. They went back to the sheet where the breeze had flipped one corner and half-covered it with sand. The ice had melted but the pop was cold enough and so was the beer. Sometimes you could feel the spray lightly on your face and Miss D said, "It feels like I'm growin freckles."

Everything was far away from everything else. Behind them the bluffs fell away to dunes and beach grass, refreshment stands and beachfront property. In between a row of striped tents where you could change your clothes. A group of teenagers picnicked on a blanket nearby, in the shadow of a smoldering log. One of them kept throwing bits of hotdog into the air, and a big white bird would swoop in and catch it before it landed.

"You see that shit?" Littlebit said. She threw her bones in the sand and lay down on the sheet with an arm over her face.

"You good, Ma?"

"Good as I get."

The gulls cried through the surf.

Jelonnek looked down the beach, where everything became vague and misted. A couple of big rocks rose out of the water there, and one of them looked to be the size of an office building. Jelonnek finished his beer and got up and headed that way. Littlebit stayed where she was but Miss D followed. He'd had two beers and didn't stop her. People flew kites, sat under umbrellas. A gang of kids were building a fortress as if preparing for an invasion from the sea. Seagulls hovered over a big scaly carcass as if tethered to it and there were dead jellyfish to avoid, transparent blobs with tendrils going yellow and brown in the sun.

They passed two women in broom skirts holding hands, one of them saying, "It's an angry coast." Miss D wanted to know why two women were holding hands, and Jelonnek said he didn't know. She asked him if they could and he said they couldn't.

It was farther than he'd thought. The rock was much bigger now but still gray in the mist, like it had yet to become real. You could see the birds flocking on and around it like bees at a hive, and there were big green patches of grass or moss. They sloshed through clear shallows between sand bars and came to a stretch of boulders covered with tiny black mussels. You had to watch your step because the boulders were slick and in between them was another kind of life, bulbous dark-green gourds that opened like a chorus of mouths when the tide came in, closed when it went back out. Jelonnek showed them to Miss D and she touched one. It opened up and she screamed and ran back up the beach. Jelonnek slipped, gashed his knee. He looked down and saw blood. Then the ocean took it away and he swore with the sting of saltwater.

When they got back to the sheet Littlebit was sitting up with her hands behind her and a cigarette in her lips. "Ready to raise?" she said. Jelonnek's arms and legs were pink. Miss D drank another pop and seemed to have forgotten all about the boulders and the terrible green things that lived in them. They let her wade a little while longer, then dumped the water out of the trash can and stuffed the sheet into it. There were a couple of beers left for the road. On the way back up the bluff Miss D said goodbye to the waves and the sand and the birds, and Littlebit told her to watch where she was going. Jelonnek kept looking back. Sand met water met sky like the seams of the world, and the world got bigger the higher they climbed.

At the top Littlebit pointed. On a cluster of rocks maybe a hundred yards off-shore, sea lions had gathered. Miss D couldn't see them for the life of her but said goodbye anyway, waving in a stiff little gesture like she was leaving home again.

Two men came to the motel in a taxi. They took a room on the second floor at the corner of the building. Jelonnek and Littlebit watched from the window. The two men wore loud, outdated clothes that looked like they'd been purchased new, and one had a ponytail. When Jelonnek turned from the window Littlebit had her face by Miss D's crotch.

"Why you sniff my privacy?" Miss D said.

"Cause you nasty. Now go get with that rag like I showed you."

Miss D slammed the bathroom door saying something. "Maybe you should go in with her," Jelonnek said.

"Maybe I'ma go for a walk," Littlebit said.

"Where to?"

"Gimme the rent," she said.

"What rent?"

"For the room. You been paid it?"

"We got time."

"Give it here," Littlebit said. "I'll take care a it."

"That's alright," Jelonnek said. He was looking in the Yellow Pages. "I'll get it on my way out."

"You don't trust me?"

"I got an errand to run."

"Then go ahead with yourself."

The old guy was in the office, his cheek bulging with tobacco. Jelonnek asked about the weekly rate. He didn't have enough cash so he tried his credit card. He'd used it up on the road but he tried it anyway. The old guy came back and said, "Better call your bank." Jelonnek paid for another day and headed downtown. On his way through the parking lot he looked up. The man with the ponytail looked back from the second floor balcony, picking his nose.

The girl at the temporary employment agency said they weren't taking applications at this time. She was very nice and gave Jelonnek a key to the bathroom down the hall. He returned the key and took the elevator down to the lobby. He asked the security guard there if they were hiring. The guard didn't know but he told Jelonnek where he could go to find out.

It was bright and warm on the street. Jelonnek walked past an old courthouse, crossed the street to a square where a pole bristling with signs told you your exact distance from certain major cities of the world. At the corner a bronze statue of a businessman with an umbrella. The square was sunken like an amphitheater and Jelonnek crossed to the other side, through skateboarders and office workers and past a recess where people spoke and listened to their echoes. The bricks under his feet had names written on them; you could buy a brick for a hundred dollars. Young people sat on the steps or leaned against the walls asking for money. "Wanna look in my box?" one of them asked Jelonnek. On his lap was a cigar box, and next to him sat a pretty girl with a smudged face. They were much younger than the bums Jelonnek was used to.

"Okay," he said. The girl opened the lid and an eye painted on the inside of the box stared back up at him.

"Cost you a quarter," the kid said. Jelonnek told him he was crazy and got going.

"I can sing you a song," the kid said.

"Have a better day," the girl yelled.

The next kid had a guitar with about three strings that made a dry buzzing sound like a trapped insect. A case was open on the ground and a sign propped against the lid requested donations with which the owner would acquire lessons and strings and become a proper musician. A spattering of change shone in the lid and there were even bills, but Jelonnek didn't add to it.

A man outside Starbucks kept asking people for the precise amount of a dollar thirty-seven. He would follow you a little ways.

But everyone else you saw was nice-looking and they drove nice cars and wore carefully chosen clothes. At the corner Jelonnek took a drink from a fountain and the water was cold, as if it came from some deep dark place.

He explained his situation at the security firm. They told him things were slow right now, but they let him fill out an application and said they'd call him if anything turned up. They even let him watch a training video. He sat at a tiny desk in a small dark room with two other people. The video took a humorous slant; a vastly corpulent guard eating a turkey leg at his post, snoring in oblivion while a pair of intruders cleaned out the premises. Only Jelonnek laughed.

When he got back to the motel Littlebit wasn't there. Miss D lay on the bed watching *The Real World*.

"She gone for a walk."

"Where to?"

"Don't start me lyin."

Jelonnek looked out the window. Later they heard a door slam from the other end of the building. Littlebit came in with a look on her face like she'd discovered something amazing and was about to share it with them. They'd seen this look before.

"Where you been, ma?"

"Around the world." She lay on top of Miss D and kissed her.

"Your mouth smell," Miss D said.

"I love you too."

Miss D looked at her. "Your eyes all bugged."

"I love you too," Littlebit said. She looked at Jelonnek and loved him as well, then loved everything in the room for the next five minutes or so. She put a cigarette in her mouth but didn't light it. She picked up the remote and clicked it at the TV with such finality that every channel she changed might also have ceased to exist. She clicked it around the room in a sort of experimental way, then aimed it at Jelonnek, said, "Smile," and threw it against the wall over his head and locked herself in the bathroom.

In the evening Jelonnek went back to the office. The young guy was there, leaning over his book with a lump in his cheek. Everyone here chewed, it seemed; Jelonnek had even seen women.

"Those two guys that checked in today," Jelonnek said. He said the room number and the night manager spat into the same coffee can the day manager used.

"I think they're up to something," Jelonnek said. "Selling dope or something."

"What do you want me to do about it?" The day manager looked at his book.

"Well," Jelonnek said. "I think . . . The police?"

"Can you prove anything?"

Jelonnek wanted to press the night manager's face into the book so he couldn't breathe, into histology or calculus till he never breathed again. Instead he went to the store across the street and bought the cheapest twelve-pack in the cooler. When Littlebit saw it she said, "I thought we ain't had the money."

"We," he said. A piece of the remote cracked under his foot. "It cost four bucks." He needed ice. He took the bucket down to the machine under the stairs and filled it. There was a room next to the machine. The door opened and a woman stood there for him. Jelonnek saw flat sagging breasts, veins, stretch marks, a belly under a belly. He couldn't look at her face. He backed away with the ice as if she might drag him inside and went up the stairs. The door slammed shut.

He sat in a chair and drank beer and smoked. Littlebit asked for one. "You had yours," he said.

"Naw she ain't," Miss D said.

"Shut up," he said.

"You ain't my daddy."

"Won't be the last time you say that," Jelonnek said.

He watched TV and drank, and after they went to sleep he was still watching TV and drinking. The show on public access consisted of a naked man sitting on the floor with his legs crossed, meditating. The beer was bitter. Jelonnek had to press the buttons on top of the TV since the remote was broken, and each time he passed the public access channel the naked man was still meditating. The beer was bitter but he got used to it and drank every can before he felt like going to sleep. He was still sleeping in the chair when another taxi came and brought visitors to the two men in the corner room.

They stopped buying fast food. They went to the store across the street, and while Jelonnek bought a loaf of bread Littlebit shoved a pack of baloney into her purse.

They filled the ice bucket and put the baloney on top.

Later they told Miss D they were going to play a game.

"Like hide-and-seek but it ain't," Littlebit said. Miss D and Jelonnek were to go hide somewhere. If Littlebit couldn't find them, there would be a surprise.

Miss D was dubious. "I wanna hide with you, Ma."

"Next time," Jelonnek said.

"I don't know."

"Well you playin anyway." Littlebit stood at the window, barefoot, wearing that long t-shirt. She kept looking past the curtain. The man with the red and white lunch pail pulled in every night around this time and limped past their window.

"What if he keeps going?" Jclonnek said.

"He ready," Littlebit said. "He more ready as you."

Miss D said, "What kinda surprise?"

Littlebit looked out the window once more and covered her eyes.

"One, two . . ."

Jelonnek gestured at Miss D and moved quickly to the bathroom. She seemed to have forgotten her misgivings. They went inside the bathroom and Jelonnek shut the door. Light from the street came through the small window but at least you couldn't see the mountain.

"Get in the tub," he said. Then he drew the curtain over the window and stood in the tub with her. He drew the shower curtain but not all the way.

"I can still see," Miss D whispered with a kind of disappointment. They crouched and Jelonnek told her not to say another word. He was practically begging.

The door rattled. Jelonnek felt Miss D stiffen next to him. It rattled again and they heard the room door shut. A muffled conversation.

"Who that?" Miss D whispered.

Jelonnek hushed her, then said, "TV." They could hear traffic outside. Littlebit's voice got louder: "Ain't nobody in there." The bathroom door opened and the room brightened and Miss D shut her eyes like it would make her invisible. The door closed but not all the way. Somebody sat or lay on the bed. The TV got louder and that was all they heard till Littlebit moaned.

Miss D stiffened again. Littlebit moaned again. A succession of harsh grunts and Miss D said, "Ma." She was still whispering like she didn't want to break the rules, but she was standing, too, and Jelonnek lunged and grabbed what he could. They fell back against the wall with Miss D against his chest, and Jelonnek was sure they could hear it over the TV. He covered Miss D's mouth and she bit his hand. Her hair was thick and dry and he pulled it till she stopped.

The man out in the room said something. He said it like he was talking in his sleep. It was hot behind the shower curtain and Jelonnek smelled Miss D. He was sweating. He kept one hand in her hair and one tight over her mouth. The breath from her nostrils was hot. Snot and tears. If Littlebit got into trouble she would call his name, that was part of the game, too.

JOSHUA COHEN

from North Vain, Bluff

North Vain

PALMROUND, PALMROUNDED, THIS SNOW, THESE FROZEN HUNKS. Balls of ice now hardened, once snow rolled, balled by cup as if to sip or sup, made from the fall that stilled his helicopter's skids. He sat like this for days waiting for an assignment: a contractor's business here to prospect oil, an opposing ecological legation always tapdanced attendance upon by its token indigeneity, Indian or Inuit, the requisite feather or fur, their red palm greased with greening—whatever would rub from the paper money, which would circulate between the same two hands or ten forever: dirty, handled, with egg batter, cum and the sperm of the nose, the register waitresses', the daughter and cook's, change from her cigarette purchase discounted if not held against her salary, if broke, from her work at the dinette that was the northern center of the country and their world. This was Alaska, the town of North Vain or village or else nowhere, in the far west though east off the coast of Russia and he was Russian, he'd come over here by flying, he'd escaped. He'd made it, his own life, and he still made it, his payload every week and payments monthly, and so could afford to sit around and wait without thinking, the only thing about him not idle his guilt. He sat at the edge of his helicopter's bay packing the previous night's fall into small round hunks as if he were young or just himself again, in vast and unaccounted Asia, and so could shape the world around to pleasure, at his forgetting or leisure, in whatever image pleased. Mil, his name was Mil and there was no problem. And this was his day, these were all his days the same until that morning. There was never any problem until that morning he killed a woman dead.

It had been the fourth or maybe, Sunday glorious Sunday, fifth day of packing this snow, of balling and cupping the winter in spring, since he'd flownup a special tire to a mining concern—that's how the thought had first come. It had fallen from the sky and his mind was as open as daylight. The tire, though, was black and was pitilessly closed and huge, intended for some truck or other monstrous dumpster of a type he didn't know, must be new. It seemed, only seemed, it'd be impossible to lift such a tire by its size, that incredible circle—the circuitous idea of a God Whose center is everywhere and so whose circumference, nowhere: infinite, snow-nowhere, ice-infinite, flaking, unfixed as patchless—but he wasn't thinking rubber. That and it had a hole. Mil packed that hole with snow. He filled it, that Monday previous, all day until departure. Amazing, snow, in that you don't have to work to shape it: snow shapes itself, is shaped. It's the same with people, humanity—after a while you don't even have to advertise or ask, they conform without question or protest, they give to the palm, go softly as their crystals compact, their edges rub up against one another, serrate each other, eventually cracking, then breaking apart, which is together, too, to harden into a central mass, a fistlike core—a pity, he thought, that he was a person, a man endowed with emotions and thoughts and not a machine or robotic as man could have only two of them, hands. Mil packed the tire's hole with snow and so had a snowball and that ball of snow was big and undirtied against the blackness, a center creamy, enormously white and immovable, stuck hard. He tried to free it then, or tumble it, kick or prod the ball on out as if it were to be the bottom stand of a snowman that would be his double though senseless, but couldn't: whether with the tire upright or with the tire lying down, he couldn't get the ball out from its shaping hole except in clumps, in fingered digs, dings and chips of nail and knuckle grooves like tire tread, a flatness, becoming unmade, a hole within a hole, with him tearingout pads, wild with the thimbles, fistfuls manic at a time in dusts and cloudy bursts and lit threads of snow as if in a rough surgical stitching of the air, but never the whole ball, never the entire—and so he, Mil, and only Mil, alone (much to the ribbing doubt of his fellow pilots, Gulf veterans retired from the military to fly missions for private insanity in this northernmost netherworld for cash or check: certified, bank), began making these smaller balls, smaller balls of snow in pyramidal avalanching stacks and then depositing them in buckets and an old tincan trough he'd found around the portapotties behind the hangar, but only after he'd dugout with fits of nail that snow from inside the tire, its inmost rim, and then had it rolled, the tire emptied and undeniably smaller once he knew what it would take to fill it, again on its side then up the ramp and into his helicopter for delivery, which was late.

Money, that's why they did it, and money was credit. Why they'd all come up here from greater Alaska, from greatest America, discharged from commissions and not, officers to privates, to pay down their helicopters' premiums while putting a little away for alimony, childsized cabins, smokes and alcohol enough to forget how much they smoked and at what price, what body cost, how little those cabins were, their bunks and ambitions both, who they married, why—the baggage of their conscience. Oilfields torched liberty in the desert. Raping the anthills raised between the legs of burka widows. Siccing missiles on ruins, sacking palace for treasure. Gigantic gray concrete cities, the sky swaying like a palm. The Arab heat, Mil couldn't imagine hot—Mil had issues with rage and difficulty imagining. Though he might have been the only pilot here not a veteran of the American force he was not the only murderer.

That Sunday he returned from flying medical supply to a weather outpost condemned to an island off Barrow. When he'd left, however, it'd been Saturday night still, refusing the hospitality of their meal and mattress. Twenty miles off North Vain, a namelessness, and the sun had no name either. Mornings like this were a mirror of terrible in that they showed you to yourself and in showing told too much. After these many years, ten since Russia, when he flew an experimental helicopter off the edge of Asia, over the strait to the Alaskan gate, sold the helicopter to the government that was itself a failed experiment in exchange for asylum, investigative suspicion and interrogative peace, this work and that ticky tiny fishing cabin up in Bluff—after so very long, he shouldn't still have been surprised. After all the sun was daily. Why should he still be taken in—not by the light but by the change, by his own reflection, startled—he couldn't help but stare: there in the windscreen, a prismatic bubble of soap or frying fat, and yet perfectly burstless, a slathering shell. And beyond that glass that was plastic was east and almost light. Mil flew effortlessly and in a daze could see the sun rising slowly and oily yet graceful. A parting, a blowsy cleave of the horizon from the whirr of his rotors—the trees in a tremble, a glisten of needles and cones—such purity fielding, further, the middle dispensation of nameless nowhere's reach: the earthen orb below only a whitetreaded, slicktreaded tire rolling forever on its polar axle to air its rounded surface, which might hide tarmac or dirt—and so going infinitely, eternally, nowhere and nameless white and slickly wet: which was snow and which ice, he was never sure. Mil never knew where the land of all ice gave way to the land of all land, when plates became the currency and not beachy shelves or sheet as the tectonic unseated, in quake and fissure overthrew the Arctic, and the blue ocean lost its nearer sky. Above, there in the plastic glass of his helicopter, its screening shield, and there projected, superimposed, as if a detailed if blurrily and faintly colored shadow—as if a dead ghost—him, his image. A reflection that was not soap, not fat, and nor was it water. And the sun's ball had not yet cleared the horizon, which was a frozen road, the highway. In it—the capture of screen's bubble as if a comic's blurb—his nature. A bush greening about his mouth and nose. The personal rotor of his moustache. He looked horrific. His tinted sunglasses making infinities of his image in their twin mirrors because his glasses were not just tinted but mirrored, too, and there was a little sun now, burned upon his face, burnt upon his faces, the eyes of his eyes. The rise of the sun was always sure, preceded by this shade of him reflected, followed by noon and lunchtime heaviness, carb ballast, lethargy, depression. Mil was, momentarily, blinded. But there is blind and there is blind, there are many makes of blindness: black blindness, which is spiritual or hereditary and Mil had no God and his parents had long been forgotten and Russian, there is white blindness, which is Alaskan, ecstatic with freedom, then there is shallow blindness, which is greedy and gluttonous, and deep blindness, too, which is irreversibly all of them together. There is only one blindness, ultimately, and it is life, whether it's to be separated into differences for understanding's sake or standing united—unseeing, unseen. The two poles, undammed by gravity, broke away in their melt into water then, once frozen again, made continent. Oceans of land amid oceans. Mil veered westward by waterways, away from such madness where, at the furthest fingertip of squint, white gave way to gray, the crazed blankness of an idle mind. A boredom glacial. There is that other species of blindness, then: the sightlessness of that that never had, that never could have, sight—which is the blindness of that that he saw: nature, insensate nature. Its greenery grew denser, a buffer this conifer fringe, then sparser, the dirt guts between the trees widening, tarred to roads allweathered, these roads of untouched snow, these roads of snows tirepacked, treaded level and iced, over the asphalt, over the dirt and revolute earth.

Only one road through is cleared, though, black. This is the horizon's road, the highway, and just off it, set back a length of trail now obliterated in weather, was the church, the tallest house in North Vain not a tower—unless a steeple might transmit its good word frequency through bells and cross and the divine were not a universal presence but rather discrete, undependable, saving only in the irregular form of waves, disgracing ebb, redeeming flow. The crucifix atop the steeple was gold, formed from the local rush that'd never panned, when claimants first struck spike here a century ago, without prospects save hope, a rich supply of earthbound faith. They found nothing but a church: just enough of a glittering nugget—it was said by a vein of patrons mortally regular at the depot dinette, the Dine-In-U-It—for them to smelt a cross from their losses to crown that house of worship established by a missionary from an itinerant temperance society. The gold was an indulgence, dues, as rapturously apologetic to themselves as to heaven. Vain clearedout, only North Vain was left, and there only bums remained, the busted—as hollow as the shattered bells, as hollow as the belltower, the fry empty with bells shattered by clappers like wagging tongues. The building itself, below, was boxy, from here, to Mil, resembling cardboard, as if an appliance had outgrown and left it, a freezer, a refrigerator crawled for milder clime. The church was that mottled color of tobacco and the fence around it kept a yard strewn with brokenglass from whiskeybottles and stray plasticbags the ministry's kids used to huff their glue: filling the shroudy depths with fumes they'd suck and snort until dizziness, dropping. The glass caught the light, bent it, throwing spectra to the sky—tangled, knotted, rainbows. There had never been a cemetery surrounding as the ice was too hard to bury through most of the year, even in spring the snow was too deep, but there was that spiky iron fence all the same keeping its yard wide and, without the dead but with the death of trash instead, incongruous. Mil had only been to this church once, inside, grounded, and didn't believe in God or Christ His son or wouldn't. He hadn't been there for belief. It wasn't his choice to go, he'd been asked, begged, then finally ordered by his employer from whom he was buying his helicopter and so, by installments, his life. In the air Mil was narrow, focused. The walls of his eyes closedin to cradle his reflection: a variety of nativity but he hadn't been reborn and it wasn't Christmastime, only summer. The wind around him was decked with candles burning in defiance, its howl the last words of saints—the clouds swelling the faces of his martyred friends, not his but the groom's whose name he remembered was Hound. There was the pilot who'd died in a wreck he did to himself, a suicide martyr in the service of Hollywood, flown down to California to fly stunts for an action movie that made a fortune for its producers, director, and stars who would survive him, then the bathwater drown and the vodka overdose, a livered nose protruding as significant cirrus. One or two were still alive and working Alaska. They were witnesses and the party both. That one day of Mil's visit to church was the wedding of their mechanic Hound to Diana, senior carwash attendant and eldest daughter of a gunsmith who rented the rear of his shop for North Vain's only public Internet (as mechanic Hound was friend to all the pilots who were his only friends). Upon the Internet wave of his future father he'd loggedin, met a woman elsewhere. He flew away the night before the wedding. Nobody knew Hound could fly, maybe least of all himself, it was surprising. It takes great hatred of the self to be able to fly a helicopter and to fly it well but instead to become a mechanic and Hound was a hateful person. He chawed tobacco and when he talked would spit and spoke only curses (which was how Mil had come to know this language, its blacker aspect). Mil stood in church that day and was embarrassed for her, prayed to himself for thrust, a lift away from there then a pornographic session aside the fire in his cabin, alone just him and the mapless placelessness of Bluff where nothing echoed and if there were any trees they would fall, when logged, without sound. The altar had switches, levers red and green, a gauge. He felt to smash it all, but her. The face of a dial cracked with condensation, the organ loft webbed by water. And then the other men, three, should've been four, two groomsmen then him but the priest, who was usually drunk, hadn't shown, had maybe, they thought like parents or police, absconded, on his own, with Hound. The best man had been sent for the Mayor who was late himself, as justice of vain peace. It was abhorrent, disgusting—being in a church for a wedding three men none of them the groom alone with the bride in her dress and them in day off civvies. It was even colder in the church than outside despite the fire from the candles lighting everything to day, to early morning. Diana the carwash attendant attending without vehicle, turned bride, was snowwhite and as flat as a griddle, and her dress was white, too, grilled lace above the spikeheel shoes that made everything about her tall and precariously tawdry. She wobbled, she leaned, was weak. Everything suggested rape on a massive scale. A spectacle of an almost ritual defilement. Martyrdom was lurid. She had breasts, a tiny pointy pair, and crying eyes, puff and wildness. She had grown older since, stunted shorter, gained weight as if she hadn't been jilted but widowed after pregnancy. Veiled in smoke and often as evangelically drunk as a priest, she'd become a shapeless skirted huddle just below him. A hunch, a roundness rolled, or rolling herself, slowly, painfully it appeared to Mil, from the road, a shovel stuckout in front of her, pincering, a mechanical proboscis. With this she was clearing the way to church and the short way behind her from the highway was cleared and underneath was muddy dirt and gravel. Mil hovered just above the tangle of light that was the church's crucifix then circled the spire at a tilt heading toward her. His face, his eyes, left his westward reflection. He stared through himself and so his reflection, he, was no more. There was only whiteness, the horizon terminant as another highway now, and this widow shoveling a swoop beneath. Mil felt as if he were steering a tire, captain of a bucket of rust: unwieldy, and this gave him the strength of recklessness with purpose. She'd been going to church daily since that aborted wedding day. Not quite nunnery, it only felt, to her, that she'd married or was related to if not God then the church, and not the Church but that cardboard box flapped with chapels so undeserving of reconstruction that, after life left, flew, they might as well have been tightly sealed, resealed, with the tongues stilled to silent bells above her.

Each morning she'd make the church and by the time the sky lit her prayers would be offered, to be refused by nightly moon, lunacy, loneliness—every morning with the shovel. It glinted at Mil, this shovel, flashed him with its nakedness, with its cold and naked metal, and Mil blinked, squinted, saw blindness again, then recovered her, that womanly spot, her black blight form, cut lower, cinched his circle tighter. He was tense in his stomach and had to piss from too much coffee at the weather station, an hour spent resting with a midnight cup emptied over the engorged controls in his lap, ogling the scientist secretary. Up there they measured storms, forecasted fronts, perpetrated a form of magic if secular. They had the mystic sky and then they had these many little skies that were screens upon which everything had the same color as in nature but different, better. Each ocean's blue was individually blue, if unnaturally comprised, constellate of pixel. Each white was ever whiter. A pattern, if popularized on radio or television, became a trend. Catastrophe was good. Ratings went through the roof, which would be rippedoff by a storm surpassing category. This was an extreme, to be sure, antipodal, nearer the Pole, and so expectations were differently backward: terrible weather was exciting to them, it was incredible not in the death it brought but with the opportunity come knocking with wind. Scientists up there might have been manipulative or smart but they were also sick with a form of diabetes or perhaps a disease of the autoimmune, probably from those massproduced, plasticpackaged, microwavable meals they ate and those energy drink mixes they mixed with purified water then drank in lieu of fresh milk or juices for flavor. Lately there was an emergency. The station's most prominent minds had taken ill, not enough for airlift to Fairbanks but sufficient to make Mil flyup late with supply. He hauled drugs and syringes, which drugs he didn't know but all syringes were uniform, all sharpnesses the same. His receivership scientist had had a passable body and, Mil had thought, an equitable mind. She wore a gauzy labcoat she took off to make coffee and under her cap had been a messy blonde (or Diana was). The ball of her head, Mil thought of it as, was large and round, then next ball came that cuppable breast, fit to the fist, but a neck between that had been strangled too thin, distended, as if overly craned, too much time spent asking, in inquiry, on research and microscope, the telescope screen, a conclusionless bobble look in her eyes, tiny together knees under a frump skirt over what were essentially sweatpants, or leggings as they were called in the catalogs she ordered from through the mail, which he delivered, too, the catalogs and what she'd ordered from them and from the Internet, didn't help or even flatter help, nothing. He couldn't look her in the eyes and those eyes became an eye in his not looking at them as they were spaced too closely together, not allowing breath to her nose. The buttocks once had been two, since sat on too much, couched, chaired at the windows or viewfinders, squished into one that would overflow her waist to include, subsume, her stomach, too, fat from the microwavable food and all the sugar that granulated her coffee, ten cups a day due to the extra shifts she had to serve thanks to sickness. Resistant to abortion, hers was the type of pregnancy you got from surrender, from grave inaction, or premature retirement, as opposed to that of the motion fucking kind. Mil had no children and obviously no wife. He had only a woman below him. He reached for the bucket just behind.

His eyes never leaving her he saw sex, heard his own Vietnam in his head, the movies he and his fellow pilots always told, breakfast special reenactments, dive-bombing white toast into coffee taken black. As for Mil (if it was his turn to tell it), he'd served communism in Afghanistan, gunningdown mules and tribes and then, once cited enough for bravery, as test pilot, bemedaled, careered. He sat around, smoked, drank, masturbated, tested new technology. He flew helicopters no one else had ever flown before as he was the best or fearless or only ordered to. Dangerous, but the hours not too demanding unless he died. With a fist of snow and his other hand packed to the cockpit's stick as if it were the arm of another possible life of his drowning he had to save or else drown himself, Mil dove. No longer a blemish on the landscape the woman, because she was a woman, had never stopped her shoveling, helicopters around here being too common to countenance, even one coming this low and near. Each thrust with the shovel she hunched forward, down to her haunches, set herself strained almost to falling, to her knees, her face, and plowed her way to God. Mil's first throw went long. Out the sidewindow against the wind, way long, a white bird whose rounded contour from speed and height he lost to the whiteness surrounding. She didn't move or rather didn't stop moving. Vain—no locals ever thought to first call it North—was just waking over the highway, between the two highways, both empty. A stretch of smoke, the entire complex—fifty odd streets, fifty off streets—of outbuildings, the entire city—town, northern nowhere—an outbuilding itself, an addon of shedding sheds and trailer regret. A smudge of stacks and latitudinal girder, the whole an abandoned factory district—you'd wonder if you were a wonderer, once you'd toured these outskirts or industrial suburbs belted by warehouses notched by wire, where Vain proper was, where the actual life. The center of this centerlessness was a large squalid litterbox square fronting a library the yellow of a malevolent moon or bad butter (its holdings included one dictionary, half an encyclopedia set, but an unparalleled map room). Even in the brightening sun the whiteness fallen wasn't enough to override a certain shadiness, an ominous reserve. Already other helicopters were stirring—one flying the Mayor to work, to be greeted on the helipad atop the Town Hall, opposite that library, by a dogpack trained to keep the tarmac free of foreign landings. The Mayor owned the heliport, most prominently, and then most everything else—the gas pumps and common mechanic business. The town being so tightly integrated the Mayor was also Hound's uncle.

Mil's second shot landed a length just ahead of her. The snowball hit hard to powder, hurling a thick mist up at her downward face. She stopped, totally, but didn't look up. Mil circled again, taking pleasure at her horror—a buzzard encased in ice yet still airborne: a frozen prehistoric buzzard he was, armed with guns of weather, supernatural rounds. Mil threw his arm forward as if castingout the already dead, diving himself in mechanical suicide, and screamed. And though she couldn't have heard his scream she now looked up. Rather she threw herself up, sloppy shoulders to ears and hairtips frayed, the pompom of the knitcap she'd kept as carwash severance. She herself now hurled a word that missed Mil but not its echo, which was physical, landing as if a cusp of mucus in the mouth, slugging down his throat the wrong way to the lungs to trouble his next breath. Hefting the shovel, which as it was metal was cumbrous and effort, she began, slowly, to turn. With momentum she twirled. And the ice and the snow spilledout from her twirl, she swirled, and was soon unstoppable. She twirled at first like women twirl in the womenmovies, in the women televisionshows, like brides twirl in the glossy fields of bridal magazines and ads folded into newspapers, as if stirred or stirring herself. She spilled herself as if into the rotation of the planet in the rotating universe as in his own head, space, Mil's, into the spilling, spinning, spiraling of all space and even spacelessness, her arms outstretched with both hands on the shovel. She circled herself around herself around her own booted tracks—spiraled as if to prey upon herself, a personal vulture of the selfsame and still living, if just for now, not much longer given the weight and the numbing at the handle. She whirled as if to make herself unto her own assailant, her own private steel death angel, a helicopter of flesh, a natural and fatty screw unwound—spinning as if to make herself, once confirmed in her humiliated flightlessness, into the church's double, it seemed to Mil, a fallen cross the shape of her shapelessness flung wide and open with the shovel as if to rise in ascension up and off the grounding earth upon this heavy and heavier rotor, under the cutting blade of its one sharp wing. She spun a whirr by its handle in the hope of lift, the shovel's mouth open to the sky to cup the gusts and sift for air but nothing, but wasted as she spun down instead as if digging with weary feet down into the earth and deeper: elliptical becoming dimensioned to orbital, a groove of a grave, her spiraling wet white debris not flung up but driven down by her steps into the earth's very core lapping at her calves, layers, strata, molten hells unwarming. She did this deeply, this mineshaft or augered fishinghole, a twirled passage toward life's other darker side or just to the sound sleep Mil hadn't had in a while. She was soaked plus with the arm tear and the lungs seized and so—she released the shovel from her hands and her body's dizzy involutions, hurling it up as if a missile or bouquet of spears, a murderous garland to do for her magic battle in the air with Mil bearing now, ultimately, down and releasing his third and final volley. The shovel disappeared into the sky—and the sky, it disappeared from her, the earth, the world. Hard, packed, the snowball, the iceball—it had struck skull and knocked her, flattened, packed her hard herself and leveled and as Mil groaned, throttling, to haul himself up with frozen hand on hand high into the air to avoid impact and so his own numb death, rising to level over Vain to circle, circle, then land, he knew that she was dead and that no one would ever know—as the weapon dispersed, dissolving into the whole and total element from which it'd come and balled—what or who had killed her.

She remained there for an entire day—a black X marking nothing but her own crossed self on a map that would be cleared again by evening, come the weather.

STEPHEN-PAUL MARTIN

Food

STOPPING IN THE MIDDLE OF A SENTENCE, distracted by thoughts about food, he closes the book without marking his place, even though it's not time for a meal, even though the sentence was holding his interest, making the claim that mainstream reality doesn't exist anymore, that at this point we can only talk about mainstream unreality, an assertion that's not as simple as it sounds, not when the distinction between real and unreal has been relentlessly blurred by the mainstream itself, to such an extent that the mainstream exists only because real and unreal have become interchangeable terms, generating a confusion so pervasive that it hardly seems to exist, functioning as a background noise that you notice only when it's not there anymore, but such moments of silence are unusual, difficult to recognize and even more difficult to sustain, provisional in a way that makes you feel insecure, like you need more control, the power to make such moments happen at will, as if the creation of silence were a skill you could learn in a classroom, but when the lesson appears on a blackboard, and the words are as precise as any professor could possibly make them, there's something that won't fall into place, something that still makes trouble, something that even experts are confused by, experts like Professor Food, a man who's been teaching long enough to know what he's talking about, long enough to know that he doesn't know what he's talking about, standing in front of the classroom with a piece of chalk in his hand, saying things he's learned to say by saying them over and over again, things he didn't fully understand until he said them, as if unspoken words were like uninflated balloons, a figure of speech he enjoyed when he first came up with it, though he's not sure now if words and balloons can really be compared, but he keeps producing the words and the faces facing him keep writing them down, concerned that what they don't write down might work against them later, though some of them are distracted by what's out-side, by colors and faces and words on walls of billboards moving closer, blocking out most of the view from the classroom windows, making the classroom clock seem larger and louder than it really is, magnified seconds made of magnified nano-seconds ticking away, or not ticking away but stretching out and curling back on themselves, serpents flicking their tongues and flashing their fangs and eating their tails, while underneath the clock a student wants to raise her hand, a blond math major wearing high heels, a lumberjack shirt and a baseball hat, an outfit that makes a statement by refusing to make a statement, making several statements at once that cancel each other out, and she's wondering why the billboards keep getting closer, wondering why the lesson is always the same, word by word and phrase by phrase not a syllable out of place, but she's not sure how smart it would be to say anything, since the first question would show that she's not focused on Professor Food's lecture, and the second question would imply that he's too lazy or too dumb to come up with anything new, even though Professor Food has already justified his teaching strategy, announcing on the first day of class that every class would consist of exactly the same lecture, word by word and phrase by phrase not a syllable out of place, since his goal was to make sure students *fully* understood the material, not just in their brains but in every cell of their bodies, and he claimed that this could only be done through repetition, as if the lecture were an elaborate mantra, hypnotically seeping through the conceptual and emotional superstructure of the mind, slowly undoing toxic patterns of thought and feeling locked into place so firmly that nothing else seemed even remotely possible, but of course there was really no question of repetition, because the lecture on second hearing would be different from the lecture on first hearing, different the third time around than the second, different heard for the fourth time than the third, different on the fifth day of class than on the fourth, and besides, Professor Food firmly believes that it's crucial for students to learn to cope with annoyance, since so much of life is annoying and you can either be pissed off most of the time or you can preserve your sanity by mastering the annoyances, in much the same way that a surfer masters a wave, but the blond math major doesn't like surfing at all, so instead of raising her hand she gets up and leaves, just as Professor Food turns and writes the word blackboard on the blackboard and the students bend over their desks and write the word notebook in their notebooks, everyone so focused that they don't know at first that she's just gone out, but the sharp sound of her high heels in the corridor gives her away, a sound so compelling that after ten seconds it's hard to tell if she's approaching or moving away, a confusion which builds as the sound continues, reaching a point where advancing and receding are about to become the same thing, destroying one of the basic oppositions that time and space depend on, threatening an even more primal condition, the distinction between possible and impossible, which means that too much is at stake, activating the occult mechanisms of universal correction, which instantly turn the blond math major 180 degrees, sending her back down the corridor toward the classroom, leaving Professor Food with no doubt that the sound is getting larger and larger, haunting him with an image of high heels punishing a floor tiled like a chess board, a design that's always made him nervous, not because it reminds him that he's never been good at chess, not because the game includes menacing metaphors like checkmate and stalemate, but because the floor reminds him of other floors with the same design, places where bad things must have happened, though he's never been able to say what they were, and he doesn't think it would help him if he could, especially since he's never been convinced that he needs any help, except that at times apparently harmless sounds affect him more than they should, especially when combined with aggressive illumination, light with a purpose, like the light that's all but replacing the afternoon sunlight in the windows, buzzing fluorescent light from walls of billboards moving closer, smiling faces clever phrases calculated colors, counterpointing the sound of high heels coming closer and closer, turning Professor Food toward the classroom door, just as the blond math major sticks her head back into the room, giggling nervously, trying to be sheepishly cute and act like nothing is going on, which loosely speaking might be true but strictly speaking can't be true, since something is always going on, even if it's on a scale too small for human perception, and the difference between something going on and nothing going on is on the verge of dissolving, threatening yet another primordial condition—the distinction between what is and what isn't— leading the blond math major to sit back down beneath the classroom clock, scribbling furiously in her notebook in response to Professor Food's description of a blond math major scribbling furiously in her notebook, not quite understanding what she's writing, and she ends up mixing Professor Food's words with her own words, half transcription half translation half misunderstanding, but three halves don't make a whole, making instead an unstable condition, like a table with a missing leg, like a story no one seems to be telling, focusing on a prominent quantum physicist, a woman whose parents got rich by writing advertising jingles, money that's helped her move to a place where jingles don't exist, a huge Victorian house on the western shores of Lake Baikal in Siberia, and she's used her family fortune to build an amazing device, something that looks like a pile of junk but allows her to reduce herself to the size of subatomic particles, things with weird names that exist for less than a millionth of a second, but a millionth of a second seems to take decades when she finally makes herself small enough to look the subatomic realm in the face, an image that she thought was only a metaphor when she wrote it in a recent journal article, but now that she's there it all appears to be just like what she left behind, people in houses waking up and eating and talking and laughing, trees bending in breeze, jazz in low-lit basement clubs, aisles of food in labeled cans and bags, rattlesnakes making figure-eights in desert sand, mystical dancers making figure-eights in desert sand, planes that look like hammerhead sharks dropping bombs on a third world country, people in observation balloons delighted by panoramas, drivers on freeways getting pissed off and giving each other the finger, out of work middle-aged men forced to take jobs delivering pizza, animated café conversations about economic instability, but she tells herself that it's all so small that no one else even knows it's there, and when her device brings her back to the top-floor lab in her Siberian house, windows facing miles and miles of the deepest lake in the world, she can't quite bring herself to begin a scientific paper, knowing that she'd be laughed off the face of the earth if she wrote what she knows, but over time the frustration of having to keep quiet about a momentous discovery drives her to contact an old college friend, an avant-garde filmmaker whose parents died in a famous ballooning disaster, and through an eager exchange of emails they plan to make a documentary film about the sub-atomic world, protecting themselves from the scorn of the scientific world by framing the film as a work of fiction, but fights over details jeopardize the project, and one late afternoon, after a vicious disagreement about quarks and leptons, the filmmaker feels like someone trapped in a prepositional phrase about food, the very same phrase that appears in Professor Food's lecture, scribbled into the notebook of an attentive young man in the front row, an astrology major with short black hair and a long white beard and a varsity sweater, someone who would surely be every teacher's dream if he weren't listening so aggressively, changing what he's listening to, transforming a detailed discussion of symbolism in ice cream commercials into a detailed discussion of movie trailers, the way would-be actors and actresses avoid waiting on tables by making stupid movies sound brilliant, thrilling, profound, stunning, breathtaking, cultivating a seductive and authoritative manner of speaking, showing that even the most vacant nonsense can sound impressive if the speaker knows how to use her voice, something that has disturbing political implications that need careful attention, except that now the astrology major is transforming Professor Food's remarks on the need to protect animals from human violence, the need for an ongoing critique of humanity's master species complex, into a playful description of puppies in cardboard boxes, offered in shopping malls throughout the nation, bringing love into thousands of homes that would otherwise be dominated by Republicans or Born-Again Christians convinced that rhetoric about national security or family values is more than just the latest official installment of toxic nonsense, more than just an indication of how brain-dead the USA has become in the past thirty years, though it's foolish to assume that the USA has ever been smarter than it is now, and perhaps a more accurate way to approach the problem is to focus on what happens when a military superpower becomes obsessed with amusing and ornamenting itself with hi-tech devices like the cell phone that won't stop ring-toning in the astrology major's pocket, the kind of intrusion that used to make everyone giggle, but it's become so commonplace that no one notices, least of all Professor Food, whose discussion of substitute gratifications appears in the astrology major's notebook as a team of mountain climbers returning from a remote summit speaking a language no one has ever heard before, an image that affects the astrology major so physically that he feels like he's walking down an urban street on a chilly day at half past noon, a sidewalk of squares that keep repeating themselves, exactly the same size and shade of grey, and he's gotten to the point where he doesn't know how long he's been walking, except that he knows he's moving south, south becoming deeper south becoming deeper and deeper south, reaching a sky-blue boundary beyond which motion is no longer possible, the place where the sky comes down to meet the pavement, something that he's always thought was an optical illusion, or perhaps an optical metaphor, but now he walks face-first into what feels like blue plate glass, and there's nothing to do but turn and walk in the opposite direction, a sidewalk of identical squares repeating themselves, a trance of motion making the north appear to recede forever, except that he's suddenly face to face with a plate glass boundary again, blue so flat it's clear that on the other side motion doesn't exist, a firm indication that north and south aren't what they were before, so he tries walking east and bangs his face against the same blue boundary, and he tries walking west and the squares of the sidewalk end at the same blue boundary, forcing him to conclude that profound changes have taken place undetected, that the open transparent space he used to take for granted has been severely compromised, but instead of just waiting there at that suddenly rigid boundary, fondling his crotch or picking his nose, the astrology major slips quietly out of the classroom as soon as Professor Food turns to write something about mountains and language on the blackboard, chalk scraping across the flat black surface with the sound of skates on ice, a sound that follows the astrology major down the corridor, past paintings of smiling men and women who gave the school money, all posing with the same mountain meadow in the background, beyond which in the corner of his eye the astrology major expects to see a blue observation balloon, bobbing pleasantly between clouds that look like brains, reminding him of a trip he once took through mountains and meadows, taking shelter from a sudden storm in a cottage empty except for three unlabeled cans of food, waiting out the storm for days, becoming so desperately hungry that he smashed open one of the cans and ate what looked like a human brain, smashed open a second can and ate what looked like a human heart, smashed open the final can and found himself inside the can looking out, but the memory collapses into the light at the end of the corridor, imagery on walls of billboards waiting outside the doors of the school, quickly convincing the astrology major that there's no point in leaving the building, that at least the classroom is still a media-free zone, an assumption that crumbles when he slips back into his seat and Professor Food's lecture becomes a commercial, flashed on a screen descending from the ceiling, separating Professor Food from the blackboard, apparently triggered by an outside source beyond Professor Food's control, an ad that begins with the sounds of battle, Custer with bullets and arrows whizzing past him, surrounded by Sioux and Cheyenne braves and hundreds of dying soldiers and horses, and a voice-over says YOU **CAN'T** ALWAYS RUN AWAY FROM YOUR PROBLEMS, as Custer looks to the sky and sees three flying saucers cutting through the blinding sunlight, suddenly becoming Tylenol tablets, and the voice-over says BUT YOU **CAN** FEEL BETTER ABOUT WHAT YOU CAN'T ESCAPE, and the tablets fill the sky with the sound of many rivers, spinning down one by one into Custer's mouth, just as an arrow goes in one ear and out the other, and the general falls with a smile on his face, the camera zooming in on his teeth, which gleam like symbols of eternal happiness, entering the astrology major's notebook as a harsh condemnation of a right-wing think-tank, the Project for the New American Century, the unelected group that secretly governs the nation, people the astrology major has never heard of, and he puts his hand up wanting to know more about them, but Professor Food calls on a finance major who's always making excuses for cutting class, a bald young man whose eyes suggest that he's permanently baffled, frustrated because he can't find the right medication, looking especially troubled now because the wall of billboards advancing in the windows reminds him of a Shakespeare play, something about a king who talks to witches, and the finance major can't recall if it's *Hamlet* or *Othello*, but he clearly recalls that woods were approaching a mad king's castle, and he also remembers the mad king's wife, pushing him to kill his way to the top, and the finance major wonders if Professor Food has such a wife at home, someone who talks in her sleep revealing her husband's murders, but the thought of Professor Food killing people is so absurd that the finance major comes within seconds of howling with laughter, stopping himself only by writing in his notebook that he knows he's inventing Professor Food, that he's always inventing Professor Food, assuming all sorts of things about his private life, assuming that he'd rather lecture than have a conversation, that he likes gazebos better than discos, that he hates politicians and thinks that voting is meaningless, that he doesn't take any drugs but uses popcorn as a drug, that his great grandparents made love three times a day for the first five years of their marriage, that he prefers puppies to children because puppies don't grow up to become people the way children do, that he wishes he could see just one cloud that didn't look like a picture of a cloud, that he dreams of living in a sparsely furnished hut on the coast of Norway, that he's absolutely convinced that no one is ever bored in his presence, that he likes frozen sunsets filled with the silhouettes of factory smokestacks, that he thinks the beach would be fine if there were no people there making noise, that he's had lots of practice in making offensive things people say to him sound acceptable, that his first wife didn't believe in ghosts and his second wife did, that he thinks people who kill animals for the fun of it should get the electric chair, that his current wife wears high heels during sex because it makes her feel taller, and the list of assumptions might keep getting longer, as if it existed only to keep getting longer, but the finance major can see Professor Food watching him, reading his thoughts, a phrase which reminds him of Professor Food's claim that all reading is misreading, that the best we can do is accept that we're misreading everything, a claim that pissed off the finance major when Professor Food emphasized it in his opening lecture a few weeks before, but now the finance major finds it comforting, since it means that mind readers like Professor Food will always be wrong, reading their own concerns and tendencies into what they think they know, never seeing beyond themselves, but the comfort fades when the finance major begins to misread his own thoughts, begins to assume that he's always misreading his thoughts, an absurdity that's upsetting at first, but soon begins to seem funny, and this time he can only shut down his laughter by leaving the classroom, rushing to the drinking fountain, only to find that it doesn't work, so he staggers into the men's room and tries to drink from the sink, only to find that it doesn't work, so he turns and drinks from the toilet, drowning his laughter, giving

STEPHEN-PAUL MARTIN   215

himself the hiccups, and he feels like he needs fresh air, but when he stumbles down the corridor hoping his hiccups aren't loud enough to get him in trouble, he sees that there's no way out, that the billboards are coming closer, that the smiling teeth in the ads are getting sharper by the second, so he goes back into the bathroom and drinks from the toilet again, drowning his hiccups, then walks back into the class like nothing has happened, just as Professor Food says that nothing has happened, but the claim that nothing has happened apparently makes a great deal happen, music suddenly playing from hidden speakers in the ceiling, big hit songs that sound like ads that sound like big hit songs, all of them playing at once to become one song, lyrics that fasten themselves to the mind like parasites, seeming at first to be about boxes of laundry detergent left on the moon, then about weeds pushing up through cracks in abandoned swimming pools, then about windows made of hamburger meat, then about dusty globes in libraries closed because of budget cuts, then about ancient ruins that serve as landing sites for lightning bolts, and Professor Food swats at the music as if he were swatting at flies on a hot summer day, snarling and foaming at the mouth and cursing wildly, making up a whole new set of profanities, replacing words so badly overused that they've lost their offensive power, words like fuck and dick and shit and cunt, but his obscene anger only makes the music louder, driving him to grab two books from his desk to cover his ears, and the words in the books are used well enough to absorb the invasive sound, though once the room is quiet again the binding snaps and the pages crumble, making two heaps of dust on the floor, a very sad sight for a lover of books like Professor Food, but he doesn't have time to think about what's just happened, not when he sees that the finance major is just about to raise his hand, probably with a question that won't have much to do with the subject at hand, like the time he wanted to know the name of the Shakespeare play with the witches, even though at the time they were discussing the Bay of Pigs, so Professor Food calls on the smartest girl in the class, a chemistry major who wears exactly the same thing every day, torn jeans and a T-shirt that features a map of Alabama, and everyone hates the way she's always got her hand up, answering questions so brilliantly that no one remembers the questions, dominating the classroom with her voice, making everyone feel inferior, Professor Food included, except he knows that no matter how forceful her ideas are, he could easily put her in her place by exposing the true reasons for most of her opinions, her recent claim, for instance, that Anchorage and not Juneau should be the capital of Alaska, since Anchorage is a larger more centrally located city, which sounded like flawless logic to the rest of the class, especially since her voice was calm and confident, but Professor Food could have pointed out that the chemistry major grew up in Juneau and hates it, has always thought of Anchorage as an escape, but not a total escape, since Anchorage is still in Alaska, still a symbolic extension of her nuclear family, revealing her inability to separate from her parents, something she tries to disguise by always wearing an Alabama T shirt, connecting herself with a hot and humid state that's worlds apart from the frozen wastes of Alaska, but Professor Food can see through the deception, which is evident in the way the two states are spelled, since Alabama begins and ends with an A like Alaska does, another sign that she can't psychologically separate from her parents, a dirty secret that once exposed would threaten the credibility of everything she says, but Professor Food knows that he himself has dirty secrets informing his decisions about what to teach and how to teach it, and he's pretty sure that the chemistry major can see beyond his pedagogical surface, that she wouldn't hesitate to make him look silly if he tried to cut her down to size, so he does little more than nod and smile when she talks in class, even though he knows that he's tacitly affirming distorted information, which doesn't disturb him as much as other people might think it should, since he believes that all information is distorted, serving the needs and interests of those who call it information, a term which insists on its own authority, its right to be right, an attitude which Professor Food is eager to place on the right wing of the political spectrum, though he knows that lefties can also be dogmatic, and some of his best left-wing friends are self-righteous people, and in his stronger moments he's willing to admit that many people would describe him in the same way, but he tells himself that you have to stand for something, even if what you're standing for is your belief that all beliefs are nothing more than patterns of syllables, a point that Professor Food frequently makes when the chemistry major gets cocky, but this time she's chewing bubble gum, blowing a gigantic bubble, popping it, yawning and looking outside, recalling what she used to enjoy looking at, beyond the wall of billboards getting close enough to spit on, beyond the old stone campus buildings covered with ivy, beyond the quaint college town, its well-preserved nineteenth-century houses, beyond the abandoned factory district on the edge of town, the jumble of blackened buildings and obsolete smokestacks, beyond the motels beside the freeway, beyond anything that the word beyond might mean to her, finally deciding that Professor Food's reduction of all knowledge to a pattern of syllables is in itself just another pattern of syllables, and she narrows her eyes and licks her lips and prepares to raise her hand, but suddenly there's laughter, not the aggressively defensive laughter of students who think they're way too cool to be thinking about Professor Food's ideas, not the secretive laughter of students passing notes or texting about things that have nothing to do with the class, but the high-pitched cackling that comes with evil experiments in dungeon laboratories, maniacal scientists in long black robes surrounded by steaming vats and bubbling alembics, a sound that bothers her because it seems to have come from nowhere, because it doesn't look like anyone in the classroom is laughing, and also because it seems to have come from a deep understanding of the lesson, something she's apparently unaware of, and she can't stand it when other people catch on faster than she does, leading her to think that maybe she's better off dropping the class, so she gets up and walks out in the middle of a sentence about alchemy in the Middle Ages, missing what Professor Food regards as the centerpiece of his discussion, the claim that the physical universe is a language words can directly affect, not so much because they allow us to construct plans that bring about actions and changes, but more because of their musical powers, the incantatory play of images riding on syllables, transforming the harmonic vibrations at the core of subatomic space-time, even if the term core is wrong, suggesting a solid center, when current speculation suggests that in the subatomic realm terms like solid and center have no meaning, and even though the chemistry major is beyond the range of Professor Food's voice by the time he starts talking about space-time, she knows all the words by heart, and all of her objections to the words by heart, the primary objection being that she doesn't think Professor Food has any business lecturing about something outside his field, though she found it intriguing at first when Professor Food began each class by denouncing specialization, claiming that it produced arrogant narrow-minded people trapped in disciplinary ghettoes, but after hearing the same argument so many times she's begun to think that Professor Food is only trashing specialized expertise because he's insecure about his own expertise, but now she's passing a room where a bald man wearing a blazer is giving advice to a long-haired student wearing a blazer, a young man gripping the sides of his chair, nodding eagerly whenever the advisor pauses, a situation that normally wouldn't hold the chemistry major's interest for more than a second, but there's a photo-realist painting of a moonlit cactus above the advisor's desk, and there's a large aquarium filled with tropical fish on a small gray file cabinet, and three feet away from the student's battered sandals there's a chocolate milkshake spilled on blood-red carpeting, and a ceiling fan is turning lethargically throwing shadows across the advisor's desk, throwing shadows across closed venetian blinds, throwing shadows across a white wooden bookcase empty except for an old black boot on the bottom shelf, and the pattern of shapes and colors and motions holds the chemistry major in place for fifteen seconds, and each of those fifteen seconds feels like fifteen minutes, and each of those fifteen minutes feels like fifteen hours, and each of those fifteen hours feels like fifteen days, but near the end of the fifteenth day the chemistry major farts, breaking the spell, and she finds herself moving forcefully toward the door at the end of the corridor, a rectangle of harsh illumination that hurts her eyes, thousands of fluorescent lights throbbing above towering walls of billboards, ads for anything and everything blocking out the college town she used to see through the window in class, not just blocking it out but replacing it, or at least that's the claim that several billboards make, ads for cell phones featuring people whose eager expressions suggest that making mobile small talk is all that matters, and the chemistry major is the only student on campus who hasn't jailed herself in a cell phone yet, another reason Professor Food respects her even though he doesn't always like her, but now she's up against more than she can handle, staggering away from the harsh blasts of light in the doorway, rushing down the hall and down the stairs to the fire exit, but only getting the door half open before the blasts of billboard light force her to slam the door shut, leaving her with no voice, not even a voice to talk to herself with, though other voices talk in her head, urging her to buy herself back from whatever she can't afford, and she staggers back into the classroom knowing she smells like someone who's dumber than she was a few minutes ago, one of the few times in her life that she's been aware of feeling anything like mental insecurity, though the feeling is quickly replaced by astonishment, the realization that something is radically different in the classroom, that Professor Food's lecture has taken an unforeseen path, and he's claiming that human beings have no moral right to exist anymore, that whatever people have done to each other for the past ten thousand years, it's nothing compared to what they've done to the rest of the planet, which means that the only responsible action at this point is for the human race to destroy itself, a claim that the chemistry major would normally find absurd, but in the present situation the claim itself doesn't seem nearly as important as the fact that Professor Food has stopped repeating himself, a change that she can't account for since it happened when she was out of the class, a gap in her understanding that makes her feel even more insecure than before, adding to her fear that she probably looks like someone missing an obvious joke, that all her classmates can see how stupid she looks and feels, but no one even notices that she's back, their eyes drawn instead to what Professor Food has drawn on the blackboard, something that might be a magical diagram, a woodcut from a medieval book of spells, a sign that conjures fires of purification through destruction, though Professor Food himself doesn't know what he's doing, only what his hand has done with a piece of chalk on the blackboard, an image drawn with artistic skill far beyond what he's normally capable of, a picture of himself drawing a picture of himself drawing a picture of himself drawing a picture of himself drawing a picture of himself drawing a picture of himself, smaller and smaller scales of representation, culminating in a picture of a blackboard that's really a mirror sketched in so carefully that it mirrors all the scales of representation, forcing Professor Food to face his own face in a distant reflection, and behind his face he can almost see the mirrored student faces facing the blackboard, as if he were nothing more than a talking mirror, getting consumed in the endless play of reflections, digested by what the students think he's teaching them, digested by what he knows he's not really teaching them, and the gap that forms between what they think and what he knows gets hot, gets impossibly hot, more than impossibly hot and it can't contain itself, flashing into quickly spreading fires that burn down the classroom, burn down the walls of billboards crushing the classroom on every side, quickly spreading all over the school getting hotter by the second, flames that sound like applause, flames that pause to enjoy what they're doing, flames that leap and dance composing a shadow play on the flat white sky, flames that seem comprised of all of history's conflagrations—Rome Chicago San Francisco Dresden Hiroshima—flames with no connection to firebirds rising from their ashes, wildly approaching what might have been there before, the college town, its tidy rows of nineteenth-century houses, the abandoned factory district, blackened buildings and obsolete smokestacks, motels with their neon signs by the freeway flashing their vacancy, as if there would soon be nothing left but the vacancy, nothing to reduce to print and pictures, nothing to cut and paste and frame and sell, only a sentence twisting and turning away from where it began, making and remaking itself through changes in speed and focus, a tale that's eating its tail, a tale untelling itself in the telling, feeding on the eyes of someone feeding on what he thinks it means, someone getting distracted and turning away from the page to find food.

Mr. Perspective Regains Perspective

First the light opens in a milky vase.
Whether he sees a slavering rabid dog
or a Madonna, still, he's looking for meaning.
Teeth in. Teeth out.
Chaste, hollow, he can't make sense
of anything. Just to know how it would feel
to give back what's given,
he smashes the vase
and his compass spreads on the ground.
He feels so purely gray-washed.
Only the crystal still rings.
Sitting with it for awhile, he dreams
of altering the earth's axis.
There is no way to catch himself in this scene.
You cannot enter, say the woods.
He enters.
Such lonely work, giving perspective
to red pines and evergreens and black claws
under the eyes of everyone.
And yet strangely not having a complete face
is why he's survived so long:
his chilling eyes insist that nothing else is unclear,
calling forth a dish towel, toy horses,
honeysuckle blossoms working with grass,
candles burning down in right corners;
he is desperate for meaning, nonetheless.
He asks for it and is given a blue sun.
What he will not burn is only a promise.

At Least Part of the Reason

Look, now, this is not my old trick again.
We keep sleeping in our chains. We can't mute
our charred appetites. We ignore the worst.
I've thought about what cannot be undone:
a young, three legged cow, shunted, shut
in a pen. (The only job I ever lost.)
Her mooing was injuring me. I made time
pass by billowing back to her. I cut
her ear tags, catheter, whatever wasn't
flesh. To touch your legs is to feel her shame.
      Deep feast.

Something more than shame: she was a beacon.
If only I could entirely forget—
for years the only voice was, *Where's your thirst?*
Swallow. Forgive yourself. The flames are broken.
But this light was like nails that split the feet.
Now I live in this light, which is the stillest
in bed. Already a worm sweeps our home.
In the rooms it eats the shadows and sets
its cold lips on my arms. It has mostly
black scales that splinter like shingles on a tomb.
      Come home.

I want to find a tomb to dig in: what can
hold out, what seeds shoot through a skull, what sweet
water cannot break. I just want to trust
the body, trust that it never shuts out sun.
I mean to be whole. I am not quiet.
How do I know if you're sleeping? I outlast
rejections. How old are we? Your hands are warm:
give me them. It isn't easy to want. To get
somewhere, I take everything off, spiders.
Once you said, "I'm not giving up." To dream
      a house.

I move above you and then the dream: carnations,
the forks shining on the table, velvet—
it all comes true, the black cord, the taste
of tears in my mouth, the hard cessation.
What you would have given up didn't amount
to much: pictures of a drowned dog, red glass.
But I wanted to show you how a stream
slips down, bursts the minerals of granite
in blood, turns veins slowly into caves, mist
and dead bats. That is, I would have become
        forceless.

I see how much like me you have become:
a woman who makes a speechless market
out of half-lit hanging blue locusts.
You wait for me to step up and buy them
and not discuss prices, as if I coveted
burned wings about to open. Who would contest,
you think, that you sell sweet and precious forms?
We have a deep thirst to bargain, and yet
I do it at my expense: it is lust
that I barter for, my head full of flotsam,
        red gauze.

In sex it's true there is mostly exhaustion.
My body's right side hotter than the left,
guilt, double vision. A travel plan is best:
simple, no clouds of annunciation,
you desolate, me as I am, a wet
lace sheet, old lamp, nothing to fight against.
But I can't understand anything, our home,
this persisting hollowness, a white slate,
why you are a little cold and so fast
as if you wanted to find rest, be
        left alone.

I talk to another more than myself

The same words: *anathema*,
bibliographic, mark

our language as fallen.
Stencils of trees to decorate trees.

At the museum, you are impressed
by ancient bronze. Metal ribs

of another. I wield a dull knife
to my way of seeing:

the cloud-thoughts, not muscles,
feel the threat. The word-hinges—

like tools of unknown origin—
exposed under the more modern way

to light old artifacts. My use of
you could distill *us*, make room

for another experiment in materials.

Bedtime story

They name it the Dream City because it hasn't been built. The park is designed to look like a park. The zoo, a zoo. The museum started planning an exhibition of inkwells to celebrate the one year anniversary of the museum before the museum was designed. This could be a fiction so wide they built a river to fill it. But it's not. The river was always there. We want the city to be the kind of city the little girl will feel nostalgic about when both happy and depressed. All her colors will be based on the colors of that city. And now the temporary is already seeming permanent: a good sign.

There is a lake and it is the third biggest in the world if we say it is. There have been drownings, accidental, all caused by over-admiration. (Lack of admiration can be equally dangerous.) The police are already stationed in the most beautiful spots to make them a little less lovely and thereby protect us.

I need protecting. I will move into any idea faster than onto a long-awaited city-to-city bus. You like this about me, but I find it a terrible quality in you. After seeing the exhibition of writings by old men in our city you say *let's become old men*. We shut the TV off and you say *let's argue*. About what. *About the Dream City*. And then we decide to put the little things off until the city is finished and we go.

ADAM CLAY

[Considered the source of these stones]

Considered the source of these stones.
They exist at the bottom of every swallow of water

and among the potatoes in a deep-bucket kept
up high.

What we desire changes from day to night.
What I hoped to exist is not a stone,

but a coin, for money
throws light across any room.

A stone, dark on the inside, darkens every room it enters.
A stone bound to drag me to the bottom.

[To endure calamity's split,
I turn to each bottle]

To endure calamity's split, I turn to each bottle
of milk cold in the well and
speak to the shards of noise
under my pillow and the eggs below the bed.

The sky looms so large from this window, but the hill
cannot be seen from this vantage.

Crowding the sky, a half-breath
demanding to be unwritten and passed over.

Eggshells in the garden. For naught. I dream
of locusts. Swarming weather hesitates,
brings with it a new definition of sorrow.

[Oft reminded of thought's quickness in a croak of noise]

Oft reminded of thought's quickness in a croak of noise
from a trustworthy messenger,

                                                  a waitress unloved.

            The gravity of liberty groans savagely

and make no mistake: I know cavaliers
dream of violence.

                        They dream of denial's twisting corridor.

I dream of dancing on the table. The glasses destroyed to ash.

What I can offer to the night: a photograph of bodies
in the river and the ravens above it forming a river all its own.

[Symmetrical silence in the dark because the dark]

Symmetrical silence in the dark because the dark
is all there is this far North. Dime-promises

hidden in the fold of a tongue

and the end of winter, what I have always yearned for,
the frozen bison in the river, the ice breaking
as if it had forgotten to eat but was remembering again.

DEREK WHITE

from Marsupial

The Connection Between Mary X. Lake and the Containment Pond

IT WAS AT THIS LAKE WHERE WE USED TO FISH FOR CATFISH. It was a man-made lake our father had surveyed and named after our mother. Unlike most of the murky lakes in Georgia, this lake was clear as a chlorinated swimming pool. A sign identified it as *Lake Germfree*, though I knew the real name. As a kid, at this lake, I always wondered what bait looked like to fish when we were fishing for them and what the fish looked like as they contemplated the bait. I dove under to find out.

When I opened my eyes I could see perfectly, but saw no fish. There were hundreds of bare hooks hanging from the mirrored surface that I was careful not to get snagged on. I took off my shorts so they wouldn't get hooked. This made sense at the time. I sensed the fish were there but could see better than me and were keeping their distance in the open water. The water was so clear it was black. As I remembered it, there was a shelf near the shore that John and I suspected was a favorite place for fish to hide. Taking a deep breath, I went down to look under the shelf. Something darted in the shadows. I went further under after it. I followed the darting shadow down a passage into complete darkness. Then it got light again and when I emerged I was in the containment pond at the Gaston sewage treatment center. It was night, but the scene was lit by powerful artificial lights. Taking another deep breath, I retreated back to the lake. When I got there, I was in a boat and the lake was now walled in with cliffs of meat (just like in the script from the movie we were engaged in). There was a staircase cut into the meat cliff but I was having a hard time paddling toward it as the waves were getting bigger. The meaty shores of the lake were receding. Water splashed on my face that tasted of salt. The salt triggered a premonition of a coming hurricane. I had to decide whether to:

a) go for the stairway cut into the meat cliff or

b) retreat back underwater to the containment pond.

I decided on (b) and hung out with some garbage men who were also there at the artificially lit containment pond waiting the storm out. Their role in this was to pick up garbage in boats to take out to a big barge in the ocean, or "wide moat" as they called it, but they were holding up at the pond because of the storm. At least that's how things appeared on the surface. I found out later they all had law degrees and were moonlighting as garbage men to "delay execution." When I asked, "execution of what?" they answered, "execution of god's will." Then one of them asked me, reading from a script, if I had called my mother.

[beat]

Then he shouted, "line."

Someone from off the set whispered, *"shouldn't you at least let her know where you're at."*

The garbage man lawyer repeated this line with more conviction.

When I didn't answer, another of the garbage men lawyers repeated the line again, "shouldn't you at least let her know where you're at?"

I kept brushing it off because I didn't want to come off as a "mommy's boy." All the garbage men lawyers started pitching in, interrogating me like I was on trial, their voices in unison, sometimes overlapping, over and over, saying, "shouldn't you at least let her know where you're at?" I realized I was listening to an old soundtrack on vinyl. The needle wore so deep into the groove it hit a nerve, waking me up.

Bernard's Inquisition

WHEN I SHOWED UP FOR MY JOB INTERVIEW, my prospective employer took me straight to his private aquarium that was in the adjoining underwater map room. I wasn't sure why he was showing me his aquarium as the newspaper posting listed the position I was applying for as "Continuity Chief for Swamp Survey Crew." The description from the *Savannah Mourning News* Want Ads said it was ". . . for a half land-based half water-based surveying position. As Continuity Chief, you will be responsible for bridging the gap in land/water data."

When I asked Bernard if I was in the right place, he told me, "our will that to get." First he wanted to show me his 55-gallon tank that was empty except for five scallops that were evenly spaced at the bottom. There were three black holes in the back wall where fish supposedly lived. "In reality," Bernard said, through some sort of voice-scrambling device, "live they in a nether tank ay, within a nether tank ay behind a nether wall, beyond a nether, beyond a nether, beyond a nether . . . " and he kept skipping until I hit him and he stopped, swallowed, and said, "wall. I sashay."

The "wall" was really a movie screen. My mind was reeling trying to figure out what he could possibly be testing me for beyond holistic comprehension. I was on my best behavior, sitting upright and acting interested, ready to field questions, and queuing up questions in my own mind to ask him. But I couldn't open my mouth. To be more accurate, I could open my mouth, but something was blocking my "voice canal," which at the time was legitimate anatomy. Bernard pulled a lever and five fish darted into the tank and rifled through the scallop shells, stripping them of any meat, or "flossing," as Bernard called it.

My stomach made a noise and I was sure Bernard noticed, but it didn't show. Once the frenzy was over, the five fish disappeared back into the three holes. I clapped to be polite, and since I couldn't speak. Then he let three snakes into the room. They were writhing at my feet, but I remained calm and courteous. I had to keep reminding myself that I was human and to be myself, but I forgot why I was reminding myself of this.

"Purse severance furthers," he said, pinching the skin on my forearm. "Must they may be able-bodied ay to seize a fold to penetrate, say ye skin. The place of pleasure legitimate ay where they may seize a catch is the strap between ye fingers."

I splayed my fingers and he was right—my hands were webbed. His hands, on the other hand, were not webbed and I was concerned he would judge me for it.

He pinched me again, and then said, "have it known ay that when ye, formally, that I evoke, ay ye do not hatch, in real skin, the contact ay? Our individual skins do not evoke naturally."

I nodded yes, thankful that although there were questions involved, his body language was leading me to the answers. When I looked down at my arm where he had pinched me, a huge chunk had molted off. He didn't notice, or if he did, he did a good job of acting like he didn't.

"Now begins the formulaic segment of the interaction," he said, pressing the record button of a small device. "Do solemnly swear you to tell nothing but the truth?"

```
JAUNE: [BEAT][I was thinking, "I do" but couldn't say it]
BERNARD: Have ye a passport?
JAUNE: [BEAT]
BERNARD: Married are to you?
JAUNE: [BEAT]
BERNARD: Have ye ever, at sea, been on a boat with men, only?
JAUNE: [BEAT]
BERNARD: Ever have ye been an armchair geologist?
JAUNE: [BEAT]
BERNARD: If, hypothetically, you were in effect under assign-
ment to survey a parcel of ground, and looking to the bottom
of the map, in the legend, it was your brother.
JAUNE: [BEAT]
BERNARD: Would ye make with the task?
JAUNE: [BEAT]
```

Even though I didn't even have the ability to answer the question, the last one threw me for a loop. I never expected to be asked if I would "survey" my own brother, if this in fact was what Bernard was asking, and if in fact John could fit in the legend of the 2-dimensional map. I moved my head in circles and up and down at the same time, until my head rolled off, waking myself up.

Atlas

"In the 17th century, Michigan belonged to Louis XIV."
—Bruce Catton, *Michigan: A Bicentennial History*

"A three alarm fire broke out at the Pioneer Hotel at the corner of Ann and Huron Streets Tuesday evening. One fireman was taken to the emergency room as a result of heat exhaustion. There were no other injuries. The manager of the hotel was unavailable for comment and a telephone call to the owner, a Mr. Davidson, was not returned. A police investigation into the causes of the fire is ongoing."
—*The Ann Arbor Times*

"Jean Nicolet was the first Frenchman to sail the straits of Lake Huron. He donned a mandarin's robes when he went ashore at Green Bay, believing he was in China." (Catton 3)

He wrote
He crossed the street
He was hungry

"Dante never dreamed of being a detective."
He didn't particularly like

that last sentence, but he
needed to begin some-
where. There was nothing
in the refrigerator. He had
eaten the last can of tuna
for lunch the day before.
The thought of going out
frightened him. That was
certainly not true.

Found text:
Birth certificates of
characters

The thought of going
out annoyed him. That
was closer to the truth.
His neighbor ate nothing
but 8 oz. cans of Dinty
Moore stew at each meal.
Wouldn't you get tired
of it? But habits like that
simplify things. He wished
he had more of them.
"Dante ate nothing but
8 oz. cans of Dinty Moore
stew at each meal." Did
that include breakfast?
Probably not.

"Some said Michilimack-
nac meant 'great turtle'
in the Ottawa language.
Others that it was the
name of a small tribe,
the Mishenemacinawgo."
(Catton 11)

Paris is the capital of
France. Population:____.
Situated in the ____ paral-
lel and longitude ____.
Although many people
wonder whether there is a
relationship between Paris
the Trojan prince and
the city, there is actually
none. The city was named
after a tribe, the Parisii.

Dear Keith,

I suspect that you must own
this book because of the care
that you have taken in fash-
ioning your own bathroom
and the fact that you have
installed a wooden bath-
tub. What does it smell like
when it is filled with water
I imagine it must have a
sauna-like scent, or perhaps
more like that of a woooden
cup when it is filled with hot
sake. That smell reminds
me of wooden sandals,
though I've never owned
a pair. And the sound of
water hitting the bottom of
the tub? Is it hollow? Dull?
In the evenings, after work,
it must be very nice to sit in
the wooden tub. I hope you
will enjoy the book.

All best to you and Todd,

Johannah

"Breakfast consisted of a cigarette and a strong cup of black coffee."

Etienne Brulé "had many adventures, obscure and apparently pointless. He lived with the Hurons and traveled throughout the upper midwest. In Pennsylvania, he was captured by the Iroquois, who would have killed him had he not cursed them in the name of God and on that sunny day, in a cloud-less sky, a thunderhead gathered and a huge clap sounded. He survived and then was clubbed to death in 1632 by the Hurons, who, according to legend, also ate him." (Catton 6–7)

In the middle of the night, I wake up. Texts overlap-ping. The rent for 2003 will total over $17,000. Enough to buy a valuable drawing (even one by Cezanne) or a really important photograph. Do you read for informa-tion or for the emotional connection to characters? What is your work about?

"Now those existentialists, they really knew something. People are completely self absorbed. No, people are completely self absorbed, emphasis on ARE, not PEOPLE. What else is there other than self-absorption? 'L'enfer c'est les autres.' How do you pronounce that? You may be able to pronounce it, but I think I really know what it means, I mean, assuming that anyone knows what it means.

My next book is written from the text I wrote on one page and then revised 200 times. Each word and its associations are explored. Any piece of text could therefore generate a book.

"What the hell does that mean anyway? I'd like to know what Sartre and de Beauvoir talked about at dinner. You're laughing, but I really wonder." But who is he talking to? The wall, the cat, himself, his wife? "When writing fiction the author must not pose questions. Rather, the author's task is to answer questions.

Questions do not further the project of verisimilitude though they may seem to." This according to Henry A. Simmons, author of *A Writer Writes*, as well as a history of the state of Michigan published in celebration of the nation's bicentennial, and *The Long Way Home*, a novel that "in scintillating prose chronicles the journey of a merchant marine as he travels around the world." Which would explain the author's obsession with sailing metaphors in, even, his nonfiction works. Why not just read *Moby Dick*? I should ask myself the same question.

Whimsical
Psychological
Comical

"The Mayor looked up at the white wall, shook, replaced, zipped, and flushed. He watched the water swirl down the white bowl, it was headed to Milan, thirty miles southeast of town, part of the finest water system in the world. What was that guy's name? Some Italian. Wanted to start

"Equinotical storms on Lake Michigan can be violent and one blew up just after the Griffon sailed, and that is all anyone knows about it, except that neither ship nor men were ever seen again." (Catton 17)

home delivery of donuts. Mechanized production, computer processed. A donut. He should focus on something people were less picky about. What flavor of donut? There must be at least a hundred. Fifty. A hundred with all of the frosted, unfrosted, sprinkles, fillings. The guy should focus on necessities. He wouldn't have to worry about fancy marketing. Guns, for instance, did not require home delivery."

story

A man and woman meet and fall in love. He takes over her identity and ambitions, and she takes on his. For many years, they do not get along.

story

A man and a woman meet and do not fall in love. There is no reason that they meet, other than the fact that he would like to get laid. They develop a friendship based on the fact that she will not sleep with him. (They both like to talk). He is from one place. She is from another. As she gets older, he gets

younger. At the end of
the book, they are each
the same age as the other
when they first met.

People just needed them.
Always needed guns.
Recreation, public safety,
peace of mind. Forget
donuts. The Mayor walked
back down the hall to his
office. Three gun stores
already and a fourth to be
opened in the spring by
the new subdivision.

"The story haunts the
imagination: one frail ship,
overborne by tempest on
an uncharted sea where
there were no other ships,
no light-houses, no harbors
of safe refuge, no rescuing
Coast Guards—no possible
chance of help for a ship
that could not make it,
nothing left." (Catton 17)

story

A random occurrence,
i.e., the meeting of two
individuals, allows this
story to be told.
(A bit like a car accident.)

story

A young actress moves
to New York and gets

involved with a man who is 20 years older than she is but who claims he is only 12 years older than she is. She is in a play at the time about a relationship between an older man and a younger woman. Her roommate is writing a romance novel about a young woman who moves to Paris and gets involved with a man who is twenty years older than she is, but who claims he is only 12 years older.

She was having a nervous breakdown. Or at least she thought she was. The idea had occurred to her in the past, but more as a possibility rather than a diagnosis. What would that mean anyhow? That she stopped being able to manage her day to day life. And what did that entail? No longer going to the grocery store or to the bank or buying tea at the store down the street from her apartment.

rain
snow
sun
overcast

sleet
unhappy marriage
extramarital affair
death
illness
unemployment
promotion
alcoholic/drug addict

engaged
married
divorced
single
never married
heterosexual
homosexual
bisexual
transsexual

novel

Take the headlines from
a newspaper from one
day and re-write all of
the articles and then
write a novel based on
those stories.

She would stop doing the
laundry and the dishes. She
would begin living with
too many stuffed animals
whom she slowly began to
consider her children and
whom she talked to in the
evenings when she got back
from whatever it was she

did in the evenings. People having nervous breakdowns probably cancelled a lot of evening engagements. Was she wealthy enough to have a nervous breakdown? This seemed like one of the first criteria, gender being the second. She knew someone who people actually described as having had a nervous breakdown and he was wealthy, yes, but he was also male, which negated her attempts at generalizing. In novels, only women have

novel

Take a newspaper from one day and write a novel using only the language, characters and plots contained in the newspaper.

artist   psychologist
professor   life guard
factory worker
teacher   mayor   priest
sea captain   photographer
writer   governor   heir
train conductor
    dressmaker
lawyer   principal
race car driver   pilot
journalist   doctor
    salesman
taxi driver   truck driver

nervous breakdowns. The male characters are alcoholic or depressed instead. What happened when generically middle class people had emotional breakdowns? She was barely middle class at this point, at least financially speaking, but she looked middle class. And what do nerves have to do with these things anyway?

actress   businessperson
police officer   athlete
hair dresser   scientist
nurse   fireman
secretary   musician
beekeeper   social worker
detective   tug boat
   operator
auto mechanic   farmer

farmer   arborist   jeweler
travel agent   gardener
store manager   tour guide
bookkeeper   stock broker
editor   accountant
   engineer
director   administrator
cabinet maker   fisherman
hotel manager   landlord

The Mayor crossed the
street. He had just left
City Hall, the second tall-
est building in town sited
in the center of a parking
lot. What happened to the
original City Hall? The
Mayor doesn't usually go
in for those historical pres-
ervationist issues. Only the
professors' wives, mainly
transplants, care about
things like that. And Mrs.
Burns who claims to have
some connection to the
town's founding families.
But he doesn't believe it.
Her family's from Indiana,
he's pretty sure. The polite
pretense of the town's
history had been added
much later, after the hoity
toity set needed some
excuse for living in the
middle of nowhere.

He ran his tongue over
his new false tooth. He
wished they would all
be replaced. He was sick
of going to that Doctor
Lowenthal's office every
other week for some tooth-
ache. Doctor Lowentooth.
And how did that dentist

know about the new jeweler in town, Davis what's-his-name. A queer for sure. You can tell from his jewelry. The Mayor and his wife had politely declined that invitation. Who knew what he did in that big house of his.

"The real magnet that drew men here had been that it offered escape; here, at the last, a man was not forced into a mold, his life constricted by the nearness and the prejudices of innumerable neighbors, and if he wanted to he could move out to the realm of the wholly lawless and live as he chose—with, to be sure, the penalty of swift death if he chose unwisely."
(Catton 31)

Would you like to live in Japan?

What is your favorite color?

Where will this novel be set?

The epigraph, as well as the text in the left-hand column is quoted from Bruce Catton's *Michigan: A Bicentennial History* (Norton, 1976).

MIRANDA MELLIS

from Materialisms

THIS WORK SYNTHESIZES LANGUAGE derived from two disparate American archives: the case files of Dr. E. M. Libby, a rural doctor of north Michigan miners and loggers circa 1900–1934, and life as a child in a Marxist-Leninist collective circa 1970s–1980s. This archive is flagrantly subjective. Other intertexts are derived from authors William Cronon and Lewis C. Reimann (see endnote). Each case is volumetric (sound and dimension) imbricating the bruised shine of fateful accidents, heists gone awry, smoke-soaked discourse, auto-cry-tique, and "enormous changes at the last minute" characteristic of bodily and earthly life's world-historical trauma. (All trauma is world-historical.) The "cases" register regimes of treatment—medical, industrial and ideological. If there is any recuperation in this operation, it is of the bald noise of expression.

No. 1998

Working in the shaft at Rogers Mine, patient fell thirty feet and landed on a timber placed across shaft.

Brought to surface acre, a monument bodily. Dissuade him. Do not ring. Fearing mental hills, mineral fires, ground waters for the entirety of called life. To incur before she died mother did lament "they are burning." The cradle is burning of civilization. This . . . memoir, enemy pleasure. They demand that you read Marx "correctly." Why don't you? You small thin tongue civility, the doctor where needed used a chisel. Oh comrade you know how to use the hammer. Of fascia sometimes upon the flesh and bone of a miner or a logger. Oh comrade why isn't it all as written? Oh redemptive mark-maker Marx. Why hast thou insufficiently. End it doctor will operate constantly. The insane philosopher will diagnose. Crest of the people who are getting hurt oh mother. Pelvis oh patient, there is nothing to worry about don't touch me there. Pain, it is sad. You are depressed but don't turn it into suffering comrade you are you and words are only. Don't suffer me so your goodness, so like malice. Your authority, so.

No. 1710

"Drifts" are tunnels drilled and dug out from the shaft to the main body of ore. At the end of these drifts were great rooms from which the ore had been blasted and hauled to the "skip," or elevator cage, and hoisted to the surface.

Working in drift in Osana Mine, he was caught between sidewall of drift and passing tramcar.

Tried to get there in time too late disaster. How to get. Outer aspect of hips and thighs shoot spun yourself shit. Of ilia to whomever, this home even, neutral push push. Patient complains of pain and lies down. Severe pain: much has been said about subject and object and region, locale, local anesthetic, locale anamorphosis, local aesthetic. Morphine I will not add, but make removals. Small, cigarette drain in low angle, its wound-made revenge pattern home spun. xo, comrade.

No. 1952

Commodities were produced by human beings facing each other in the tumultuous relationship whose name was market: farmers and grain traders, cowboys and cattle barons, lumberjacks and lumbermen, miners and managers all struggling over who would control the product of their collective work.

Shoveling ore in stope at Chicagoan Mine, a large mass of ore fell striking patient and knocking him down.

Who would control their collective? Misreadings, posters of death, ideology, coinage. Shame produced by human beings misrecognizing each other in the tumult whose name. Don't drive through blame town without visiting authority. Necrotic tissue of doubtful vitality. The children laugh they screwed, drilled and screw. Cast with windows to permit inspection no one is watching. Will return to work as a miner. Will return to anger.

No. 1830

They fastened lighted candles or carbide lamps to their waterproof miner's hats.

Working in shaft of Osana Mine, a piece of rock, falling down shaft, struck patient on head.

"I have no pictures from that time; my life was erased." Angles of laceration. Force of semi-conscious iterations, repetitions. Elevate, insinuate, make a gesture ascetic mistaken under the edge of a fragment the fragment raised, seized with forceps pain vs. concept. Who is under the bed? Dura lacerated. Closed with fine catgut. Bone fragment trimmed to firm seating replaced in bony defect of skull. Silkworm gut. Dressings retained by firmly applied cap. Convulsions resume hard labor. Return to iron for visit, procure money to see the doctor, strikes would not be allowed to stop production, diseases are a kind of strike, too. The mother laborer, whose, patient abed, whose body refuses to work, to work properly on behalf of the collective. Who will not, will not stop for that? Nor would the mines stop, stop for that. Stutter, strike, scatter, stutter. How can you hold a limit responsible: a limit cannot go beyond.

No. 1633

Hand drilling was the method used for boring holes into the ore or the rock overlaying the ore. One held the steel drill while the other struck the drill with a sledgehammer, the drill being turned after each blow. At the end of the day miners placed sticks of dynamite into the holes with fuse and dynamite caps attached. When all the holes were "charged" word was shouted to all men in the mine to clear out. At a set time all the fuses were lighted and the miners ran out to the shaft. Each man carefully checked to see that his partner was with him and in a safe position. Great explosions sounded throughout the mine, echoed and reverberated and rumbled to the surface until they could be heard for a mile or more around. Many were maimed or killed each year. Mining laws to protect the men were few and seldom enforced. "Get out the ore, damn you. Never mind the risks."

Believing it to be a missed shot, patient picked up stick of dynamite that had been fused and lit, which exploded in his hand at Dober Mine.

Severe shattering. Loss of distal, loss of entire. Numerous small pieces. "The alterity of the detail, in the excess of the part retained as a part," and embedded or remaining fingers, data marked with asterisks, report made to Oliver Iron Mining Company.

The italicized sections that appear below the case numbers are drawn directly from—or paraphrase—one of two source texts: Chapter 3, "The Iron," from *Between the Iron and the Pine* (Ann Arbor, Michigan: Edwards Brothers, 1951), a biographical account of pioneer life in the mining and timber town of Iron River, Michigan, in the late nineteenth and early twentieth centuries, by Lewis C. Reimann; and Chapter 4, "The Wealth of Nature: Lumber," from *Nature's Metropolis: Chicago and the Great West* (New York: Norton, 1991), by William Cronon. The case studies prefaced by lines from Reimann are No. 1710 and No. 1830; the remaining italicized passages are drawn from Cronon.

JILL MAGI

from Nival

Nival (ni′vel): of or growing in or under snow.

( )

A walk into what has eclipsed us.

Cutwork   absorbing

"I feel barren"

                      setting up—

( )

Fallen into   above.

pry
pockets of blue
open—

rain   toward

                    "I did not expect—   "

( )

Neap tide fossil.

Folded stone

teasing the boundary of blindness.

( )

From the cell—   electrical.

Retracted, she lost her humor.

( )

Spokes light the wheel. Hub,
a fascicle. Impulse to collect—

          December dream
a Cooper's hawk.
Yesterday, five
buffleheads,
the merganser pair,
swoop of a cormorant
drawing the horizon
          us,

( )

Warming—

                                        enough god—

if

( )

Concave side of quiet

taking rooms out of confines

                              January enwreathes.

( )

potter wasp

equipoise

hollow-balance

"I am nothing absolutely."

floating rib

story

( )

Great black back gull coasting
northeast

I hold clouds
in windows   delight
in what is false.

Wisp to vein to
table-sky.

( )

Anchor-pulled

whorled.

Imbricate prayers

imagine edges.

( )

Wall-expansion   after

                    grief   porous.

(Marginalia sustained the binding.)

( )

What is the substance of shadow?
(Atrium of disaster-sense.)
What is between the twenty-second and third hour?
(Crux. Roomage on all sides burns glister—
temperature spike in the space
between winter and kiln.)

( )

Ideas about curled iron.
(About is around.) Month
vines its way

                        capillary bed.

( )

Canyoned

silhouette / tidemark

                                     ("I am—   ")

mirror   a moiré effect.

( )

Tree of bowls

turned

          to hold—

( )

Arrow-cloud.

Drill bit traces   read "remove/place."

Marital sculpture.

( )

       required to say
that we came to an amicable agreement. Truth
on the hinge
            (sutured rock, signatures.)

( )

Ivied house. Endless chatter.

Lived house. Still

questions pond in the crook of a mountain, wintered.

( )

      opening inching from

right to left

         glass / sky

                —unaware, leaning on left to right.

( )

A bottle gourd is not round.
A battle ground may be partially.

My apsis   your form.

(Take away this   )

( )

Dripstone

                              / mass.

PATRICK MORRISSEY

Variable Songs

Each attempt to seek
    a ripple in the structure
  interval moving across

water sounds against walls. Not
    a room but a chamber
  bound by a tremor in the ear-

drum, into which one casts
    small variables, breaths to ring
  the surface, to sound a depth.

• • •

Breath's flung tapestry,
    diaphanous cathedral
  evening thrown through

with light sung upward.
    Behind the screen, the stone
  structure stands, gathering

its meaning. Within its with-
    held cavity, a rigorous
  silence expands and arches lucent.

• • •

The tongue occupies
    a silence at the heart
  of the sentence. If I

look long enough my mouth
       opens to expose a sung
    negative: *if I, if I.* Syll-

ables fall into a small
       heap of conditionals,
    so many attempts to see.

• • •

As seeing would have it
       the landscape impresses
    a surface behind the eye,

invisible optic
       pulse persons numerous
    and things, the curious

thing between us the day's forms
       printed in relief explain each
    other each single instance among.

• • •

Earth become information
       the news always arrives to
    a body placed in a public

clearing in which one occasion
       of sensitive life attunes it-
    self. The dailies, the differences

one wakes to find make the city
       one lives in. Walks across
    bridges, under arches of language.

SARA MICHAS-MARTIN

Ars Poetica

Alone, the student
scrubs the shadows, blends
        and subdivides.

           The look of mercury
reflected in the eye. No,

        no a beauty that's criminal.
A gold studded pasture, bodyscape
      with wings.

The accuracy of wine bottles,
said the professor,
is the last thing I care about.

Other's pallets bloom in their stalls.

     His field
turns cistern then is scraped away.

      Put thumbtacks in circulation, plaster
of paris, iodine in the linseed. Push

to another terrain.
      Eyelash glued to bottom lip.
      Juice stains on blazer. Wreckage,

inner wreckage, pylons and silos
of wreckage.

      His shirt heavy
      from the deposited paint.

Much better
when he smoked.
                    can I leave now, can I
go home.

His nose against the canvas—dirt soup.
From six feet, cacophony.
Hunger
with the bottom rotted out.

        No entry.   No mileage gained.
Daylight arrives
and it's sickening.

Fall already. He sees a swath of red
in the line of trees—
someone overdressed,
a raised hand.

Elsianne Walks Between Quiet Rooms

This is not a dream kind of dream.

Spanish moss has taken us over,

gone down the jawlines,

around the necks,

and pokes from our sleeves.

Not even the chairs creak anymore.

Walking around a grieving household

makes you think it could be picked up

in the palm and put in the oven.

Come on, little house. Say something.

Father, Mother, Sister, Sister, Sister, Dead Sister.

New poems from the gilda cycle

The mirror is magnetic
like a puddle of shadows

repelling reflection

but gilda bathes

for her length
to settle

she wears your body like a shirt

saying
this beautiful long sleeve shirt

but she folds

as fumes
from marching

a flock of sheep
held at her door

        lost
        in the frame
she is locking

as she empties

the earth startles

        wind teething
        its broken hills

threading herself
malignant

they held her down

to add the pigment

      oil and the white
      opaque

      that flails

in bone

saving her
from

a landscape
too wide

she has found light flawed

and stands
a street post

      alone in the sky

her electric hum

      metronome

      to quivers
      and caws

STEFANIA HEIM

I Compromise My Self

after Luigi Pirandello

1. MY WIFE AND MY NOSE

Both pending.
Both slightly to the left.

2. FOLLOWING THE STRANGER

A number of times, leaving
The station, I noticed
Someone else leaving, too.
I have to decide: are you
Plausible? All movements
Are suspicious. I marry
My eyes to the glass.

3. UNCOMFORTABLE VICAR

Among
The similarly
Obsessed.

4. MARCO-OF-GOD AND HIS WIFE, DIAMOND

The judge needs time. He is also the doctor.
Someone has been working for weeks.
She read old books in Florence.
She lived there for a long time.

5. COMPLICATIONS

This thing
Is total.

6. GREEN WOOL BLANKET

I am surprised to see
All of that touching
Still going on.

Remind me
How to be comfortable
Constantly
In my clothes.

Furious Water

Reason to believe the ships
Will return. Want to

We are getting out the
Big sticks

We are bracing
For the next kiss

Sails across the face
Of wind. Or leaning in to it

Washed, sad, we are
Otherwise inconstant

Our wildly associative
Self-serving way

And what lengthens
In summer isn't nearly enough

PAUL WINNER

Anoth. Dict. of Rec. Ideas (Abbrev.)

A

AMBITION: Often "naked" or "noble." Preferable in people of new acquaintance to features such as sincerity or kindness.

B

BIAS: A sin of ignorance. Everyone else operates from it.

C

CLICHÉ: That which forms the readily recognizable elements of art, visual or narrative. When in doubt of its existence, identify regardless.

D

DIPLOMACY: A quaint form of sincerity on the geopolitical scale. (see AMBITION)

E

EXERCISE: More noteworthy, though less effective, taken up late in life.

F

FANFARE: With what most everything enters into discussion. Very much needed to get public's attention.

I

ICONOCLAST: Look in the mirror, rebel.

K

KINDNESS: Evidence of a weak constitution, poor education, and provincial thinking. (See AMBITION)

L

LINGUA FRANCA: Latin for "groupthink."

M

MACHIAVELLI: Used in its adjective form to describe political operations your side wishes it had thought of.

N

NATURE: A Romantic state known for purity of heart and clarity of sight. If not for the bugs, somewhat preferable to exurban sprawl.

NIGHTMARE: Try coupling with "Orwellian" or "public relations."

P

PETIT-BOURGEOIS: Whoever does not understand one's humbly proffered and clearly reasoned commentary.

S

SPORT: Physical link between bourgeois and proletariat. Usually one's interest in following matches is directly proportional to one's inability to play them as a child. Try to form opinions of any kind on the subject. (see LINGUA FRANCA)

SWEATPANTS: What one wears anticipating, or often in place of, bodily improvement.

T

TASTE: What one yearns to accumulate in place of hard currency.

W

WATER: Petroleum of the twenty-first century. Lower atmosphere of the twenty-second.

WEALTH: Always relative. Claim to be unmoved by it.

Z

ZEITGEIST: Defined through purchase habits. Like Arafat, never stays a night in the same place.

DONALD BRECKENRIDGE

from You Are Here

An Older Lover—Act 1

THREE STAGE LIGHTS WENT UP IN A SLOW TWENTY COUNT as the scattered conversations around me concluded. The man and woman seated on the beige folding metal chairs were facing each other. He was wearing a dark green suit, "I think we'd be able to tell the difference," glasses with thin black frames and black leather shoes. She was wearing a sleeveless low-cut short black dress, "How so?" fishnets and black patent leather pumps with three-inch heels. A couple that happened to be seated in the audience were being portrayed onstage. They just had dinner in a dimly-lit West Village restaurant that had recently been awarded two stars in the *Times* and praise for its romantic ambience, esoteric wine list and above average French food. "It's in their body language," he was halfway through his third glass of Crozes-Hermitage, "now don't turn around." The woman discreetly turned and studied the young fashionable couple tucked into an oversized booth across the dining room. "It isn't *that* obvious." Cindy had found most of the actor's costume on the racks and in the bins of the Salvation Army on Flatbush Avenue last week. His short brown hair had been set with styling gel, "I didn't say that it was obvious." The rings on her left hand caught the stage lights as she accompanied her question with a gesture, "Are you sure that you're not projecting your own insecurities?" "Please," he furrowed his brow, "they're trying too hard." The actress who was portraying the wealthy, childless divorcee in her mid forties, "You really like watching people," had purchased her dress online and wore it during almost every rehearsal. Her thick hair was cropped into a bob and had recently been dyed magenta. He'd been too distracted by their conversation, "they are like a Diane Arbus photograph," to do more than half-heartedly pick at the herb encrusted roast chicken she suggested he order for his entrée. Her cheeks had been heavily powdered and the dark red lipstick carefully painted on and around her lips gave her face a corpse-like pallor. He then added, "Without chemistry." She had been instructed to carry herself with warm outspoken urgency, "my husband was like that," to compensate for their difference in age, "when we—" He nervously blurted, "Like what?"

"Just like you silly," she cleared her throat, "he really enjoys watching people."
He shifted in the metal chair, "I guess it's not all that uncommon," that creaked
beneath him. The wine and the warmth of their repartee had almost invalidated
the cloying embarrassment he felt whenever the tall gay waiter hovered over
their table with his incessant questions about the food: if it was seasoned to their
liking, how well the wine he recommended paired with their entrées and, most
recently, while taking their plates away, if they had given any thought to dessert.
"Do you know her work?" Tilting her head to the left, "Who?" He regarded her
expression before saying, "Diane Arbus." "Of course," she has a quick wit and a
half dozen credit cards nestled in her calfskin wallet, "I'd love to own one of her
photographs." He imagined the art on the walls of her apartment in a nearby
prewar building. A black and white Warhol silkscreen hung above the couch in
the living room where a longhaired chocolate colored cat just woke from her
evening nap. A framed poster from G. W. Pabst's *Diary of a Lost Girl* hung on
the wall above the Mackintosh table and chairs in the dining room. He com-
mented on the framed, autographed poster from a Kiki Smith retrospective on
the kitchen wall opposite the sink as she mixed their drinks. She handed him
a scotch and water with a wink while asking if he'd like to see the etchings on
the ceiling in her bedroom. Cindy was biting her lower lip in frustration while
scribbling . . . *Diane Arbus . . . where is your focus????* in her wire-bound notebook.
The actress turned to observe the couple in the audience before claiming, "He
is nothing more than the latest way for her to wear her hair." Cindy wanted to
know, and wanted the audience to be clearly aware of what her character's emo-
tional investments were. He smiled, "And for him?" Cindy repeatedly insisted
that although they were portraying nameless caricatures they had to remain in
the moment at all times. "And for him . . . " after another careful look over her
shoulder she stated, "she is nothing more than a new pair of shoes," in a cool
matter of fact tone. Over the coming weeks she will reach the conclusion that
their relationship must have constituted an interesting life experience for him
and will occasionally wonder how he will portray her in his fiction. "Are you sure
that you're not projecting your own insecurities?" She swallowed hard, "sweet-
heart," while searching his face, "I didn't mean anything by that." He noticed
how the crows-feet etched around her dark brown eyes were starting to show
through her makeup. "Then why did you ask me that?" Knowing if she strays too
far from the persona he began fashioning for her long before they actually met,

"you're being so sensitive," that this date and any subsequent encounters will be total disasters. He shrugged, "Aren't women into that?" "Oh it's for my benefit," she is incapable of being alone and afraid of being hurt in another relationship, "well that is very flattering."

There were many days when she was unable to get out of bed and subsisted on whole-wheat crackers, warm mineral water, the fickle affection of her cat Esther and sleep as the afternoons dragged into late mornings while the shifting blue glow from her bedroom television covered her pale face and bare limbs like a warm muted blanket. He will later insist that this relationship was simply an exploration of the roles and preconceived notions of romantic love. The unlikely vow they took later that night, upon her faintly perfumed sheets, was to love one another with as few inhibitions as possible and without any emotional strings attached until the end of the year.

While placing her elbows on the table, "Don't you want to know what she is thinking right now?" "Sure," he shrugged, "why not?" "Well she is hoping that everyone here will notice how beautiful she looks in that new dress," before glancing over her shoulder, "although she is a bit disappointed that there aren't that many people here yet . . . which is odd especially considering that *Times* review," then rested her chin in the narrow palm of her left hand, "but maybe if they linger over dessert she'll get a larger audience." "Oh really," he squeezed his knees, "and how do you know that?" During their first date last Thursday afternoon in the rear of a dimly lit Tribeca café, he had carefully floated the idea of his experiment past her. "She is a real type." It happened after the first awkward pause in their conversation, after they had exhausted an extensive list of writers that he admired. He stole another glance at the couple across the restaurant as the skepticism in his voice, "I guess," betrayed him. It was just after she had finished her second cup of chamomile tea. She shifted in the metal chair, "I was once very close to a woman like that." As the opening strains of Bruckner's 6th were piped in through the café speakers, he politely asked her if he could talk about himself. "Do you think you still have anything in common with the woman sitting across from us?" She batted her eyelashes while confessing that she found him fascinating and assured him that nothing would be more interesting than learning more about him.

What followed was a carefully prepared and well-rehearsed twenty-minute monologue that began with a detailed description of his unhappy childhood and concluded with his proposal concerning romantic love. He was an only child of divorced parents, he had endured a stifling upper middle-class suburban upbringing and attended a private liberal arts college in the northeast that was well known for its creative writing program. She was informed that his professional prospects were quite good and that although he was so young a few of his stories had already been published in quarterly journals and monthly magazines and achieved, to a certain degree, critical acclaim. He had recently made the acquaintance of the assistant to a highly sought after agent and believed that it was only a matter of time before his first collection of short stories would be picked up by a major publishing house for a hefty sum. He then speculated that, even though the major houses weren't publishing many short story collections from young writers, with the help of his soon to be agent and a handful of well placed and carefully tended relationships with powerful editors it could easily turn out to be a bestseller. With watery blue eyes widening behind fashionable frames, he wistfully described the power he would soon be wielding in the publishing industry. Claiming that he had everything he wanted, everything he hoped for in his young life had been attained and yet he had never experienced love. She stopped herself from remarking that *so few of us, especially people like us, ever do experience love* and simply nodded before gazing thoughtfully at the urine colored dregs in the bottom of her tea cup. He appraised her silent response before confidently adding that he was certain that with her—and only with her—a woman twice his age—could he truly come to understand just what it meant to be in love. This was because she had known love, as any woman as beautiful must have on countless occasions, and because, and here he paused long enough to prepare the delivery, she had thus far lived a full, and by her own acknowledgment, an interesting life. She was silently flattered by all of his false assumptions.

"It was just neglect that ended our relationship," both hands were now cradling her chin, "and the less time we spent together," as she sighed, "the more I realized how little we had in common." He leaned back in the chair while asking, "And how long ago was this?" A slight smile creased her lips, "when everyone I knew had a ton of money and when you were just staring high school." He wiped his palms on his knees before delivering the next question, "And how did you become friends in the first place?" She folded her pale hands on the table, "we were never really friends," and tilted her head to the left, "we were lovers." "I didn't know that you were—" "I'm not really," a blush dimmed her powdered cheeks, "it was just a phase." "Like the way you wore your hair?" "Exactly," she smiled through his last line, then quickly added, "the skirts that spring were very short." The following Wednesday afternoon she called him at the bookstore because she had somehow managed to get early dinner reservations at that new French restaurant in Chelsea on the same day it was reviewed in the *Times*. He swallowed hard before placing both feet on the stage, "What was it like?" And then he briefly described a two-act play being performed that night on the Lower East Side and asked if she wanted to do that after dinner. "I prefer men." She said it sounded more interesting than that movie she'd been reading so much about before brightly suggesting that they should go back to her place for a nightcap afterwards. Clearing his throat, "Physically?" He clutched the telephone receiver with both hands while being told that she simply loved the short story he gave her last Thursday, then added that it was well written. "Physically I guess, but we can talk more about that later." He leaned forward, "How many women were you with?" She asked, "Encounters or relationships?" and before he could respond she confessed, "I was either very lonely or deeply cynical." He placed his elbows on the table, "Why, can't it be both?" They had met at the Strand three weeks ago. "I suppose it would depend on what day of the week you asked me." They were standing on opposite ends of a display table when he caught her eye. "Isn't that how you described your second marriage?" She had been thumbing through a remaindered copy of *The Satyricon* before acknowledging his attention with a discreet nod. "Now be very careful you . . ." while waving a narrow index finger in front of his face, "young man."

JOANNA HOWARD

Seascape

IN THE HAUNTED COTTAGE BY THE SEA, I settled into the seaman's berth. The captain was long since dead from his own hand. I came from the west in widow's garb with a trousseau in cedar. Drawn to the sea, again. The sea that captivates men with motherly arms and swimming dark womb is no place for a lady.

In the beginning, I only heard laughing. His portrait in brooding oils hung in every room. The balcony's French doors swung open of their own accord. I had been very lonely for a very long time. Below the bedroom's balcony, dark waters spilled into a narrow cove. The deck chairs, clothed in damp canvas, faced seaward on their precarious stage. Through nights I kept watch. Shadows and flashes in the movement of the night waters. Nightmares disband in sweet lingering insomnia. I was very good at looking straight ahead.

In time we lulled each other. He crept out of his painting and moved among his own things. The rooms doubled their size. The house shifted carefully, and the air inside grew thick and pendulous, and the furniture swelled near to bursting. Nothing was mine, but was done up according to demand in scrimshaw and leather, blue velveteen, and papered walls. I preferred the traditional black, though all of my underclothes were convent made in silk and lace. I undressed behind a painted screen, and felt a slight breath—certainly feigned—on my shoulder. We had not yet been introduced.

I was getting lovelier in the days that followed. Men in two-seater cars drove up the hill and down again. I took no suitors. Another courtship had begun. In our bedroom, his figure slipped out from the shadows and hardened its form, square and unshaven. He appeared as though he might speak. Here began the affectation of the living: breath, glance, speech from the mouth. Sounds came rough and unsorted. I fell deeply asleep, and in my dreams the sea air and its vapors, gaining force, stirred the bed clothes, and I awoke bathed.

The memory becomes very sweet, and the hands of the clock spin forward. Most days, he came and disturbed the contents of the room. His voice drew together in scraps and curses, and with it a certain perspective. I attempted to record his advances. He held together in a dashing form, and his sweater buttoned at the shoulder. Now, gaining voice, he had quite a lot to add. I accustomed myself to an unvarnished point of view. Language that meant all too clearly what it said. Periodically, his name burst with violence into the air, which I repeated to myself in a whisper, removed away to the darkness of the closet. Even there I was well accompanied. I was plunged into community. In the late afternoon, the fog came down from the cliffs, and settled in so close around the house it blocked even the view of the balcony's rail from the lounge where I sat, most often, near to fainting. It brought him in close as well, out of the haze, and fluid and silent, he knelt at my elbow. There was no time to be lost in admiring him.

Though his temper was cooling, I felt, if not quiet wanted, that I was waiting in line. Outside, the short lawn collected a periphery of spectators. Three bombshell silhouettes in ragged black crepe, slipped up among the beach grass, watchful, and distrusting. The captain refused to comment. In modern times, I might have had competition, but ours was an arranged affair.

Some years passed, and the road lay still, and broken with weeds. An auburn hound, with feral eyes, followed me through the house, and slept at my feet. I draped my shoulders in tartan. I spoke often and in all directions to a captive audience. In wakeful hours, with the light high over the water, I waited for the night that disrobes. A certain fear crossed my mind. How long before the past, in finally forgiving, would open up and give him passage? It was enough for me to live at the water's edge, on the spirits' line, and wait to be overtaken.

I woke and slept. In sleep's reverie, taking his arm, I found it opaque and firm. We walked up the steep incline from the beach to the cottage. We began together in step, my wild dog held close. Moving along the path, the captain was at our height, and then moving apart from us, far ahead, and above. The air wavered, and I dropped into fever.

That day, the sky and the sea met at a narrow seam. Like the hinge in a dream which, closing, changes the register. The room kept silent. Beyond the French doors, the horizon held steady. All I could see was what I could see.

I cast about inside the house, held as I was to the hope of his return. In this way, I haunted. I catalogued my memories, and counted among them several of his that had passed between us. I might have thought it unlike a thing to posses in itself a soul and a memory. Years passed, but I kept current in the blush of love.

I married the place. This was the more lasting of the two liaisons. Loving so solitary a horizon, when one has been abandoned, proves some compensation for absence. If a lesson follows, then don't look for truth in dark waters. The thin scrim of my captain's cottage kept all picture windows facing seaward, and so in passing from glass to glass, I followed that unchanging vista, a reminder of the one who never abandons.

KATE SCHREYER

Tapestries

Of the additional, of the added and added.
To be turned into a tree or a Chimera.
The endless wish to. Standing. Sitting.
In the night weaving and weaving the day.
The weak, pulling the hair out.
Dyeing the hair into a face. Gardens
of tapestries. Sarah and her age.
Procne the bird. The brain blossomed through
the ages from the center out. The first
black lake is circled and circled
by the body, by the eye behind the eye,
reptilian, fluttering, that was your own
to carry. Half forgotten, valley, tower, gut,
in the recession of space where movement,
a lie, is the biggest lie. There is the mirror.
There is always a mirror to stop in.

The Clothesline

Like one bird leading fifty birds into a tree:
clamor then silence, the morality
of keeping up. When the rest were expelled,

when the rest were made to wander
off in their bodies, thatched over now,
the snake was allowed to stay.

That was what staying meant, and being
the last. I could see it in each bird.
In that careful season, I pinned myself

in my dress, and later, my dress
to a clothesline. The days billowed,
stiffly. The days as a hymn, sung

as the words appear, line by line, the mixing
of verses. Good sun. Good
and goodness. My tongue in my mouth

sounding as if I was being played
by being struck. The birds in the morning,
possessed by wind. The fluff that scattered.

A sounding, with a padding of silence,
a mistake that echoes, terribly
on and on, deliciously on.

Quarantine

One eyelid, frozen open, so that to sleep
you must blindfold yourself. Night,
the water gums at your feet. In dreams,
soldiers come and tell you how to live.
They hold globes in their shadows,
know about trenches, will coat on you wings,
and kerosene, if what you say is true.

Catalogue Entry for Aging

The night we met, I contracted a childhood disease.

The discoloration resembled that of turmeric or a fig tree.
I measured the color's expansive, wide distance: Inner thigh to the edge of the mattress.

Tonight, a man on the phone poses an inquiry re: two boxes of books by Leon Trotsky.
I cover the mouthpiece, laugh with my co-worker.

Dear Sir or Madam: I am stunned by how easy it is to be a Very Bad Person.

There are apologies I am too

The night you leave, I write *tourist* across my stomach with regard
to everything I've ever done. Later, I read cities could conserve by

shutting off their lights. There are apologies I am too
close to understand. How I pass my days? Try to go to sleep. No

room can numb someone with blue across her back.
Or, replace everything that's lost. You have to pass the time.

BRANDON SHIMODA

from Lake M

silence
at the bottom of a valley
bearing to the surface of a former lake

a throat

songs drawn
of guardian ash

other bone   uncrossed

will remain
or be removed
from phantom tides

take   —   leave

the ashes
deliquesce

Everything you want of her

    she sends

by censoring post

thin, translucent fingers
on the fold
           a scale of lip
upon the seal

her shaking hand unlining

She gives herself up

    cell by cell

You take her in to your own

    eroding

Drought drawn retractions

emulse in the craquelure grass

    Everything shakes

A draught of stolen perfume
leaps out
of a wooden bowl

hovers in the fine
bone air
a single glinting

marrow cell
finger prints on the obtuse
neck glow

in the side-drawn light
wood spins on
its hollows

down in the dirt

a lip

                bouquet

       a (stirring) salt

I am here   because I saw

in the waves

an epoch of flags

unfolding

a gown I wear   where I was

suspect

the people   inlaid

the sequence   brushed, branching

rose   the slope

the fruit

heart and reckless

are the mouths

about

the dress   into

's

bulbs in the flash pillar
burn   wandering ghosts
among manna ash
evaporate through the wires

    black as the extent

laid in half
    to life   in an arborescent hall
    fireflies, an aureole

willows bow
the luminal pulse
her faceless head   each coal tress
    glowing

in you
luck runs dry
running for your waiting maid
leaking onto the peony bed

monument　　—　　tempo

　　　　　rosette

　　　　　spikes　　on which you see her

spread　　—

　entwining the tertiary light

　　　　　　the amyloid folds

　　　　　　the pond behind the eating hall

　　melting a hole

　　　　in

　　　crustration

　　　and yes

OISÍN CURRAN

from Mopus

WILLIAM THE SILENT TUGS ABSENTLY AT HIS EYEBROW and says, Well that's enough about the end. Can't just keep going over the same ground again and again. Let's try and move on. Or back. Here I can't afford words without consequence. What I'd like is an empty verb, a husk of noise to use just once and have it weightless on my tongue. Instead each word's another priceless item wasted. Another misplaced segment of the key to my release.

He opens his book to a marked page and ponders it. He says, According to the book it's quite simple.

He reads aloud, By bringing the beginning of the reverie into proximity with its end, a closed circle is formed. Or more accurately, a noose. It is simply a matter of drawing the daydream out through its own slip knot until it's cinched to the vanishing point. In this way anything can be cancelled out, even a life.

He puts the book down and looks into the distance. He says, But how does one do this, exactly? For instance, I've made my own double, and my daydream of the double moves backwards, more or less, while my original goes forward as best he can. My thought is that they will meet—one at his end and other at his beginning—but I can't quite see how to do this.

He pushes his glasses back up the bridge of his nose and looks at the table full of bread crumbs left by Bluebottle and Asa. He says, Where are those intruders now? Those bubbles of the earth.

> **Bluebottle:** I was no more than a shift in a pattern of light.
> Asa peers into the lightness of trees. Pockets of sun, or mini-spotlights that cross and bob, weave, what one calls, Dappled Light.
> I seem to remember this, whispers Bluebottle and nobody hears him.

—— —— ——

Bluebottle and Asa rest on tree stumps by the side of the road.

Asa: I didn't like all that back there—the barking, the voice.

Bluebottle: It's this war. You never know what's going to happen. They must have been ghosts. A dog and a man.

Asa: But what was the man saying?

Bluebottle: He spoke in a ghost language. I understood nothing.

Asa: (*carefully*) Do you think that might've been your dog? The ghost of yours?

Bluebottle: (*quickly*) Impossible. Mine's tracks go on. Look.

He points to the gravel shoulder where the paw prints continue.

Bluebottle: I think they were ghosts from some other world, not ours.

They rise and stretch.

Bluebottle: My dog never barked at me.

They walk into the mountains, not stopping as the sun goes thudding down. Everything falling, even the air. Bluebottle unzips before a tree.

Bluebottle: I'm peeing blood again.

Asa: Do you still have stomach pains?

Bluebottle: As we speak.

He stumbles into the inky forest and throws himself headfirst on the ground, nose digging into pine needles. Asa stands guard and then sags against a tree and in the night drops down by inches to the ground. He might dream of sleeping in his bed at home, and there dream of fishing quietly in a mountain brook.

When he wakes he finds that they've slept near a wide stream cutting through the forest. He bathes in it, shivering, then rouses Bluebottle who strips and floats sleepily, naked in the freezing water. He looks down at the stream-bed pebbles considering his size, the water he displaces, how much air he breathes. His skin is hard and dense. He dives, rises in a rush of breathing and climbs up to the grass.

Donning his clothes, he stretches and looks around at the sharp-edged morning.

Behind a birch, the face. Her face. Her eyes drill into him. Then she disappears.

Bluebottle runs after her.

Asa: Bluebottle?

Bluebottle: Give me back my dog!

Asa sprints after him through the trees, through fluorescent leaves that wander down around them.

Suddenly the forest gives way and they fly out onto the road.

Nobody there. The road curves away through trees, empty in either direction.

Bluebottle: #?!@+=?%!!!

Bluebottle paces up and down. Asa wants an explanation.

Bluebottle stops pacing and looks down into the roadside ditch. Paw prints in the mud. He strides off down the road, on the trail again. Asa sighs and follows.

They walk and walk. Down past the Dead Lakes. Down past pylons, pawn shops and fast-food joints. They walk through fifteen traffic lights, then back into the trees. On the other side of the woods they enter the Organized Territories. They walk on, past fields of potato rows. Then trees again. The stars pop out and dragonflies give way to moths. As they pass by, residential developments boot up their defense systems, and in the forests, the skidders and bulldozers and four-wheelers all fall silent for the night.

The next morning they wake up in a potato field, stiff and hungry. They return to the road and pick their way through the fumes, the cigarette butts, the weeds and empty soda cans, until they come to a diner.

Worn linoleum floor, booths upholstered in hot vinyl. A portly mustachioed waiter seats them. Asa points vaguely at the menu. Bluebottle's head slumps on the table top. His eye is level with patches of sticky ketchup and salt crystals scattered on formica. He feels that today the world is corked inside a bottle. Sounds have short echoes. Mute light slips from a glass of water.

The waiter lowers two plates before them and exits.

Asa: (*quietly*) Mary, mother of Martha.

He stares down at a slab of gristle and fat.

Bluebottle says nothing and starts eating. To distract himself he concentrates on the chrome of the napkin holder where he notes the wobbly reflection of a hold-up in progress. Men in balaclavas gesture silently with sub-machine guns.

He turns to observe their technique but the thieves have de-materialized.

Bluebottle: Surgical.

Asa has seen nothing. He's reading the newspaper. Gagging on a chunk of fat, he turns the page and the table erupts in a flurry of crackling paper.

Asa: (*reading*) WAR HEATS UP, *Operation Yes Yes deployed. Transchronical orbiters positioned to fire indifferent heat waves upon Future O8Q-T115 (FAR3, the Third Future Anarchist Revolution). Megalomaniacal FAR3 commander (the "Anarch") threatens Armageddon or similar retribution. Meanwhile the crack Anti-Apocalypse Squad infiltrates sects, cells and cabals that fulminate against the cosmos in any and all time fields.*

The waiter leaves the bill.

Bluebottle: (*whispering*) I have no money.

Asa checks his pockets.

Asa: I have a dime.

Bluebottle and Asa leave the diner at a clip, chased vigorously by the waiter until they hurl themselves onto the flat bed of a supplies truck resting at a traffic light. The waiter jumps on too, but they shove him off. The light turns green and they're away.

The truck drives to a train station's loading dock. A security guard waves the driver on and the truck moves into the darkness, turns two corners and descends a ramp before Asa and Bluebottle slip discretely off into the shadows.

The brake lights of the truck recede and disappear. Now the shadows increase. What light there is comes down through layers of grating. As they stumble on, even that light peters out and in a short time they're completely lost.

Bluebottle: I can't go on.

Asa: (*in despair*) Stop here.

They sit on a train rail and rest, pondering their position in silence. Far above them they hear the roar of a train leaving the station.

Asa: This sister of yours, this ghost—

Bluebottle: Listen.

Out of the darkness, a small engine. A baggage cart. A man with a beard steers the vehicle and stops when he catches the two travelers, huddled and pale, in his headlights. He waves for them to climb aboard, and gratefully they do.

He drives them into the bowels of the train station, down rain-soaked elevators, through corridors lit by torches, deep into the maze of public transport, until, turning a corner, they see a square of light that grows with their approach. They enter the light and it blinds them. The driver parks in the glare which, little by little, settles into form.

Bluebottle: Hell.

A room made of human bones.

A chandelier of vertebrae and femurs hangs low over the bearded man. A few battered desks piled with papers indicate that the room is an office of some kind. The driver explains to his superintendent what he discovered in the tunnels. Bluebottle and Asa eye the place with fear. Skulls of children have been mortared into mosaics. There's a couch of patellas. Tibias and taluses on the far wall, arranged in the pattern of a giant sun. Here, underground. Sepulchral echo. Anti-sun.

In a far corner, huddled on baggage carts, they see a tattered band of people. A woman rises from the group, brushes off her coat and strides over to them. She introduces herself and her friends.

Yeoh: We are refugees from the mining cities of the West. Agents from the present struggled there with the ghosts of God's Future (Future 27B-T116) and the cities disassembled—our grandparents have dematerialized and already our parents are fading into thin air. The same fate will befall the rest of us unless we can exit this era very soon. We seek asylum in the distant past and search for a train to The Port Resonant in Midwinter and a machine thence. These good baggage handlers have given us shelter, though it is illegal.

Bluebottle: I'm looking for my dog. Have you seen him?

He describes you, your height, weight, color, disposition.

Yeoh: Yesterday it boarded the train to Midwinter in the company of a young woman.

The bearded man hands out doughnuts the size of dinner plates, shows them to the baggage carts and bids them sleep.

They doze fitfully among the bones, the coming and going of uniformed workers, the ticking of the time-clock, the rustling of refugees. Bluebottle dreams that he has captured a murderous criminal, only to find that the man's skin is toxic to the touch, so that he, Bluebottle, is irreversibly dead because he seized his arm.

Bluebottle wakes trembling with fear. He doesn't dare move. He remembers that maybe even Asa is dangerous, certainly everyone else in the room will kill him. He is pinned to the cart by panic until someone leaps on him, forces his mouth open and pours fire down his throat.

It's the man with the beard. His name is Jerzy. Jerzy jumps back and the room bursts out laughing. Asa is next. He wakes sputtering, head in flames. The room is full of refugees and workers swigging lava at the end of their days. And when they die, Bluebottle thinks, their bones will further ornament the walls.

Now the refugees, fifteen in number, men, women and children, ages seven to forty-two, lead Bluebottle and Asa from this place with the intention of boarding a train.

Bluebottle: We have no tickets.

Asa: No money.

Yeoh: No problem.

Tito, a dignified young man with a long scarf, flashes a wrench, which is whipped out again once they're all on the train and jammed inside a toilet. A trapdoor in the ceiling is unlocked and everyone shoehorned into the airspace above. Bluebottle tries to say, Help, but he can't speak because he can hardly breathe. For the next thirty-five hours he's stretched out like a flying superhero, his face in the heel of somebody's boot, the stench of the toilet pickling his nose. Through a tiny vent-hole he sees that they are chugging out into a dimly lit landscape of dusty fields. He hears singing on the train, a dirge drifting through the cars below them. The refugees tremble at the step of the conductor.

Bluebottle's body is out of fuel early on. He starves, he sweats, he freezes in his sweat. Not all of us will live through this, he thinks. He has a vision of the end of the world: burning plains, skeletons, a hot sky. Years go by, the train stops; the train starts again. This repeats. I've already lost my mind, he thinks. I've already died.

Then, through the vent-hole, Bluebottle has a brief glimpse of a city before they enter the darkness of another train station. As the train scrapes to a halt, somebody grabs Bluebottle's heels, drags him down through the trap door and shoves him out a window.

We must scatter, says Yeoh.

Bluebottle stumbles alone through tunnels. Somebody runs into him in the dark, whispering, A candy bar, a carrot, I'm dying.

Bluebottle: Asa, it's me.

Asa: Are you edible?

Bluebottle props up his friend, but then falls down.

Bluebottle: We're in terrible shape.

Asa: I'm not even a shape. I'm a cramp.

They follow train tracks and a speck of light and come, at last, to an arched opening on the day. They cross snarled tracks and weave between arriving and departing trains. With their last strength, they climb a wall and drop down onto a sidewalk on the other side.

Bluebottle collapses. He lies back on the pavement and looks at the buildings rising from his forehead. Steel sky. Grainy pavement at the back of his head, and through it he can hear the planet sizzling at its core.

Asa leans feebly against the side of a building. He watches the pedestrians watch Bluebottle as they pass him by. Rummaging in his coat, Asa finds a hat, which he places upside down next to his friend, then retreats to the wall again. Coins rattle into the hat.

In another pocket, Asa finds a stub of a pencil and the newspaper from the diner. He reads, circles something. Reads. Circles. A drop of rain on the newspaper.

He looks at the sky, watches a cyclist wobble down the street, looks down, reads more, circles.

Asa: We need money.

He gathers up the coins that were dropped in the hat, drapes his friend's arm over his shoulder, hauls him up and they stumble through the rain. The coins are pushed into the turnstile of a city bus where the passengers sit very still, their flesh waxy in the steel light of Midwinter's afternoon.

Bluebottle: (*whispering*) Are they ill?

Asa: No, comatose, I think. Workday's over.

Four job interviews later, Asa and Bluebottle enter a door under a shabby sign: The Artmobile.

It's nearly empty inside. A gray carpet, white walls, a few windows facing the street. Behind the desk a young face with lizard eyes. The eyes belong to Walton, president and CEO of The Artmobile. He explains his company: it's a job for art lovers he says, art lovers who have no conscience. Who are willing to sell paintings door to door.

Bluebottle: A job for hucksters. Scammers.

Walton: (*calmly*) If you like.

Asa: (*sighing*) We're desperate.

Walton: You're hired. Come back tomorrow afternoon.

Asa: Could we stay here? We have no place and no money yet to rent one.

Walton: As it happens, I have company apartments. As it happens there's a vacancy. It will cost you eighty percent of your income.

(*He searches in a drawer and comes up with a key. Bluebottle and Asa look at it, at each other.*)

Walton: Your hesitation is rhetorical. I don't have time for rhetoric in real life—only in sales pitches.

Twenty minutes later Bluebottle and Asa find the building and puff up six flights of creaking spiral stairs to one room with two beds, a sink, a coin operated stove, bathroom in the hallway.

In the refrigerator Bluebottle finds four carrots, two rotten. He cleans the other two and they sit on the beds, cracking off big hunks and slowly chewing. They gaze through the window at the wet light of the city. Asa finishes his carrot and falls back on a lumpy pillow and whining springs and is quickly asleep.

Bluebottle looks over at Asa, rises and goes to the window. Old brick in the watery dusk, briars and thorns. Great circular roof of a concert hall shimmering in the distance. The city spreads out, out.

Something moves in the tangled gardens below. A thief? Maybe a dog. White? Humble. Its body a radiant heater. Bluebottle backs away from the window and sits on the bed. A horn sounds in another street, across the city a mournful siren. He crumples to the sheetless bed.

The next morning Asa consults the darkest corners of the cupboard, finds onion skins stuck to honey spots, two sprouting potatoes and three turnips. He carves out the rotten bits, sticks a coin in the stove and boils away.

Bluebottle comes drifting out of sleep as Asa drains the turnips and sets them on the table next to a salt-shaker. Bluebottle wanders to the window on the other side of which it rains. A dark morning. He sniffs at the turnips, massages his empty stomach and sits down to eat.

One after the other they make the pilgrimage through the hallway to the bathroom and back. Then they go to work.

In a back room of the Artmobile, they sit on plastic chairs and endure a Sales Workshop.

Walton: They've let you in their house, you're following them down the hallway, they're letting you inside. Their house is their mind. You own the house and everything in it. You kneel before them, but you own them. You unzip the portfolio, you unzip, and you're stripping, but you own them, it's a game, you're stripping them, and painting by painting you show them how to strip themselves. Of their money. You, Bluebottle, show us what you can do.

Bluebottle: Hello I am a bohemian exhibiting the work of my friends door to door offering this unique opportunity to view Art on delivery here for instance is the perennial favorite Mediterranean Fishing Boat executed in warm reds and as I speak I elide imperceptibly from the shabby interior of the Artmobile to the glamorous streets of Midwinter where I stand on your step as you peer at me over your door chain and if you would only just let me in I am absolutely confident that I will be capable of pressuring you with my hard-sell soft-sell variation so that in a matter of minutes you'll find yourself buying not one not two but quite possibly three of these pieces of shit plus the frames for a minor surcharge of twelve dollars all of which is roughly three hundred thousand times the amount the starving ghosts get for painting these by the dozen in our POW sweatshops a sad fact upon which I choose not to dwell so if you would just let me inside the door behind which you skulk with good cause as if behind a shield because if you do let me in all this will come to pass and I can pay my rent and eat and I know because I've seen it happen many times before. Surrender.

Pelletier of Pelletier's Antiques: No thanks. (*closing the door*) Good night.

Bluebottle: How about a pretense of culture? I see evidence of it. The Van Gogh repro in your hallway? Come on. These paintings actually have paint on them.

Pelletier of Pelletier's Antiques: Not at the moment. But thanks for dropping by. Good night.

(*The door closes and locks*)

Bluebottle: (*to the door*) Why would I drop by? To chat? I knocked on fifty-three doors in two hours tonight with no strikes no sales no money no rent do you have any idea how demoralizing how demanding how demeaning I mean I'm not coming for the firstborn I'm just a simple grifter purveying low-quality knockoffs but every door tonight has the X marked in chalk while the cold swamp of your sidewalks crawls into my shoes into my toe knuckles into my plantar wart my shin-splints my pointless resentment but one thing's for certain: I Did Not Drop By.

Every night the sellers of the Artmobile march out into the dark to the car and drive for miles through the city lights. The bridge is illuminated by ships that pass beneath, cables floodlit. Stars are invisible. Bluebottle's brow rolls and thumps against the window. There's little talk. Metropolitan fire, lanes and lanes of traffic snakes. Insert car body, remove it, move on. Honks, bumps, headlights flash, language of metal and light. Bodies here inserted, here removed, onto lesser streets of lesser flames.

#65 Boomerang Ave: (*sipping a highball*) I can do better than that, take a look at my oeuvre. (*gesturing at paintings on the walls*) Hobby. Retired. Horses. Alone. On mountaintops. At the races. Groomed. Surprised myself I have to say. Rather talented. Don't go in for that dauby stuff. A nice clean line that's what I like. Now these you have here, quite third-rate. You should be ashamed.

Bluebottle: Give me your work. There's a market for static chevals and self-portraits of the bilious hunters who pose astride them.

Down! says William the Silent, Down you rebel dog! He pounds on his wheelchair. He looks at you and says, Not you, this blasted machine. He fiddles with a brake lever and pounds on it again before giving up. He says, My situation is desperate and yet I'm in a good mood.

Paterfamilias

AFTER COMPULSORY RELOCATION TO HORNVILLE, Misery's family lived in a skyscraper made of living flesh. The building's eyes served as windows that were barely transparent, and although it was said that the heavens were out there, no one could see them. The people who lived in the building wore internal helmets injected into their ears by the doorman, who was also a skilled surgeon. On any given day, one was either deaf to the world, or everything was painfully amplified, but it was worth it. The human head was indestructible. When people died, the government shot their heads into the sun.

Most families wore matching belts that could be ported to one another at the hip, enabling shared sensations. The heavy buckles served as ballast, keeping its wearers balanced for a time, but over the years the spine was affected and many families were paralyzed with their chemistries permanently linked, their bodies frozen in prayer circles.

Misery wrote to her father and asked him if he remembered those years; that she had refused to wear the belt or pray; that she had refused to enter the underwater temples. She called him her father but she couldn't remember his name. On a rainy spring day before they moved to Hornville she recalled her brother breaking his own arm. Their father had suggested this punishment after Jake broke the family transport's headlights and the boy had obliged without expression, calling it his first magic trick. That evening, their mother drove him through the fog to a local bone man, signaling out the window with a flashlight, and the next day, having removed the cast and reopened all his stitches, Jake renamed himself Gutbane.

Their father had liked working in the yard barefoot and Gutbane had gotten his revenge, burying knives beneath the grass hilt first. He and Misery pulled all the leaves off a buttonwood and pasted them to the side of the house. At the top of the tree, they carved the highest branches into spikes as protection against carnivorous birds. Facing into the wind was useful for their training in the wind tunnel that their father had built in the basement, and within which they struggled as he threw books before the fan, an activity he called "home schooling." He built a cannon from which he shot their pets, claiming the pets were sick.

The last time Misery ported their religion had just been banned, and authorities hinted that the area would soon be rezoned. They would have to move to Hornville, and Gutbane threw a tantrum and wanted his new permanent teeth pulled. The pain rushed into Misery through her belt as each tooth was ripped free by their father, who was willing to help for a small fee. Gutbane put the teeth beneath his pillow, having heard that a banker might come, but the next morning the teeth were still there, so he and Misery repositioned them in his mouth, molars in front. Father regarded his son's awkward smile, but said that this wasn't going to work. He needed wood glue. They were ushered out the door, but instead of going to school, they took advantage of the season's first snowfall and made a snow cave, feeding icicles to a snow baby that had real teeth.

She wrote her father by means of mechanical mail, trying to find out his new address, which she believed might be underwater, perhaps New Gate Island. She imagined swimming there and wondered what she would do if she found him.

> Dear Dad,
> Do you remember the toy-bred goat that Gutbane killed? After he killed it, he named it Quarry after the pit we led it into, down the long winding trail to the only patch of light, your silhouette waving from above the cliffs. Gutbane removed its small head and dried it as a cactus pot, but you crushed it, saying you needed the skull powder. At the top of an enormous silt mound beside the quarry was a crater filled with mud and charred bibles. Gutbane and I would sprint across this crater and up a small embankment and jump out into the night, never knowing where we'd land.
> Remember the high-speed trains always passing invisibly, never going the other way? Once an older boy gave us a ride on his motorbike, Gutbane in the sidecar, and we moved quickly enough to see a caboose. The boy crashed the bike into a cornfield, mowing down stalks and smoking a glass pipe, explaining between puffs that this was the best way to get high. We emerged behind the river and he gestured toward the floodplain. There were some weeds over there. He said he was planning on opening up a business back there.
> Misery

Dear Daughter,

You were always an odd sort. I remember you put a spike through your lip. Before we could reinforce your head, your mother dropped you on it, which in a lot of ways made things easier. I remember your brother was a determined sleepwalker and often you led him by the hand. We would find you both under his bed or outside beneath his favorite tree, Gutbane talking to his imaginary man.

I don't remember corn, but I remember Gutbane struggling to gum his hard cereal flakes after you two removed his teeth. He fell back on his stool and broke the window. It was difficult to potty train the boy. He would sit on the pot for hours while you stood by with a stopwatch.

Was it the fiber of that age? After you and Gutbane ran away, I drove a truck that was powered by shit. We sat on processors connected to the engine and learned to live that way. Now my back is ruined and I report to a long line of stalls. Relief is a spastic affair and requires way too much paperwork.

Have you met any men on your travels?

Old Man

Misery thought about the day that she and Gutbane ran away from school for the first time. They had poisoned their pet cactuses and the teacher had pinned black Fs to them. Gutbane couldn't perform the long division, so they disappeared under thorns and over logs, entering a park where they lay on the grass. Dividing the playground was a newly widened road on which two-story vehicles crept by, their antennae jostling the traffic lights. Misery and Gutbane were unable to cross this road and so they waited. It wasn't dark, but these vehicles were driving with their lights on, moving slowly through the red traffic light and toward the setting sun.

Old Man,

To answer your question, I was briefly with a fellow that I met in the public showers. His skin resembled corrugated cardboard, and he had a borderline personality that bled into my own. Things seemed okay until one day I noticed a large metal stain on his cheek.

"What the fuck is that, Jim?"

"I had to blowtorch my meds."

"Meds?"

"You know, the stuff that I take to keep sane? That keeps me from going psycho?"

"You might go psycho? You had to blowtorch them?"

"They're liquid and coat the interior of my helmet. If I forget to take them they harden. I have to blowtorch them."

"But on your face? Couldn't you do it in a bowl or something?"

But that wasn't the real reason we broke things off. What happened was that we began to communicate in notes, never using speech, much like you and me. We met in public confession booths and crumbed notes through the slot like balls of bread. Even living together we wrote things off from separate rooms, sending messages across the apartment via fax. I'm guessing that one of us must have run out of paper.

Over, and out,

Misery

After she and Gutbane ran away for the last time, Misery disappeared into the woods. She lived in the forest eating mushrooms and bark, writing little notes on the bark and eating them.

"Dispositioned in a wilderness transformed into a habit, I realized that everything is subject to transformation. I became a mushroom. I became a tree. Don't ask me for specific details. The years mishammered into a warped dwelling on the outskirts of anything peopled, with me its sole resident and architect seen squinting through the holes and cracks. These shambles would have collapsed on the vibrations of a sneeze, had those environs been capable of it. I swear the damned forest was dust free. The shack squatted without foundation or ascent and provided such a poor excuse for shelter that I had to erect a second smaller dwelling inside, one that could be seen without, a flimsy tent that flickered and glowed at night."

She wrote in tiny script on peels of bark. Then ate the notes.

"When I returned to the city, the hydrogen smokestacks were busier than ever, sending radiation through the neighborhood and into the yard where it transformed the flowers. Time was unraveling and I remembered when a certain car crashed, killing its driver, an event that Gutbane had witnessed. Clinging to the bare branches of his favorite tree above the road, he had watched the car smash into it below. He had seen the long approach and the sudden swerve, the vehicle smashing into the tree in which he swayed, the driver's face exploding in a cobweb of glass, the windshield ballooning to accommodate. Father had come outside with a bowl of popcorn."

She wrote to her father:

"In the grips of a convincing smog, I decided to exit the woods. I destroyed my shack, which tried to make the first move, thrusting out a corner edgewise, then schooled the entire area, putting handfuls of pebbles in their place. Now that we have started our correspondence, it's as if a whole new structure might be built, simply for the sake of being razed again: a remotely shared abode of sustainable material and carpentry, albeit one whose glaring fenestration will probably reveal it to be fleeting? Are you living underwater now?"

Having returned to the city, she lived in a tent, noting that the transports had grown to three or more stories high. The traffic lights were too high to see from down there, and if one was caught in the path of one of these vehicles, an internal helmet was no guarantee. "Without a body," went an ad, "the head is sun fodder." People wore prophylactic collars that exploded into balloons, surrounding all but a person's head. She was understandably afraid to cross the street.

> Old Man,
> I am currently living in a tent pitched over a manhole that releases periodic issues of steam. Have you ever dreamt of horses colliding with the street, falling under parachutes made of their own skin? Regarding my escape from a lush wilderness teeming with peelable bark, daylight disclosed itself evenly, defying my judgment of momentum, but with swiftness I found my way. The leaves instructed the day with high rustling, a maze of bramble stepped forth as my guide. I had a device that measured the stars behind my sunglasses and I used it to plot a glitter map by which I found my way. Knowing that proximity to others is a hazard, when I reentered the city, I stuck to myself like glue.

Remember Gutbane's lack of teeth and the manmade tornado twisting round our house? If that house was ticklish it would have fucking exploded. They were rezoning but we hadn't left yet, and after the first artificial storm, blind baby squirrels lay scattered among sticks speared deep into the ground. Gutbane flashed his gums and rode his bike over the babies and they squished. Then a neighbor girl appeared, having just learned to ride, but when we asked her to leave, she refused, saying that our driveway was God's driveway too. Across the street, behind the library, a train passed on an invisible track. You came outside and asked if anyone wanted to play baseball.

Remember Gutbane with his high fever and hives, repeatedly striking out in a game in which the ball was never pitched? The ball rested on a rubber pole, but his swinging cast kept missing.

Where are you living now, Dad? Underwater? Have you heard from your son? How is Mom?

Regards,

Misery

Gutbane helped their father tie the ropes. Misery had tried to run away so she had to be tied to the flagpole. There was a pattern of afternoon on her sleeve. It depicted the driveway in miniature, on which was an outline of a body with a bird inside, pecking at the remains of a fortune cookie. Their driveway was wider than most and ended at a gully as it had originally been planned for a road that was never finished. Gutbane had once beaten her doll at the bottom of the gully, at her encouragement. She had pointed to the naked doll on a stump, handing him a stick. After he had beaten it, one of its eyes had remained frozen open.

Daughter,

You asked about Gutbane and mother. Regrettably they are not of this world. For a while Veta was in an asylum as you may or may not know. After her release, Gutbane returned, and while they were out buying milk one night they disappeared, much like you. It's my belief that they joined a cult of auto-cannibals and ate themselves. I'm pretty sure that's what happened, anyway, to answer your question. Sorry to break the news, but maybe you already knew.

Yours,

Dad

While Misery tended to take existence with a dash of pepper, she found her father's latest news unpalatable. She tried to remember her mother, but recalled only a dim image of a woman batting at furniture with a stick. She became more determined to track down her father and began looking into public records. One night, she climbed into the manhole below her tent and steam welled up around her nostrils. In the dark she recalled Gutbane and how, as a result of a birth defect, he could pull his eyes a full inch from their sockets, moving them around between his fingers, something he often did in front of the mirror at night. He would stare into the mirror as Misery rapidly flipped the light on and off. He would transform into his imaginary man.

Gutbane used a magnifying glass to set flame to a parade of red ants, placing the charred dots on his tongue, not swallowing until he had a mouthful. He made a plane by stunning flies with sprays of aerosol, then gluing their legs to a paper cross, so when the flies awakened, the cross lifted. He stole a boomerang and they were amazed by how it actually worked. Instead of flying in straight line as they imagined, then returning, it moved in a circle, approaching on its return from behind.

Late summer. They would not leave the public pool when the emergency siren sounded, so Father dove in with his clothes on. He punished them in the moldy locker room where an old woman was sick. Misery gave her a lifesaver, thinking it would help, but things looked grim. When they found the lifeguard, he said that his shift was over, and also this was not his job. Later, by the train tracks, they found a bear trap among the rotten fruit trees, a television crushed between its claws. They watched their father launch their yellow-eyed dog.

"I was strapped to the rusty flag pole and climbed for what felt like hours, inching up the knot in increments, until at the top I pulled free and slid back down, chafing my hands and then falling, hearing my ankle snap, hearing what sounded like the wind clapping cymbals in the clouds. I saw the flowers transform and could smell the odorless music. Sometimes I will picture my bleeding hands around Father's neck, about to choke him, or I imagine the still-knotted end of the rope and gazing through its fraying aperture. I imagine running with it tied about the planet, dragging the planet to make time spin backwards, but this is already happening. I can see that now. In my mind black grass sways for miles of recall, parting on memories that feel like dreams. When I left the sewer that night, I found a message in my mechanical mail."

How to get to the entrance to my house. It has no door and I've painted all the windows black. Sometimes I come home on the left-hand side, which is familiar to only me. Go around to the right and climb the shaded hill to the ocean, then walk ten blocks along the seawall. This is what I call the Atlantic approach. Listen for crickets until you see the last dune, then simply climb and start swimming. You'll be close.

Paterfamilias,

I was able to find your address by more conventional means. I arranged a flight at an old-fashioned airport. In the plane, seated beside a recently trained pilot, I realized that it doesn't matter if we're awake or asleep. Either way, I don't want our reunion to be compromised. I've always had this fear of inversion, so I asked if our jet could fly upside down. The pilot was a very nice man. He explained about the strength of the wings and how they could be bent upwards and wrapped around the hull. How the heavy aircraft glided on its descent and would not simply drop if its engines failed. When landing, a jet doesn't use its engines, only gravity, then water, then finally black space. He was very helpful and I was even tempted to ask for his phone number, but what I needed to know was if the jet could fly upside down. I figured that if it could, then I would find you. That things would happen relatively painlessly. I have a few of Gutbane's knives and can use them. Anyhow, we passed through a cloud and I was given my answer. As you read this, I can see you through your windows, which are not as black as you think. The answer was yes.

DAVID GOLDSTEIN

from Millar's New Complete & Universal System of Geography

A Perspective View of The Hague, a celebrated Town in Holland

Birds or incoming aircraft overhead.
To survive as a tuft of disheveled hair,
as a lady the size of a soul
if the soul were a penny.
To survive as a limpet, which is to survive
with one's whole being.

The engraving has a mandolin on its roof
preventing your third skin
from escaping. Let the world
wag as it will, says the boatman,
his voice muffled beneath afternoon.

One of the people inside me
is behind a column in the picture.
In the new country he was a charioteer
whose head ends in a tree.

The place: Perspective.
The time: Trapped sky in the form of canal water.
The scene: The clock in the back of the deserted house.

On the border you will find the part of yourself
played by a gray wreath.

A General View of Paris, the Capital of France, taken from an eminence in the Village of Chaillot

A charming rococo piece,
quite in the mood, if not the style,
of a child's tarred head.

The supreme refinement,
the threshold, the eminence,
the bone spur of Chaillot.

(The Seine finds nothing familiar.
The pillow creeps into its ark.
How could you not understand me?
Between us lay only the dark.)

I am standing in Chaillot
on an eminence,
in the open air of my blank gaze.

I have journeyed (formal) the scholiast's journey
and now I see (bang) the Universal System
that was called upon to hang a lock on my lips.

In the foreplay a monsieur and his deux dames
return from the branching-off place.
The afternoon haughtily holds its clouds.

From the background the dark garden
surges up.
Inspectors cannot always watch us.

An Accurate Prospect of Vienna, the Capital of Germany

I will tell you how it is in Vienna, the capital of Germany:
A constant wind blows off the engraving.
In the foreground
Hawkins has a scar.
There are forehooves of three goats.
The donkey carries his sky-blue wariness
in his reins.

Plié, owner of the donkey, plié,
now is your time.
You are the color of a donkey's baggage,
of the river behind you,
of the roofs of the town.
Every accurate prospect ends.
The clouds are most delicately realized.

A Perspective View of Dresden, the Capital City of Saxony

The quoins lock tight around you
in the dream where you are made of menilite
and I am a blue tent.

The delicate engraver
died long after completing his vision:

four spires, a bridge,
soldiers on charade,
a cloud in the form of a tree,
a square prism of space
forcing the air out of all directions.

You locked up all the Meissen china
before I arrived.

Dresden, why do you fear me?
It is deep midnight
although you think it is spring.

Repugn, and live!
Live, city of the barred soul,
Live, bright river,
Live, boycott!

Three Jews to settle at each railway station.

Dresden, my balk, my privation.

Poem for Hoa Nguyen

It follows from an envelope
locked latch & reading

in the tub while
you're scubbing somebody's
spidery hair.

Is it a poem if it's
all sleepy & has
crooked teeth—

if the gunpowder is
buttoned to a longing
for Texas autumn?

Little moviehouse for
we who stick to everything
& quotient & spirit &
drawbridges sharking the traffic.

I'm on the phone all
about this—I'm yellow
in the green light
& hoping the drunk stories
stay well enough inside

mesquito swamp tripping & the nets
foil good song & away into
the city narrowing.

Poem for G.C. Waldrep

Without any history of night
we go towards

a bound booklet of
verse to lesson us:

Station of labors, spotlit
station of horseways

A livery,

a mole going through the mulch
apart from the shorn hands
we play.

Station beyond the
orchard ghosts, young
white mare, young

city going through us
finely like silt—us or that city
alive in treacherous

hollows for traincars more train
cars an

occasional footbridge wooded.

Poem for Sasha Steensen

Cotton Mather standing under
where

the owls fall through

paroxysm & a barnful
of your work waiting askance

for your flashlight,
Gordon's (my favorite) face
& what

will your daughter haunt of
these archives?

night finally, one of just
poems & cigarettes & porch drinking
& there's no more Vegas or
gradesheets

just Oriana's hilarious yawns & we're
filed down, fled back.

STEVE KATZ

from Time's Wallet

My Bridge

EMBEDDED IN MY GALLERY OF VISUAL NOSTALGIA, like an unforgettable dance movement, is the shallow arc of the span of the George Washington Bridge before the lower roadway was added. It was a mile-long elegant convex gesture of engineering, yoking New Jersey and New York City. My youth never kept me from sitting with the old folks on the terrace at the west end of Jayhood Wright Park to gaze on this phenomenon of grace. It made me sing. It made each day precious. Life turned gross and full of dreary practicality when they built the lower roadway. They also threw up a high-rise to obstruct the view from the terrace. At that time, though we lived far from the Lower East Side, I could lie in bed in the morning and listen to the cry of the ragman. "High cash clothes, high cash clothes," he chanted as he plied the streets of Washington Heights as if it were way downtown. And there was a knife sharpener who came by less frequently, but sometimes added to the music of my mornings. He rode his bicycle, pulling the carborundum wheel and implements behind. "Scissors sharpened. Knives sharper. Sharp here. Sharp here." Housewives rushed to meet him with their cutlery in canvas bags. His wheel screeched as sparks and water droplets flew. Then there was Manny who pulled his horse-drawn cart up to the corner of Ft. Washington Avenue and 173rd, and sold vegetables and fruit. Manny was good to the horse, that always had his muzzle in a leather oat bag hung over his ears. My mother wouldn't go near the beast, and didn't want me to either. A horse had bitten her when she was a kid, and she lived in fear of them. I worked for Mr. Manny occasionally. He'd give me a penny a delivery to carry bags of vegetables and fruit to the old ladies in apartments around the neighborhood. They fearfully cracked the door and sniffed me out before they opened. Some would tip me, maybe a nickel. We were poor. I was nine. Any money was a lot of money.

Once they hung the lower roadway my childhood slowly coarsened. No cause and effect, except in my private economy. I could hardly look at the bridge anymore. It was dull and clumsy. It was first proof for me that in America commerce trumps beauty.

One day, when I stepped out of my building, a teenager riding a delivery bike, one of those grocery bikes with a big box on two wheels in front, called out, "Hey kid." He gestured for me to come over. "Want to make a quarter real easy?" A quarter to me was a fortune. "Yeah. What?" "Just come with me. I'll give you a quarter." That was six maybe seven egg creams at the Russian's candy store on Broadway and 173rd. It was two fistfuls of Clark bars. For the quarter I let him lead me into a big building on 173rd and Haven Avenue. The interior was a labyrinth of corridors and turns. I followed him past apartment after apartment till he stopped near the back of the building. Everything around me was beige.

"Okay, kid." He handed me the quarter. I felt it to be sure it was real, and put it in my pocket. "Close your eyes," he said.

"Why?"

"All you got to do is hold onto my finger. Close your eyes."

It seemed very strange. Hold a finger for a quarter? Close my eyes? I was an honest kid. I had his quarter. I held his finger.

"Now I'll give you another quarter. Keep your eyes closed."

Four bits? Who was this guy? I had struck it rich, but something was weird. "Now grab my finger again."

He guided my hand and laid his finger in it, except I knew this wasn't his finger. It was hot and snaky. I'd never held a snake, but I was sure it felt like this. He moaned a little. I let go when we heard some voices in the hallway. And he sprinted out of there, leaving me alone. He never gave me the second quarter. He was back on his bike when I left the building. He shouted to a friend of his walking up the street, "This kid jerked me off for half a buck." I wanted to tell him he never gave me the second quarter, but I kept my mouth shut. I was disappointed, humiliated, and ready to go to Broadway for an egg cream at the Russian's. The experience was traumatic. I'd been exploited, my innocence stolen. But what city kid wants to hold on to innocence? This was a real experience. I learned something. I'm straight as a road in Nevada. I learned that you've got to be alert. The delivery boy still owes me two bits, and I'll never get it. The real trauma was the loss of the beauty of the single-span George Washington Bridge.

Caffeine

I WAS FIFTEEN WHEN MY FATHER DIED. He'd been sick for seven years already, was rarely home, usually bedridden in some dreary veterans hospital in the Bronx, or upstate at some rest home. That was treatment for a heart condition at the time—stay in bed! Without a father to help me into my future I felt like upcoming life had been placed on the other side of a thick high concrete wall too slippery to scale, and I couldn't bust through it, but against it I constantly pressed the enigmas of my rising adolescence.

Mr. Jacobs, who was the father of my classmate, Vernon, and his little brother, Hubby, was office manager of an import-export company, Amtria (American/Austrian) Trading Company. Because he took pity on me, or maybe sought to take advantage of me, he gave me a job at the Broad Street office on Saturdays and on some late afternoons. It was probably illegal for them to hire a fifteen year old.

I was a gofer, a messenger, the kid to blame when things went wrong, generally an office boy. If coffee spilled, I wiped it up. I opened envelopes. I stuffed envelopes. If a file was missing, I hunted it down. I cleaned windows, tidied the desks. My favorite task was to leave on a postal trip, or to deliver a document, or to buy office supplies, just so I could get out into the population on the streets.

That winter the canyons of Wall and Broad Streets were cold, full of snow and slush, winds that cut like knives. I sloshed around in galoshes, kept the papers dry under my mackinaw, moved invisibly among invisible people breathing ghosts into the air. I walked past the steps of the stock exchange, rested at the foot of skyscrapers. Everyone inside the buildings looked competent and busy, in identical suits and ties, women prim and neutral. It was on one of the most frigid, blizzard days that I discovered coffee. Returning to the office after a delivery, I let the wind blow me into a Chock Full O' Nuts. All praise goes to William Black, who founded this chain of black-owned businesses, and to the great Jackie Robinson, who signed on as personnel manager. I straddled and settled down on one of the stools at the counter. It was all blue and yellow in there, and it smelled of coffee and sugar. The waitress, a light brown woman with straightened hair streaked with blonde, asked me what I wanted. I hadn't thought about it, didn't even know why I was in there. "Regular coffee?" she asked after I didn't respond. I heard someone else order a light coffee, so I said "Light." "What else?" "A donut," I said. I was proud to get that out. "Whole wheat?" "Yeah." "Sugared?" I nodded affirmative. The storm mixed it up outside, snow blowing horizontally down the canyons. People skidded on the sidewalks, were whipped akimbo, out of control in the wind. I felt warm, snug in the Chock Full O' Nuts. I wanted to return to the office never.

The waitress brought my donut and my first cup of coffee. I checked the other people at the counter, sipping comfortably. The cup was heavy. The cream swirled through the dark liquid. The acrid smell was a tough barrier. I tried to sip, but it was too hot. The waitress who seemed to know I was a virgin, enjoyed watching me. "Put some sugar in it, sweetheart." She dumped in some sugar from the dispenser, then heaped my teaspoon, handed it to me, and I dropped in more.

It was cool enough now to taste. The sweetness made it familiar and welcome, the bitterness gave it an edge and mystery, the cream and the warmth made it feel like protection from the cutting slants of wind on the street. Perfect! I bit the donut. It was soft and crunchy. I haven't tasted anything like it since. The world looked great. My first cup of coffee was beyond delicious. The clutter of storm outside flew down the street on wings of jubilation. "Good stuff, huh, sweetheart." "Thanks," I said. I laid down a tip and stepped out to part the wind. The snow melted off my face. I headed back to the office, ready for anything.

Near the termination of my career with Amtria Trading Company the office called and asked me to come in on a Sunday. They were moving, and needed me to help with the furniture. I had sprained an ankle shooting hoops in the schoolyard, and didn't feel ready to do heavy work, not on a Sunday. I told them about my injury, and that I wouldn't be in for a week. When I did return Vernon's father greeted me with my pay envelope, which contained a pink slip. "You have outlived your usefulness with us," he said. The shock backed me into a seat. I was fired. It was the first time I had ever been hired, and now I was fired.

I left the office. It was my last day on Broad Street. I headed for the Chock Full O' Nuts. The waitress recognized me and brought a light coffee and a whole wheat donut, and I sat there like a workingman with the workingman's blues. I was fifteen years old, and I had outlived my usefulness. How was it possible? I drank the coffee. This time it made me a little jittery. The donut was good. I was dizzy. Fifteen years old. Outlived my usefulness. I'd read Dylan Thomas. I'd read T. S. Eliot. I'd read Archibald Macleish. Do not go gentle, must not mean but be, this is the way the world ends. It was then the first time I ever realized I would have to be a writer. If you are fifteen, and have already outlived your usefulness, you'd better wise up and become a writer. There was nothing else I could do.

Stowaway

"**Y**OU'RE STOWING AWAY, RIGHT?" The words fell from my mouth. It was three A.M. I was working for an outfit that hauled college students aboard Italian ships, this one the Vulcania, from New York to Southampton. No one said it, but I think it was a USIS operation. I had just got the advance from Holt for *Peter Prince* and I was on my way to Istanbul, to Israel, to Italy. It was a long crossing on a slow ship, eleven days from New York to Southampton. On the way the kids got to take seminars in the various cultures they were about to visit. My official title was assistant shipboard director. My duties were mostly as night security officer. I was assigned to patrol the corridors at night with the sergeant-at-arms, do bed checks in the dorm rooms, and deal with any conflicts. I spoke Italian, so I could be liaison with captain and crew, and Aldo, sergeant-at-arms. Aldo was an undersea demolition expert, once with the Italian navy. He was handsome, well put together. Every night he'd get stranded in the room of a Midwestern Catholic men's college, the boys on their way to some Vatican-sponsored retreat. I was on my own after that—open every door, say hello, don't spoil the fun.

This was the first night out of New York. Three A.M. I spotted her in the lounge, curled up in an easy chair. "Stowing away?" I repeated.

"O wow," she said, uncurling and sitting up. "I felt you walking there." She stretched and yawned like a cat. "I probably needed you to know. I sent it out to you."

"I'm the cop on this ship," I said.

"This is so far out. Wow."

She told me her name was Teri. She was one of those acid waifs of the sixties. She was traveling light, wearing very little—some baby-blue leather Capezios over black mesh stockings, dark blue micro-mini, black mesh panties, see-through red net blouse. The backs of her wrists were soiled from rubbing the heavy make-up around her eyes, smeared now to make her look like a tired clown.

This was my first big decision in my official capacity. "You can go down and sleep in my cabin for tonight," I said. There were two beds. Unlike my usual self, I had no interest in jumping on her. I felt no lust, nor was there anything paternal. With my modest success, and an understanding wife, I was indulging in a respite from family. If I had a desire to protect anything, it was my curiosity about the girl's situation.

By the next evening she had organized her scene, found new accommodations in the cabin of a Dutch couple, managed to get some other clothes. She made a lot of friends very quickly. Most people thought she was part of the staff, the activities organizer. When she checked back with me again, she told me her whole story. She had been communicating by ESP for a couple of years with a guy in London. She wouldn't say who it was. To connect with him she always dropped acid. In their last exchange he told her to get on this ship and sail to Southampton. Compliance was her part of the game. I doubt she could have told him to do anything. He instructed her to bring no money, and to leave her passport. It was a tough story for me to digest, but here she was, a stowaway. What was my official position? What kind of cop was I? Every hour she gained in shipboard notoriety.

One of the situations I had to police was a surfeit of pot. Many of the students packed plenty of it, thinking to sell it on the way. This was the first and only time I had ever worked in "law enforcement." I was determined to use a soft touch. My job here was to keep the information from the crew. They didn't want to know, anyway. No one wanted an international incident. The kids had to do something with this glut. A shame to waste it, but nobody needed to get busted trying to carry it through customs. They were frisky, but they weren't stupid. On the third day out we hit a storm. Seasickness kept them in their bunks. Visions of the Andrea Doria going down danced through their heads. I didn't get seasick, and did my rounds just the same. A scent of vomit drifted through the corridors.

I decided it wasn't my job to check the private cabins that couples had rented, but I stopped outside one of them. Something felt peculiar here, an outlaw vibe. I opened the door. Here was Teri. She didn't get seasick either, as long as she had something to do, she said. Her "to do" found her happily rolling joints, surrounded by pot and rolling papers, like a kid in a mud puddle. She had cleaned up, was dressed in jeans and a pink sweater, and had the shining face of a high school cheerleader. She had solved the problem, as much as it could be solved. Once people got their sea legs she showed up at the end of each meal with a tray full of tightly rolled joints, serving them to anyone who wanted to smoke. She was very gracious, no stranger to manners. My job as cop, I figured, was to hush this up, because if they busted anyone in Southampton, they'd have to bust almost everyone. I didn't even tell the shipboard director, with whom

I hardly spoke. He seemed very straight. If you dressed him in a dark raincoat, black oxfords, Foster Grants, you'd know where he worked.

Maybe it was Teri who had snuck into my cabin to fill my vitamin C jar with white crosses, a superdose of amphetamine. I swallowed one every morning with my other vitamins and felt fantastic, robust, smart, equal to the swelling Atlantic. It took a few days for me to get what was happening. Meanwhile I bounced around on deck, singing to the dolphins that played in the wake. All the women were incredibly exciting and beautiful, and I flirted with great panache. At the seminars I read from my new book, *Creamy and Delicious.* I talked Italy. I talked Europe and the benefits of travel. Who needed to sleep? I was oceanic. I was gabby and boring. After I made my rounds I went aft to howl at the algae that lit up in the foam. I listened all night as Paul Blackburn, great American Black Mountain poet, courted Joan, his future wife, in the next cabin. He told me the problem was cracking the corset. He said he liked men who stayed up and talked all night. He liked women who knew when to shut up.

I ignored Teri, lost track of her until we were about three days out of Southampton. One afternoon she sought me out. "I don't have any money, and I don't have a passport," she said, blithely. "I think I have to drop some acid and see what he tells me to do." I felt as if she were asking my approval, although my disapproval wouldn't have made any difference.

"Sounds okay," I said.

She kissed me on the cheek, and we never spoke again. I held off till the end because I didn't want to disembark until I saw how she managed. She looked presentable, like someone had gifted her with a modest skirt and sweater, and a small case for her other stuff. I watched her persuade the officer at the top of the gangplank, and then talk her way past the customs officials below. They totally let her through. She was safely in Southampton, talking with Peter and Sylvia, a couple that had befriended her. Then she was gone. I disembarked, exchanged information with the lovely Ellen D'Alelio, whom I hoped to meet in Italy, after I'd been to Turkey and Israel. I left my alleged shipboard charges to their various mischiefs.

I thought about Teri frequently, as one of the heroines, victims, of the acid culture. I wouldn't have heard of her ever again, except that I ran into Peter and Sylvia in Istanbul, and they had kept track of her for a while. They told me what they knew over sweet coffee at the Pudding Shop. The story is like some hippy apocrypha. She got off the ship and through customs by claiming she had

STEVE KATZ   321

already been through once. She had returned to her cabin to get something she had forgotten, and her husband, to whom she pointed in the waiting crowd, had her passport and her bags. I could imagine how persuasively helpless she seemed. She went to London and became one of the acid princesses of Carnaby Street, working in a store that sold hippy gear. She reached the critical point in her acid transmitted ESP when she was urged by her communicant to join him. Peter and Sylvia got the rest of the story second hand. The voice on the other end of the ESP was Paul McCartney. None other. She dropped some acid, went to his house, somehow got into his garage, and sat in a car and smoked all her pot until the time was right for her to enter the house, which she did in the wee hours. She found her way to an empty bedroom and went to sleep. In the morning someone woke her, and taking her for a girl friend of Paul's brother, told her breakfast was ready. Teri joined Paul and Linda at breakfast. She passed on the ESP story, and was quickly expelled from paradise. It sounds like it could be true. It sounds like it could be false. This is the whole story, I swear to g-d.

LYNN CRAWFORD

The Stubborn Aunt

for Gina Ferrari

T HE FAMILY (MOTHER, FATHER, TWO BOYS, ONE GIRL) IS CLOSE KNIT.
The parents work hard, far away, and for extended periods. During them,
a maternal aunt—the youngest in her family—watches the siblings. She is an
attentive caretaker: makes sure they have the necessary clothes, supplies; makes
sure they have healthy meals; makes sure they are enrolled in school and reason-
able extracurricular activities. Because she believes a degree of frustration is es-
sential for character development, her relationship to the children can be oppo-
sitional. If they ask for milk she gives them juice; if they read, or do schoolwork,
she insists they play outdoor ball games or, in bad weather, practice music.

The siblings understand some of their aunt's ideas do not benefit them or
her, but agree to keep this to themselves; agree not to bother their parents,
already so overwhelmed by their pressured profession.

One early spring, after a bitterly cold winter, this aunt stands up from shell-
ing beans on the front porch swing and collapses. She hits the side of her face on
the hard cement floor, lets out a piercing scream. The bowl lands on the swing
without spilling a single bean. The children run from different activities and
locations (one clears debris from the front yard garden; another practices baton
tosses in the driveway; a third scrubs potatoes in the kitchen). Together they
carry her to the living room couch, make tea, read her poems and entries from
their journals (she requires they fill a minimum of one page daily). Still, she re-
mains unconscious. A lump grows, puffy and discolored, on the side of her face
where she banged it. The children, believing she can hear them, promise her that
when she wakes up, they will walk her to a favorite place, the garden, not yet in
bloom, and make her favorite soup: rice and red pepper.

Meanwhile, they set the table, cook the shelled beans and scrubbed potatoes
in butter, oil, salt and pepper; hope the smell will wake her up. When it becomes
clear that she will not, cannot wake up, they call the doctor. While waiting,
they place her on the down cover of their parents' four-poster bed (where she
sleeps), remove her insulated slippers, massage her nylon-clad feet.

Not long after, the doctor arrives with his nurse. They examine the patient, take vital signs, find nothing identifiably wrong, even after thumbing through a weighty diagnostic reference book. They note, but are not alarmed by, the growth on her face.

The children offer them a meal, the bean and potato dish, but the visitors decline.

"You will need that food," the nurse tells them. Then, "Is your house always this neat?"

The children nod, and explain that their aunt is a careful housekeeper and has taught them, individually and together, to keep a careful house, too.

Over the next few days the children helplessly witness their aunt's transformation. A once sturdy, carefully groomed woman, is now still, gray, motionless. Yellowish liquid dribbles from the corners of her mouth.

One late afternoon, the children, the doctor, his nurse, standing in a circle around the aunt's bed, note that she is exceptionally pale, that her body is cold, unmoving.

"It is her time," the nurse says. "She has stopped breathing."

The doctor nods his head in agreement. He gently touches his long fingers to her neck artery.

"This is it," he says. "This is her time."

The children are stunned, and very sad. They love this aunt. True, at times they wished she were not taking care of them, even wished she would go away and let them take care of themselves. But they never wished for her to fall, to get sick, to get so sick. They never wished for her to die.

"We cannot cremate her until your parents return, but we can prepare her for cremation," the doctor says.

He, his nurse, the children, carry her out back to the spacious garden shed, and lay her on a clean work surface there. They stand around the aunt in the darkening evening light. There is a crease in her forehead and her hands are clenched.

"How do we really know if she is dead?" ask the children.

"She has no pulse," says the nurse.

"Boys, let's build a fire," suggests the doctor. The nephews gather wood for a bonfire. They use shovels in the shed, evenly hanging from sturdy pegs, to help the doctor dig a hole for the blaze. The nurse and the niece put the aunt in a good dress (silk, yellow). They comb her shiny blond hair, rub lipstick along her lips and into her cheeks.

Now all they have to do is wait for the parents, but no one knows when the parents will come. The doctor gives the aunt a transfusion to keep her dead body fresh. When he finishes the shot, he looks down at the niece, who carefully watches him. He takes in her small size, her curly blond hair, is shocked to notice a yellowish bruise on her neck. He questions her; she answers.

"It is from our aunt. Last week, in the middle of the night, she came into my room, pulled my arm, told me to get up and help her clear the garden. She said, 'Get up, get up now, get up now, time to garden,' and at first I just could not because I was so tired. So she pulled my hair and grabbed me by the neck. I choked, I could not breath. My brothers were sleeping in the other room. I got up and went outside and worked with her in the garden. She wanted us to clear away debris from winter so we could get things ready for spring. She made me hot chocolate, gave me raisin buns with butter and honey on them when we'd finished."

The two brothers move toward and hug their sister. "You should have told us," they whisper, stroking her hair.

"But you know her, we all know her, she cannot help her opinions, or behavior," the child answers.

"Look at her now," says the nurse. They stand around the aunt, lean over to watch her in the darkening evening light. There is still a crease in her forehead and her hands are clenched. The niece stands to her aunt's right.

The right arm shoots up, straight into the air.

It stays raised.

"Push it back down," instructs the nurse. "Push her arm back down."

The girl stands, frozen.

"Do as she says," says the doctor, "push the arm back down."

The child pushes the arm down. Again, the arm shoots up.

"Push it back down," repeats the nurse. "Her arm will come up as many times as she hit you and my guess is she hit you a lot."

The child repeats the exercise again and again.

After a time the aunt's arm stops shooting up. It rests on the table, palm down, next to her hip.

"She did not hit me that many times," says the child.

"Now, one more thing," says the nurse, ignoring the comment, "take this branch from the garden and hit her on her neck on the exact same spot where she choked you last week. Find that spot and hit that spot hard. This will allow your aunt to rest in peace."

The nurse pulls the stick from her deep uniform pocket, and hands it to the girl. The child takes it in her palm, raises it high, and hits her aunt very hard once, twice, three times on the neck, then stops striking. A heave comes from the aunt's chest. Her forehead smoothes, her hand unclenches, the bruise on the side of her face fades.

The doctor puts his hand on the young girl's shoulder.

"People in this town treated your aunt very badly when she was a child, but she never told anyone. I knew, others knew too, and we never did a thing. Your aunt had it tough, and we in this community are all to blame. I am sorry you were hurt because of our failure to be good neighbors."

It is night. Dark, starless. The group circles the aunt. Some time the doctor will tell the children what happened to their aunt as a little girl, but not now. He does not want to tell, and they do not want to listen to, those stories now. What they want to do is circle her, hold hands and breathe with each other, listen to the fire crackle behind them, wait for their parents, remember every little and big thing about the aunt that they can.

"suddenly as night"

With the wind came water, a door
"honest, and therefore
unmanageable."

When a gap opens,
he thinks it comes to him from God.

Well, you've gotta have your cookies, I know.
You gotta have your cookies
and your gun.

Meanwhile, I'm in the middle of writing my poem
about the city. Talking to the drapes. 100 bricks a day.

The pattern
is present in the room. More water!
May I not move you?

Contributors

ROBERTA ALLEN is the author of eight books, including two story collections, a novella-in-shorts, a novel, and a travel memoir. She teaches at the New School and in private workshops. Her novel *The Dreaming Girl* is forthcoming from Ellipsis Press. • STEPHANIE ANDERSON's chapbooks include *In the Particular Particular* (New Michigan Press), *The Choral Mimeographs* (Dancing Girl Press), with two more forthcoming. She lives in Chicago. • JASON BACASA lives in Los Angeles. He performs music under the name Jackson Durkacz. • ANDREA BAKER is the author of *like wind loves a window* (Slope Editions) and the chapbooks *gilda* (Poetry Society of America) and *true poems about the river go like this* (Cannibal Books). • JESSICA BARAN currently resides in St. Louis. Her poetry and art criticism has appeared in *Tusculum Review*, *The Village Voice*, and *The Riverfront Times*, among other publications. • JESSICA BARON is the author of a chapbook, *The Best Word for the Job of Mourning* (BlazeVOX). She lives in the high mountains of Colorado, where she writes, works, and teaches. • SHANE BOOK is directing a film based on his first poetry collection, *Ceiling of Sticks* (University of Nebraska Press), winner of the 2009 Prairie Schooner Book Prize. • DONALD BRECKENRIDGE is fiction editor of *The Brooklyn Rail* and co-editor of the InTranslation website. He is the author of the novels *6/2/95* (Spuyten Duyvil), *YOU ARE HERE* (Starcherone Books), and *This Young Girl Passing*, forthcoming from Autonomedia. • MICHAEL CARLSON is the author of *Cement Guitar* (University of Massachusetts Press), which won the Juniper Prize. He teaches 5th grade in Brooklyn. • JOSHUA COHEN is the author of five books, including the novels *Cadenza for the Schneidermann Violin Concerto*, *A Heaven of Others*, and *Witz*, which is forthcoming in 2010 from Dalkey Archive Press. He lives in Brooklyn. • JULIA COHEN has ten chapbooks out or forthcoming, and her first full-length book, *Triggermoon Triggermoon*, will appear in 2010. She is poetry editor of *Saltgrass* and assistant editor of *Denver Quarterly*. • ADAM CLAY's second book, *A Hotel Lobby at the Edge of the World*, is forthcoming from Milkweed Editions. He co-edits the magazine *Typo* and teaches at Western Michigan University. • LYNN CRAWFORD lives outside of Detroit. Her fifth book, *Simply Separate People, Two*, is forthcoming from Black Square Editions. • OISÍN CURRAN's *Mopus* was published in 2008 by Counterpath Press. He grew up in Maine and lives with his wife in Montreal. • CLAIRE DONATO lives and writes in Brooklyn. Her poems have recently appeared or are forthcoming in *Black Warrior Review*, *Boston Review*, *Denver Quarterly*, and *Octopus*. • FARRAH FIELD's first book of poems, *Rising*, won Four Way Books' 2007 Levis Prize and was published in 2009. She lives in Brooklyn. • COREY FROST lived in Montreal for many years and is now an enthusiastic resident of Queens. He has published three books, including *My Own Devices: Airport Version*, a collection of stories. • David Goldstein is the author of the chapbook *Been Raw Diction* (Dusie, 2006) and a founding member of the Wa-kow! artist collective. He teaches at York University in Toronto. • Andrew Grace's third book, *Sancta*, is forthcoming from Ahsahta Press in 2012. He lives in Cincinnati with his wife and daughter. • Kate Greenstreet's second book, *The Last 4 Things*, is new from Ahsahta Press, which also published her book *case sensitive* in 2006. Her most recent chapbook is *This is why I hurt you* (Lame House Press). • Sarah Gridley is the author of *Weather Eye Open* and the forthcoming *Green is the Orator*, both from University of California Press. • Emily Gropp's poetry has appeared or is forthcoming in *Bloom*, *Denver Quarterly*, *Fence*, and *Whisky & Fox*. Her manuscript *Sleeping with Phosphorus* was recently selected as a finalist for the Fence Modern Poets Series. She teaches 8th grade in Pittsburgh. • Evelyn Hampton co-edits *Dewclaw*. Her writing appears in *Birkensnake*, *Denver Quarterly*, and other venues. • Jennifer Hayashida is the translator of Fredrik Nyberg's *A Different Practice* (Ugly Duckling Presse) and Eva Sjödin's *Inner China* (Litmus Press). She is on the faculty of the Asian American Studies Program at Hunter College. • Stefania Heim's poems have appeared in chapbook form from Hand Held Editions and in many publications. She is co-founder and co-editor of *Circumference: Poetry in Translation*, and a doctoral candidate at the CUNY Graduate Center. • Lily Hoang is the author of the novels *Changing* (Fairy Tale Review Press), *Parabola* (Chiasmus Press), and *The Evolutionary Revolution* (Les Figues Press). Her novels *Invisible Women* and *Unfinished* are forthcoming later this year. She is an associate editor at Starcherone and an editor at Tarpaulin Sky. • Joanna Howard is the author of *On The Winding Stair* (BOA Editions) and *In the Colorless Round* (Noemi Press), a chapbook. She is an editor for Tarpaulin Sky and lives in Providence, where she teaches at Brown University. • Dan Hoy lives in Brooklyn and is co-founder of *Soft Targets*. His recent publications include *Glory Hole | The Hot Tub* (Mal-O-Mar), co-authored with Jon Leon, and *Basic Instinct: Poems* (Triple Canopy). • Thomas Kane is the editor and co-translator of Tomaž Šalamun's collection of poems *There's the Hand and There's the Arid Chair* (Counterpath). His work has appeared in *McSweeney's* and *Bat City Review*. • Steve Katz started the trouble with *The Exagggerations of Peter Prince* in 1968 and published *Kissssss: a miscellany* last year. Many books came between. The first volume of his memoirrhoids is forthcoming as *Time's Wallet* from Counterpath Press. • Karla Kelsey is the author of *Knowledge, Forms, the Aviary* (Ahsahta Press), *Iteration Nets* (Ahsahta), *Little Dividing Doors in the Mind* (Noemi Press), and *3 Movements* (Pilot Press). • Joanna Klink is the author of *They Are Sleeping*, *Circadian*, and *Raptus* (forthcoming from Penguin in 2010). She teaches at Harvard University. • Jennifer Kronovet is the author of the poetry collection *Awayward* (BOA Editions) and is co-founder and co-editor of *Circumference: Poetry in Translation*. • NORMAN LOCK is the author of the novels *Shadowplay* (Ellipsis Press) and *A History of the Imagination* (FC2), among many other works, including novellas, brief fictions, and stage plays. He lives in Philadelphia. • JILL MAGI works in text and image and is the author of *SLOT* (Ugly Duckling Presse, forthcoming), *Threads* (Futurepoem), *Torchwood* (Shearsman), and numerous small, handmade chapbooks. She runs Sona Books, a chapbook press, from her apartment in Brooklyn. • JUSTIN MARKS's first book is *A Million in Prizes* (New Issues Press). He is a co-founder of Birds, LLC, and lives in Woodside, Queens, with his wife and their one-year-old son and daughter. • PETER MARKUS is the author of a novel, *Bob, or Man on Boat* (Dzanc Books), as well as three short books of short fiction. A new book of stories, *We Make Mud*, is forthcoming in 2011 from Dzanc. • EUGENE MARTEN is the author of *In the Blind* (Turtle Point Press) and *Waste* (Ellipsis Press). He lives in Harlem. • STEPHEN-PAUL MARTIN has published twenty-two books of fiction, non-fiction, and poetry. His most recent collections of fiction are *Changing the Subject* (forthcoming from Ellipsis Press in 2010) and *The Possibility of Music* (FC2). He teaches at San Diego State University. • ZACHARY MASON is a computer scientist specializing in artificial intelligence. The second edition of his first book, *The Lost Books of the Odyssey*, came out with Farrar, Straus and Giroux earlier this year. He lives in California. • MIRANDA MELLIS is the author of *The Revisionist* (Calamari Press) and *Materialisms* (Portable Press at Yo-Yo Labs). She is an editor at the Encyclopedia Project, and lives and teaches in San Francisco. • SARA MICHAS-MARTIN's work has appeared in *American Poetry Review*, *Forklift, Ohio*, *Jubilat*, *Field*, *Threepenny Review*, and elsewhere. She lives in San Francisco and teaches at Stanford and Goddard College. • PATRICK MORRISSEY's chapbook *Transparency* was published by Cannibal Books in 2009. He lives in New York. • RYAN MURPHY is the author of *Down with the Ship* (Otis Books/Seismicity Editions) and *The Redcoats* (Krupskaya). • EILEEN MYLES lives in New York, though not this spring; right now, she's in Montana. *The Inferno*, a novel about the hell of being a female poet, will be out very soon. • BRYSON NEWHART's fiction has recently appeared in *No Colony*, *Anemone Sidecar*, *Thieves Jargon*, *Lamination Colony*, *Sein und Werden*, *Defenestration*, *5_trope*, *Caketrain*, *elimae*, *Tarpaulin Sky*, *The Dream People*, and *BDtDaEAtC*. • LINNEA OGDEN is a teacher living in San Francisco. Her work has appeared in the chapbooks *Another Limit* (Projective Industries) and *Long Weekend, Short Leash* (Taproot Editions). • CAMERON PATERSON lives in North Carolina. His poems are forthcoming in *Permafrost* and *California Quarterly*. • JOHANNAH RODGERS's book *sentences*, a collection of short stories, essays, and drawings, was published by Red Dust in 2007. She teaches at CUNY's New York City College of Technology and is a contributing editor at *The Brooklyn Rail*. • JOANNA RUOCCO co-edits *Birkensnake*, a fiction journal, and is the author of *The Mothering Coven* (Ellipsis

Press). Her collection of short fictions, *Man's Companions*, is forthcoming from Tarpaulin Sky in 2010. • ELIZABETH SANGER'S work has appeared in *Conjunctions*, *Phoebe*, *Meridian*, *Touchstone*, *Past Simple*, *Typo*, *Verse Daily*, *Drunken Boat*, and *Saranac Review*. She lives in Florida with cats. • ROB SCHLEGEL is the author of *The Lesser Fields*, winner of the 2009 Colorado Prize for Poetry. New work is forthcoming in *New American Writing* and *LEVELER*. • ZACHARY SCHOMBURG is the author of *The Man Suit* (Black Ocean) and *Scary, No Scary* (Black Ocean). His translations of Andrei Sen-Senkov have been published in *Circumference*, *Mantis*, and *Aufgabe*, among others. He lives in Portland and co-edits Octopus Books and *Octopus Magazine*. • KATE SCHREYER lives in North Carolina. • ANDREI SEN-SENKOV, the author of eight books of poetry, was born in Tajikistan in 1968. He now lives in Moscow, where he is a medical doctor. • BRANDON SHIMODA'S collaborations, drawings, and poems have appeared in books and magazines, on magnetic tape and vinyl, on walls and online. He was born in the valley and lives now in the shadow of a chief hanged for murder. • PETER JAY SHIPPY is the author of *Thieves' Latin* (University of Iowa Press), *Alphaville* (BlazeVOX Books), and *How to Build the Ghost in Your Attic* (Rose Metal Press). He teaches at Emerson College in Boston. • JOANNA SONDHEIM'S chapbooks *The Fit* and *Thaumatrope* were published by Sona Books. She lives in Jackson Heights, Queens. • MATHIAS SVALINA is the author of *Destruction Myth*, published by Cleveland State University Poetry Center. • BRONWEN TATE is the author of the chapbooks *Souvenirs* (Dusie), *Like the Native Tongue the Vanquished* (Cannibal Books), and *Scaffolding* (Dusie). She is a PhD candidate at Stanford University and can read and knit at the same time. • G.C. WALDREP is the author of *Goldbeater's Skin* (Center for Literary Publishing), *Disclamor* (BOA Editions), and *Archicembalo* (Tupelo Press), which won the 2008 Dorset Prize. He lives in Lewisburg, Pa., and teaches at Bucknell University. • DEREK WHITE is the author of *Marsupial*, a novel. He runs Calamari Press, edits *Sleepingfish* magazine, and blogs at 5cense.com. • JARED WHITE'S chapbook of poems *Yellowcake* appeared in 2009 in the hand-sewn anthology *Narwhal* from Cannibal Books. He lives in Brooklyn. • JOSHUA MARIE WILKINSON is the author of several books, most recently *Selenography* (with Polaroids by Califone's Tim Rutili). He lives in Chicago and Athens, Ga. • PAUL WINNER'S work has appeared in *Tin House*, *Maisonneuve*, *Seneca Review*, and *The Paris Review*. • DAVID WIRTHLIN is the author of *Houndstooth* (Spuyten Duyvil) and *Your Disappearance* (BlazeVOX Books). He is currently at work on a PhD from the University of Denver and is editor of *smallHABITS*. • MICHAEL ZEISS is a writer living in Woodside, Queens. He works as a consultant for non-profit organizations. • LENI ZUMAS is the author of the story collection *Farewell Navigator* (Open City). She has taught at the University of Massachusetts, the Juniper Summer Writing Institute, Hunter College, and Columbia University.

Harp & Altar is an online literary magazine founded by Keith Newton in Brooklyn, N.Y., in 2006. Andrew Ackermann designed the website and oversaw its production. Eugene Lim, whose fiction had appeared in the first issue, joined soon afterward as fiction editor. The work in this anthology was selected from the poetry and prose published in the first six issues, dating from the fall of 2006 to the spring of 2009. Michael Newton, who has frequently written gallery reviews for the magazine, was the book's designer. Although many contributions to *Harp & Altar* were unable to be published here—including criticism, reviews, translations, art, and photography—every issue is fully archived at www.harpandaltar.com. *The lyf so short, the craft so long to lerne.*